What Do Unions Do?

WHAT DO UNIONS DO?

RICHARD B. FREEMAN

&

JAMES L. MEDOFF

Basic Books, Inc., Publishers   New York

Library of Congress Cataloging in Publication Data

Freeman, Richard B.
  What do unions do?

  Includes bibliographical references and index.
  1. Trade-unions—United States.   I. Medoff, James L.
II. Title.
HD6508.F73   1984   331.88'0973   81–68407
ISBN 0–465–09133–4

To Martin Segal, Sylvia Freeman, and Herbert Freeman

To Frances Darman, Syvia Medoff, and Edward Medoff

CONTENTS

ACKNOWLEDGMENTS

IN WRITING THIS BOOK we have benefited from the contributions of many individuals. For valuable assistance with the research, we thank Molly Abraham, David Belluck, Greg Bialecki, Vincent Carey, Jon Fay, Alan Garber, David Yermack, Wayne Gray, Harry Holzer, Casey Ichniowski, Donna Jackson, Joyce Jacobson, Jonathan Leonard, John Maki, David Mandelbaum, Jane Mather, Laura Nelson, David Neumark, Karen Parrish, Jeanne Quesnai, Eric Seiler, Greg Tang, Pam Thomas, Martin Van Denburgh, Janet Walker, and Jonathan Wiener.

Useful comments and suggestions were provided to us by many of our fellow professional economists; we are particularly grateful to Katharine Abraham, Charles Brown, Gary Chamberlain, John Dunlop, and Martin Segal for their generous inputs.

Our research has been funded by grants from the National Science Foundation to the National Bureau of Economic Research.

R. B. F.
J. L. M.
December 1983

What Do Unions Do?

CHAPTER 1

A New Portrait of
U.S. Unionism

TRADE UNIONS are the principal institution of workers in modern capitalistic societies. For over 200 years, since the days of Adam Smith, economists and other social scientists, labor unionists, and businessmen and women have debated the social effects of unionism. Despite the long debate, however, no agreed-upon answer has emerged to the question: What do unions do?

On the one side, many economists view unions largely as monopolies in the labor market whose primary economic impact is to raise members' wages at the expense of unorganized labor and of the efficient functioning of the economy. These analysts stress the adverse effects of union work rules on productivity, the loss of employment in the organized sector due to union wage effects, and the consequent crowding of the nonunion sector with displaced workers. Consistent with this view, managers frequently complain about inflexible operations and work disruptions due to unions, while many social critics paint unions as socially unresponsive, elitist, non-democratic, and crime-riddled institutions.[1]

On the other side are those who believe unions have beneficial economic and political effects. Industrial relations experts have long stressed the ways in which collective bargaining can induce better management and higher productivity. These specialists note that unions can increase the development and retention of skills, provide information about what occurs on the shop floor, improve morale, and pressure management to be more efficient in its operations.[2] Unionists point out that in addition to increasing wages, unions provide workers both with protection against arbitrary management decisions and with a voice at the work place and in the political arena. Even the managements of some organized companies have cited positive impacts of unions on their business. Consider, for example, this statement by Thomas Murphy, then Chairman of General Motors, on the fiftieth anniversary of the "Battle of the Running Bulls," one of the turning points in the struggle to organize the company by the United Auto Workers:

The UAW may have introduced the sit-down strike to America, but in its relationship with GM management it has also helped introduce . . . mutually beneficial cooperation. . . . What comes to my mind is the progress we have made, by working together, in such directions as providing greater safety and health protection, in decreasing alcoholism and drug addiction, in improving the quality of work life.[3]

During the past twenty-five years, however, the negative view of trade unions has become increasingly dominant. While there are notable exceptions, many on both the right and left now doubt the social relevance and value of America's organized labor movement.[4] The widespread, one might say textbook, picture of U.S. unions today is of institutions adept at advancing their own interests at the public's expense. Economists concerned with quantifying the economic effects of collective bargaining have focused almost exclusively on the monopoly wage impact of unions, developing a large and valuable literature on the differences in wages paid to organized and unorganized labor.[5] Because monopolistic wage increases are socially harmful—in that they can be expected to induce both inefficiency and inequality—most economic studies, implicitly or explicitly, have judged unions as being a negative force in society.

When the research for this book was begun ten years ago, there was very little quantitative evidence concerning the impact of U.S. unionism on outcomes other than wages. Whereas adherents to the monopoly view of unions could cite numerous quantitative studies of union wage effects, those stressing the nonwage impact of unions were limited to citing specific cases and personal observation.

It was this shortage of statistical evidence concerning what unions do beyond raising wages that set the stage for our research. The recent availability of computerized data files, which contain vast amounts of information on thousands of individuals, establishments, and companies, offers the opportunity for quantitative analyses of many of the nonwage effects of trade unions to parallel the analyses of the wage effect of unions, and thus for broadening the forum of the debate on unionism. Our quantitative analyses and those of our colleagues elsewhere in the social sciences have, indeed, yielded new findings that, taken in conjunction with case-study evidence and the observations of industrial relations experts, provide a new picture of the impact of unions on the economy and on the broader society.[6]

This newly emergent picture of what unions do has important implications for the assessment of unions by labor and management and by the general public. The average unionized worker will see that unions generally "deliver the goods," by providing higher wages and benefits as well as a voice at the bargaining table and on the shop floor, but that some of "the goods" have a social cost. Many nonunion workers will recognize that, because of the threat of unionization, their wages and working conditions are better than they might have been, although generally not as good as they would be under collective bargaining, while others will find that their economic position is worse as a result of unionism. Employers of unionized workers will see that while unionism is associated with a lower rate of return on capital and less managerial flexibility, the extent to which a union is a liability or an asset depends crucially on how management responds to it. Nonunion employers will learn that while the benefits of being union-free generally exceed the costs of union avoidance, the former are often overstated and the latter are often understated. Finally, the general public will see that in the economic sphere, unions reduce wage inequality, increase industrial democracy, and often raise productivity, while in the political sphere, unions are an important voice for some of our society's weakest and most vulnerable groups, as well as for their own members.

The "Two Faces" Debate

The meaning of the results of our study of U.S. trade unionism can best be understood by recognizing that unions have two faces, each of which leads to a different view of the institution: a *monopoly* face, associated with their monopolistic power to raise wages; and a *collective voice/institutional response* face, associated with their representation of organized workers within enterprises.

The Monopoly Face

Most, if not all, unions have monopoly power, which they can use to raise wages above competitive levels. Assuming that the competitive system works perfectly, these wage increases have harmful economic effects, reducing the national output and distorting the distribution of income. The analysis of unions as monopolies focuses on the magnitude of the union markup of wages and traces the ways in which this markup causes firms to lower employment and output, thereby harming economic efficiency and altering the distribution of income.

Despite the attention economists give to the monopoly face of unionism, analysis of union monopoly behavior is much less fully developed than is the analysis of monopolistic enterprises. The principal reason is that unions are not the simple monopolies of economics textbooks but rather collective organizations of workers with diverse interests. Unlike the monopoly firm that sets prices to maximize profits, unions rarely set wages; they bargain over wages with employers. Unless one believes that the process of collective bargaining is a sham, the wages obtained by unions must be viewed as the joint responsibility of management and labor: the stronger management resistance to union wage goals is, the smaller union wage gains will be. Moreover, unions' ability to raise wages is limited by the fact that, all else the same, higher union wages will induce employers to reduce employment. Some members gain when wages are very high; others lose. Despite decades in which unions have been part of the economic scene, economists lack an accepted maximizing theory of union behavior that would predict the results of bargaining within the union over wage goals. Under some circumstances a union may seek a high wage at the cost of employment; under others, it may be more moderate in its wage demands to preserve jobs. This union concern is quite distinct from the worries of a monopolist, whose sole goal is to maximize profits, regardless of what happens to the number of units sold.[7]

Analysis of the monopoly face of unionism must confront the important issue of the source of union monopoly power. If unions operated in perfectly competitive markets, and if *all* they did were to raise wages ——— above competitive levels, unions would have a very difficult time surviving, for organized firms would necessarily have higher costs of production than other firms. One way unions could survive in such markets would be by organizing the entire industry or sector. If production costs are higher for all establishments in a sector, output and employment will be lower than they would be in the absence of unionism, but the sector will survive. Alternatively, if unions operate in markets where firms have different cost structures (for reasons unassociated with unionism), unions could survive by organizing firms with the lowest costs of production, raising wages at the expense of above-normal profits or "rent."[8] Perhaps most importantly, union monopoly power is likely to be closely related to the market power of the sector it organizes. When unions organize noncompetitive firms, they are able to raise wages without endangering the life of the firm. In sum, from the monopoly perspective, unions are likely to exist in industries where new firms have difficulty entering and/or where some enterprises have cost advantages over their competitors.

The fact that union monopoly power is likely to be important only when unionized firms either completely dominate a market or operate in a non-competitive market has created an interesting intellectual anomaly. Some economists of a strong free-enterprise bent, who one might expect to be strongly opposed to unions, are in fact rather indifferent. They believe that markets are competitive enough to give unions little or no power to extract monopoly wage gains.

The Collective Voice/Institutional Response Face

As Hirschman pointed out in his important book *Exit, Voice, and Loyalty,* societies have two basic mechanisms for dealing with social or economic problems.[9] The first is the classic market mechanism of exit-and-entry, in which individuals respond to a divergence between desired and actual social conditions by exercising freedom of choice or mobility: the dissatisfied consumer switches products; the diner whose soup is too salty seeks another restaurant; the unhappy couple divorces. In the labor market, exit is synonymous with quitting, while entry consists of new hires by the firm. By leaving less desirable for more desirable jobs, or by refusing bad jobs, individuals penalize the bad employer and reward the good, leading to an overall improvement in the efficiency of the economic system. The basic theorem of neoclassical economics is that, under well-specified conditions, the exit and entry of persons (the hallmark of the free-market system) produces a situation in which no individual can be made better off without making someone worse off. Much economic analysis can be viewed as a detailed study of the implications of this kind of adjustment and of the extent to which it works out in real economies. As long as the exit-entry market mechanism is viewed as the *only* adjustment mechanism, institutions like unions are invariably seen as impediments to the optimal operation of the economy.

The second mode of adjustment is the political mechanism that Hirschman termed "voice." "Voice" refers to the use of direct communication to bring actual and desired conditions closer together. It means talking about problems: complaining to the store about a poor product rather than taking business elsewhere; telling the chef that the soup had too much salt; discussing marital problems rather than going directly to the divorce court. In a political context, "voice" refers to participation in the democratic process, through voting, discussion, bargaining, and the like.

The distinction between the two mechanisms is best illustrated by a specific situation—for instance, concern about the quality of schools in a given locality. The exit solution to poor schools would be to move to a different community or to enroll one's children in a private school, thereby "taking one's business elsewhere." The voice solution would involve political action to improve the school system through school-board elections, Parent Teacher Association meetings, and other channels of communication.

In the job market, voice means discussing with an employer conditions that ought to be changed, rather than quitting the job. In modern industrial economies, and particularly in large enterprises, a trade union is the vehicle for collective voice—that is, for providing workers as a group with a means of communicating with management.

Collective rather than individual bargaining with an employer is necessary for effective voice at the workplace for two reasons. First, many important aspects of an industrial setting are "public goods," that is, goods which will affect the well-being (negatively or positively) of every employee in such a way that one individual's partaking of the good does not preclude someone else from doing so. Safety conditions, lighting, heating, the speed of the production line, the firm's formal grievance procedure, pension plan, and policies on matters such as layoffs, work-sharing, cyclical wage adjustment, and promotion all obviously affect the entire workforce in the same way that defense, sanitation, and fire protection affect the community at large. One of the most important economic theorems is that competitive markets will not provide enough of such goods; some form of collective decision making is needed. Without a collective organization, the incentive for the individual to take into account the effects of his or her actions on others, or to express his or her preferences, or to invest time and money in changing conditions, is likely to be too small to spur action. Why not "let Harry do it" and enjoy the benefits at no cost? This classic "free-rider" problem lies at the heart of the so-called "union-security" versus "right-to-work" debate.

A second reason why collective action is necessary is that workers who are tied to a firm are unlikely to reveal their true preferences to an employer, for fear the employer may fire them. In a world in which workers could find employment at the same wages immediately, the market would offer adequate protection for the individual, but that is not the world we live in. The danger of job loss makes expression of voice by an individual risky. Collective voice, by contrast, is protected both by the support of all workers and by the country's labor law: "It shall be an unfair labor practice for an employer by discrimination in regard to hire or tenure or employment or any term or condition of employment to encourage or discourage membership in any labor organization" (National Labor Relations Act, Section 7a of the 1935 law). Court interpretation of U.S. labor law makes a sharp distinction between collective and individual actions at the workplace: even nonunion workers acting in a concerted fashion are protected from managerial retaliation.[10] However, the nonunion protester acting alone and not seeking a union is "terminable at will" and must speak very carefully.

The collective nature of trade unionism fundamentally alters the operation of a labor market and, hence, the nature of the labor contract. In a nonunion setting, where exit-and-entry is the predominant form of adjustment, the signals and incentives to firms depend on the preferences of the "marginal" worker, the one who might leave because of (or be attracted by) small changes in the conditions of employment. The firm responds primarily to the needs of this marginal worker, who is generally young and marketable; the firm can to a considerable extent ignore the preferences of typically older, less marketable workers, who—for reasons of skill, knowledge, rights that cannot be readily transferred to other enterprises, as well as because of other costs associated with changing firms—are effectively immobile. In a unionized setting, by contrast, the union takes account of *all* workers in determining its demands at the bargaining table, so that the desires of workers who are highly unlikely to leave the enterprise are also represented. With respect to public goods at the workplace, the union can add up members' preferences in much the same manner as a government can add up voters' preferences for defense, police protection, and the like to determine social demand for them. In sum, because unions are political institutions with elected leaders, they are likely to respond to a different set of preferences from those that prevail in a competitive labor market.

In a modern economy, where workers tend to be attached to firms for many years, younger and older workers are likely to have different preferences (for instance, regarding pension or health insurance plans versus take-home pay, or layoffs ordered inversely to seniority versus cuts in wage growth or work sharing). The change from an approach that focuses only on workers at the coming-or-going margin to one that considers all employees is likely to lead to a very different labor contract. Under some conditions, the union contract—by taking account of all workers and by appropriately considering the sum of preferences for work conditions that are common to all workers—can be economically more efficient than the contract that would result in the absence of unions.

Finally, as a collective voice unions also fundamentally alter the social relations of the workplace. The essence of the employment relationship under capitalism—as stressed by such diverse analysts as Karl Marx, Herbert Simon, and Ronald Coase—is the payment of money by the employer to the employee in return for the employer's control over a certain amount of the employee's time. The employer seeks to use his employee's time in a way that maximizes the profitability of the enterprise. Even in the case of piece rates, employers monitor employee activity to assure the quality of output, prevent the wastage of materials, and protect the stock of capital. As a result, the way in which the time purchased is utilized must be determined by some interaction between workers and their employer. In the absence of unionism, the worker has limited responses to orders that he feels are unfair: the worker can quit, or he can perhaps engage in quiet sabotage or shirking, neither of which is likely to alter the employer's actions. In the union setting, by contrast, the union constitutes a source of worker power, diluting managerial authority and offering members protection through both the "industrial jurisprudence" system, under which many workplace decisions are based on rules (such as seniority) instead of supervisory judgment or whim, and the grievance and arbitration system, under which disputes over proper managerial decision making on work issues can be resolved. As a result, management power within enterprises is curtailed by unionism, so that workers' rights are likely to be better enforced. Consider, for example, a firm that decides to fire senior workers immediately before they become eligible for pension rights. In the nonunion setting, a firm may be able to get away with such a maneuver; in the union setting, it is unlikely to have such power. Economic theorists of all persuasions have increasingly recognized that unions' ability to enforce labor agreements, particularly those with deferred claims, creates the possibility for improved labor contracts and arrangements and higher economic efficiency.[11]

Management's Role in What Unions Do

The two views of unionism lead to fundamentally different analyses of what management does in response to the existence of a union. In the most basic monopoly analysis, in which unions can simply raise wages, management's responses are limited. It can reduce employment, substitute capital for labor, or hire more skilled workers to raise labor's productivity. Since management is assumed to be doing everything just right in the absence of unions, these adjustments are socially harmful.

By contrast, the voice/response face directs attention to the possibility that, because of incomplete information, lack of coordination in an enterprise, and organizational slack, management can respond to unionism in more creative ways, which may be socially beneficial. This view is consistent with modern theories of the firm, in which management is taken to be not a simple all-knowing profit-maximizer, but rather a mediator of the interests of relatively permanent employees, stockholders, and consumers.[12] The greater the imperfection of markets, and the further real-world management is from a computer programmed by the Invisible Hand, the greater are the possibilities for management's response to unions to improve the operation of the economy, and thus the greater the validity of voice/response insights into what unions (and unionized managements) do.

If management uses the collective bargaining process to learn about and improve the operation of the workplace and the production process, unionism can be a significant plus to enterprise efficiency. On the other hand, if management responds negatively to collective bargaining (or is prevented by unions from reacting positively), unionism can significantly harm the performance of the firm. If management acquiesces to exorbitant union wage demands, the organized sector may suffer serious economic decline. If it reaches sensible agreements with labor, all parties may benefit. At the worst, if management cooperates with racketeers who suppress union democracy and offer "sweetheart" contracts, the organized sector will be a sorry place indeed.[13] The important point is that just as there are two sides to all markets, demand and supply, there are also two sides to all collective bargaining arrangements, management and unions. Industrial relations practices and economic outcomes depend on the policies and actions of both management and labor. The reader who believes that the industrial relations and personnel policies of management can affect the outcome of the economic system will find our results more believable than the reader who believes that all enterprises are *always* operating with perfect information in a way that makes profits as large as possible.

The Issues in Question

Table 1–1 provides a capsule summary of the differences in how the monopoly and voice/response faces of unionism affect three major economic outcomes: the level and composition of national output (effi-

TABLE 1-1
The Two Faces of Trade Unionism

	Union Effects on Economic Efficiency	Union Effects on Distribution of Income	Social Nature of Union Organization
Monopoly Face	Unions raise wages above competitive levels, leading to too little labor relative to capital in unionized firms. Union work rules decrease productivity.	Unions increase income inequality by raising the wages of highly skilled workers. Unions create horizontal inequities by creating differentials among comparable workers.	Unions discriminate in rationing positions. Unions (individually or collectively) fight for their own interests in the political arena. Union monopoly power breeds corrupt and nondemocratic elements.
Collective Voice/Institutional Response Face	Unions have some positive effects on productivity—reducing quit rates, inducing management to alter methods of production and adopt more efficient policies, and improving morale and cooperation among workers. Unions collect information about the preferences of all workers, leading the firm to choose a better mix of employee compensation and a better set of personnel policies.	Unions' standard-rate policies reduce inequality among organized workers in a given company or a given industry. Union rules limit the scope for arbitrary actions in the promotion, layoff, and recall of individuals. Unionism fundamentally alters the distribution of power between marginal (generally junior) and more permanent (generally senior) employees, causing union firms to select different compensation packages and personnel practices from those of nonunion firms.	Unions are political institutions that represent the will of their members. Unions represent the political interests of lower-income and disadvantaged persons.

SOURCE: Based on R. B. Freeman and J. L. Medoff, "The Two Faces of Unionism," *The Public Interest* 57 (Fall 1979): 75.

ciency); the distribution of income; and the extent of economic equality and political freedom. On each of the issues, the monopoly face implies social losses while the voice/response face offers potential social gains. And on each of the issues, as illustrated in the quotations that follow, there has been considerable debate over which face is dominant.

Efficiency

. . . their activities necessarily reduce the productivity of labor all around and therefore also the general level of real wages; because, if union action succeeds in reducing the number of workers in the highly-paid jobs and in increasing the number of those who have to stay in the less remunerative ones, the result may be that the over-all average will be lower. It is, in fact, more than likely that, in countries where unions are very strong, the general level of real wages is lower than it would otherwise be. This is certainly true . . . where union policy is strengthened by the general use of restrictive practices of a 'make-work' character.[14]

. . . a strong union, guided by farseeing men who have a grave sense of responsibility, is found to enable a few minutes' quiet conversation to settle innumerable petty disputes that in old times would have caused much delay and worry and loss of mutual feeling. . . . In such trades we may conclude confidently that Trade Unions on the whole facilitate business.[15]

As monopoly institutions, unions reduce society's output in three ways. First, union-won wage increases cause a misallocation of resources by inducing organized firms to hire fewer workers, to use more capital per worker, and to hire workers of higher quality than is socially optimal. Second, strikes called to force management to accept union demands reduce gross national product. Third, union contract provisions —such as limits on the loads that can be handled by workers, restrictions on tasks performed, and featherbedding—lower the productivity of labor and capital.

By contrast, the voice/response face of unionism suggests important ways in which unionism can raise productivity. First of all, voice at a workplace should reduce the rate of quitting. Since lower quit rates imply lower hiring and training costs and less disruption in the functioning of work groups, they should raise productivity. In addition, the likelihood that workers and firms will remain together for long periods of time should increase the incentive for investment in skills specific to an enterprise, which also raises productivity.

14

The fact that senior workers are likely to be relatively more powerful in unionized firms points to another way in which unions can raise productivity. Under unionism, promotions and other rewards tend to depend less on individual performance and more on length of service. As a result, feelings of rivalry among individuals are likely to be less pronounced in union plants than in nonunion plants, and the amount of informal training and assistance that workers are willing to provide one another is greater. On the other hand, however, a greater reliance on seniority in determining who gets jobs can reduce productivity by placing individuals in jobs for which they are less qualified than other workers. Which of these effects dominates is an empirical question.

Unionism can also improve efficiency by putting pressure on management to tighten job-production standards and accountability in order to preserve profits in the face of higher wages. Because unionized management can be challenged by the union, moreover, it will tend to discard vague paternalistic, authoritarian personnel policies in favor of practices in which explicit rules govern behavior. After making comprehensive case studies of management in over one hundred unionized firms, Slichter, Healy, and Livernash concluded: "The challenge that unions presented to management has, if viewed broadly, created superior and better-balanced management, even though some exceptions must be recognized."[16] Management's ability to do a better job can be greatly helped by the union, which can perform helpful roles, such as explaining changes in day-to-day routine.

Finally, through the voice/response mechanism, the collective bargaining apparatus opens an important communication channel between workers and management, one likely to increase the flow of information between the two and possibly improve the productivity of the enterprise. As Reynolds (Yale) has observed, "Unions can do valuable work by pointing out improvements that perhaps should have been obvious to management but were not, and that, once discovered, can be installed with a net gain to the company as well as the workers."[17] Union impacts on the composition of compensation packages—on the balance between working conditions or fringes and wages, for example—have often been cited as reflecting, at least in part, the greater flow of information about worker desires. If, for a given dollar of labor cost, workers are better off because the division of the dollar between wages, fringes, and work conditions is more nearly optimal, social productivity, broadly defined, is higher as a result of union activity.

Distribution of Income

If unions raise wage rates in a particular occupation or industry, they necessarily make the amount of employment available in the occupation or industry less than it otherwise would be—just as any higher price cuts down the amount purchased. The effect is an increased number of persons seeking other jobs, which forces down wages in other occupations. Since unions have generally been strongest among groups that would have been high-paid anyway, their effect has been to make high-paid workers higher paid at the expense of lower-paid workers. Unions have therefore not only harmed the public at large and workers as a whole by distorting the use of labor; they have also made the incomes of the working class more unequal by reducing the opportunities available to the most disadvantaged workers.[18]

Summing up these diverse consequences of collective bargaining, one can make a strong case that unionism has at any rate not worsened the wage structure. We are inclined to be even more venturesome than this, and to say that its net effect has been beneficial.[19]

One of the most striking implications of the analysis of the monopoly face of unions, greatly stressed by opponents of unionism, is that union wage gains increase inequality in the labor market. According to the monopoly argument, the workers displaced from unionized firms as a result of union wage gains raise the supply of labor to nonunion firms, which can therefore be expected to reduce wages. Thus, unionized workers are likely to be made better off at the expense of nonunion workers. The fact that organized blue-collar workers who are more skilled would be higher paid than other blue-collar workers even in the absence of unionism implies further that unionism benefits "labor's elite" at the expense of those with less skill and earning power. Since many people have supported unions in the belief that they reduce economic inequality, evidence that unions have the opposite effect would be a strong argument against the union movement.

The voice/response face suggests very different effects. Given that union decisions are based on a political process in which the majority rules, and given that the majority of workers are likely to have earnings below average in any workplace, unions can be expected to seek to reduce wage inequality within firms. Furthermore, union members are also likely to favor a less-dispersed distribution of earnings for reasons of ideology and organizational solidarity. Finally, to reduce managerial discretion in the wage-setting process, unions seek equal pay for workers in the same job rather than pay according to the manager's perception of individual merit.

Social Organization

I do hold that large and powerful labor unions are integral elements in a total institutional complex whose development is everywhere antithetical to eco-nomic freedom, to political liberty, and to world peace.[20]

In the last analysis the major thrust of labor's activities has been to increase the political participation of poorer segments of society and to provide a coordinated and coherent political voice to workers who would otherwise be largely disorganized. Whatever one may think of the political platform that results from this activity, it is hard to deny the value of these endeavors in a democratic society. It is precisely because issues of policy are so often controversial that the nation has based its system of government on the vote of all interested members. Under these circumstances, one can hardly disapprove of the efforts of any organization to broaden the participation of all interested groups in the political process.[21]

The monopoly critique of unions as social organizations is harsh. It holds that much of union monopoly power arises from the coercive and potentially violent acts of union activists to disrupt production through strikes and related activity. Some claim that the essence of union monopoly power is the power of forcefully preventing nonunion workers from obtaining jobs at organized plants and of coercing workers to join in strikes.[22] Monopoly power is also said to foster corruption and undemocratic behavior and to lead to high dues or entry fees, so that the dominant faction in the union reaps the rewards of the union's market power. In addition, it is believed that unions use their control over the supply of labor to extort funds from firms—especially small, weak ones. The archetypical union in this view is a gangster-ridden Teamsters local. In the political sphere, unions reveal their monopoly face through efforts to obtain special-interest legislation that strengthens union power to extract monopoly gains. The prime lobbying activity of unions, often in alliance with business, is to obtain governmental regulations that restrict competition and raise prices and wages for the sector, at the expense of consumers.

The voice/response view is that unions are democratic institutions operating on behalf of their members and that their political activities are part-and-parcel of modern democratic states. Unions are expected to be democratic because they require the approval of a majority of workers, who elect the leadership and determine policy through conventions, referenda, or change of leadership. In the United States, both union constitutions and the law, particularly the Landrum-Griffin Act (1959), require unions to operate under democratic rules. The union is often said to represent its "median" member, since in a political organization the views of the median person will, under some circumstances, dominate. Within the political sphere, unions are viewed as representing the general working population, devoting much political muscle to promoting legislation that would be of no more material gain to unionized workers than to other workers. For instance, organized labor was active in pushing for the passage of the Public Accommodation Act of 1964, the Voting Rights Act of 1965, equal-employment-opportunity legislation, anti-poverty legislation, and the Occupational Safety and Health Act of 1971. It is argued that though unions fight for self-interest legislation—as do other groups in our pluralistic society —they have scored their greatest political victories on more general social legislation and thus are more effective as a voice of the whole working population and the disadvantaged than as a vehicle for increasing the power of a monopoly institution.

The Debate

Social analysts who focus on only one of unionism's two faces have strikingly different pictures of the institution. According to those who see only the monopoly face, unions are undesirable impediments to the social good; according to those who see only the voice/response face, unions make many valuable contributions to the functioning of the economy. Those in the first camp hail the decline, from the 1950s through the 1980s, in the percentage of wage and salary workers unionized in the private sector in the United States as a desirable development that will increase productivity and reduce inequality. Those in the second camp view the dwindling of private-sector unionization as an

18

undesirable development with serious negative economic and social consequences.

Since, in fact, unions have both a monopoly and a voice/response face, the key questions for understanding the impact of private-sector unionism in the United States relate to the relative importance of each. Are unions primarily monopolistic institutions, or are they primarily voice institutions that induce socially beneficial responses? What emphasis should be given to these two disparate faces to obtain a realistic portrait of the role trade unionism plays in society?

The Study and Its Findings

To answer these questions, we have studied a wide variety of data that distinguish between union and nonunion establishments and between union and nonunion workers, and we have interviewed representatives of management, labor officials, and industrial-relations experts. Although additional study will certainly alter some of the specifics, we believe that the results of our analysis provide a reasonably clear and accurate picture of what unions do—a picture that stands in sharp contrast to the negative view that unions do little more than win monopoly wage gains for their members.

Our most far-reaching conclusion is that, in addition to well-advertised effects on wages, unions alter nearly every other measurable aspect of the operation of workplaces and enterprises, from turnover to productivity to profitability to the composition of pay packages. The behavior of workers and firms and the outcomes of their interactions differ substantially between the organized and unorganized sectors. On balance, unionization appears to improve rather than to harm the social and economic system. In terms of the three outcomes in table 1–1, our analysis shows that unions are associated with greater efficiency in most settings, reduce overall earnings inequality, and contribute to, rather than detract from, economic and political freedom. This is not to deny the negative monopoly effects of unions. They exist. They are undesirable. But they are not the only ways in which unions affect the society. Our analysis indicates that, in fact, focusing on them leads to an exceedingly inaccurate representation of what unions do. In the United States in the period we have studied, the voice/response face of unions dominates the monopoly face, though we stress that an accurate portrait must show both faces.

Following is a capsule summary of the more specific findings that underlie this broad conclusion:

1. On the wage side, unions have a substantial monopoly wage impact, but there is no single union/nonunion wage differential. The union wage effect is greater for less educated than more educated workers, for younger than for prime-age workers, and for junior than for senior workers, and it is greater in heavily organized industries and in regulated industries than in others. It increased in the 1970s as unionized workers won wage gains exceeding those of their nonunion peers. Most importantly, the social costs of the monopoly wage gains of unionism appear to be relatively modest, on the order of .3 percent of gross national product, or less.

2. In addition to raising wages, unions alter the entire package of compensation, substantially increasing the proportion of compensation allotted to fringe benefits, particularly to deferred benefits such as pensions and life, accident and health insurance, which are favored by older workers. These changes are, on balance, to be viewed as a social plus.

3. The claim that unions increase wage inequality is not true. It is true that unions raise the wages of organized blue-collar workers relative to the wages of unorganized blue-collar workers, and thus increase that aspect of inequality. But they also raise blue-collar earnings relative to the higher white-collar earnings, thus reducing inequality between those groups. Moreover, by adopting pay policies that limit managerial discretion in wage-setting, they reduce inequality among workers in the same establishments and among different establishments. Quantitatively, the inequality-reducing effects of unionism outweigh the inequality-increasing effects, so that on balance unions are a force for equality in the distribution of wages among individual workers.

4. By providing workers with a voice in determining rules and conditions of work, by instituting grievance and arbitration procedures for appealing supervisors' decisions, and by negotiating seniority clauses desired by workers, unionism greatly reduces the probability that work-

ers will quit their jobs. As a result, unionized work forces are more stable than nonunion workforces paid the same compensation.

5. Unionism alters the way in which firms respond to swings in the economy. In cyclical downturns, unionized firms make more use of temporary layoffs and less use of cuts in wage growth than do nonunion firms, while in cyclical upturns, unionized firms recall relatively more workers and nonunion firms tend to hire new employees. In a decline that threatens the jobs of senior employees, unions negotiate wage and work-rule concessions of substantial magnitudes.

6. Union workplaces operate under rules that are both different from and more explicit than nonunion workplaces. Seniority is more important in union settings, with unionized senior workers obtaining relatively greater protection against job loss and relatively greater chance of promotion than nonunion senior workers. In addition, management in union companies generally operates more "by the book," with less subjectivity and also less flexibility, than does management in nonunion companies, and in more professional, less paternalistic or authoritarian ways.

7. Some nonunion workers, namely those in large nonunion firms that are trying to avoid unions through "positive labor relations," obtain higher wages and better working conditions as a result of the existence of trade unions. The average employed nonunion blue-collar worker may enjoy a slight increase in well-being because the threat of unionism forces his or her firm to offer better wages and work conditions, but the average white-collar worker appears essentially unaffected by the existence of blue-collar unionization. Some workers, however, may suffer from greater joblessness as a result of higher union wages in their city or their industry.

8. Paradoxically, while unionized workers are less willing to leave their employers than nonunion workers, unionized workers often report themselves less satisfied with their jobs than nonunion workers. Unionists are especially dissatisfied with their work conditions and their relations with supervisors. One explanation is that unions galvanize worker discontent in order to make a strong case in negotiations with management. To be effective, voice must be heard.

9. The view of unions as a major deterrent to productivity is erroneous. In many sectors, unionized establishments are more productive than nonunion establishments, while in only a few are they less produc-

tive. The higher productivity is due in part to the lower rate of turnover under unionism, improved managerial performance in response to the union challenge, and generally cooperative labor-management relations at the plant level. When labor-management relations are bad, so too is productivity in organized plants.

10. Unionized employers tend to earn a lower rate of return per dollar of capital than do nonunion employers. The return is lower under unionism because the increase in wages and the greater amount of capital used per worker are not compensated for by the higher productivity of labor associated with unionism. The reduction in profitability, however, is centered in highly concentrated and otherwise historically highly profitable sectors of the economy.

11. Unions have had mixed success in the political arena. Legislators representing highly unionized districts or receiving considerable union campaign support tend to support unions' political goals in the Congress, but legislators representing less unionized districts or receiving more support from business and other interest groups often oppose union political goals. In the important area of major labor legislation, bills opposed by unions have been enacted while bills favored by unions have been voted down. In general unions have managed to *preserve* laws augmenting monopoly powers in specific sectors but have not been able to use the law to *expand* their monopoly power. Most union political successes have come in the areas of general labor and social goals that benefit workers as a whole rather than unionists alone.

12. The picture of unions as nondemocratic institutions run by corrupt labor bosses is a myth. Most unions are highly democratic, with members having access to union decision-making machinery, especially at the local level. While corruption exists in some unions, its occurrence seems to be highly concentrated in a few industries.

13. The percentage of the U.S. private-sector work force that is in trade unions has declined precipitously since the mid 1950s. The decline is due largely to a dramatic increase in the amount and sophistication of both legal and illegal company actions designed to forestall the organization of workers, and reduced union organizing activity per nonunion worker.

Some of our findings are controversial. They challenge the prevailing negative assessment of the economic and political impact of unions. Not surprisingly, they have engendered considerable critical comment.

It is therefore important to understand the strengths and weaknesses of the evidence on which they are based.

The distinctive feature of the evidence presented in this book is that it is derived largely from quantitative analyses of data from many sources. Some of this information is from samples of thousands of individuals or establishments, some from companies, and some from industries.[23] While labor economists have been using similar data for over a decade to estimate the effect of unions on wages, it is only in the past few years that we and others have used this sort of information to examine the effects of unions on the nonwage outcomes central to the voice/response face of unionism.

Quantitative analysis of computer data files of the type we have undertaken has the advantage of providing numerical estimates of the magnitude of union effects and of covering a sufficiently large number of workers and firms to permit generalizations about overall economic effects. Analysis of this sort also has problems, however, and we believe the problems should not be concealed by the quantity of the output.

The chief difficulty with our (and other social scientists') quantitative analysis is that the data we study are not generated by an "ideal" experiment in which we have altered one factor while holding all else of relevance fixed. (In the case of unionism, such an ideal experiment would involve unionizing a randomly chosen individual, establishment, or industry while allowing no other relevant changes to occur, and observing the resultant outcomes.) Rather than coming from such a controlled experiment, our data are based on either comparisons of union/nonunion individuals or firms at a moment in time (cross-sectional analyses) or comparisons of the persons or firms as they change union status over time (before/after, or longitudinal, analyses). Both comparisons are imperfect, for several reasons. First, despite our statistical efforts not *all* other relevant factors are held fixed. Second, our variables invariably suffer from measurement error because of faulty responses, coding mistakes, key punch mistakes, and the like. And third, individuals or firms with similar measured characteristics are unlikely to be unionized on a random basis. If individual or firm X gets organized and individual or firm Y does not, there is probably some difference between them that explains their different unionization history. This uncaptured "pre-union difference" may explain part of the outcome difference that we attribute to unionism.

The problem of controlling for all relevant factors except the one under investigation is particularly severe when we try to estimate the voice/response effects of unionism, because these effects are presumed to operate on top of, or in addition to, the monopoly effects. When the two effects operate in the same direction, failure to control adequately for the monopoly impact of unionism can lead to an erroneous conclusion that union-nonunion differences are due to voice/response rather than to monopoly behavior. For instance, we expect the higher wages that unions win for workers to reduce quits, and we also expect the greater voice that unions win for workers to reduce quits. To isolate the reduction in quits due to voice/response, we must accurately measure the reduction in quits due to monopoly wage gains. If we do not, estimates of the union voice-induced reduction in quits may be illusory, the result of poor statistical experiments rather than the reflection of true behavior.

How did we deal with these problems?

First, we based our conclusions on comparisons of persons or establishments that are as similar as possible. We did this by performing multivariate statistical analyses in which we controlled for a wide variety of other factors ranging from the demographic characteristics of workers to the industry-occupation-regional locus of jobs. In particular, when studying voice/response effects, we always tried to control for the union wage effect and all reactions to it.

Second, we used as many different data sets and types of data as possible. If one survey lacked a certain control, we sought others which contained it. While we could not replicate experiments as natural scientists do, we could perform the same basic analysis on several different data sets, obtained from different samples, by different sampling procedures, and with different survey instruments.

Third, we performed various statistical checks on our findings, which allowed us to estimate how much results might vary if some variables were, say, better measured, or if one had information on factors not available in a particular data set.

Fourth, we conducted special small surveys designed to obtain answers to specific questions which could not be addressed with existing information.

Finally, we discussed our results with labor, management, and neutral participants in industrial relations and compared our statistical findings with their perceptions and with the findings of case studies. These efforts to prune our statistical results of potential biases do not, of course, guarantee that all our findings are correct: some certainly are, while others unfortunately may not be. The most we hope is that our overall assessment of unionism as an institution with important voice/-response as well as monopoly wage effects is close to the mark.

In the remainder of this book, after briefly setting out in chapter 2 the institutional background of the American industrial relations system, we present the detailed results of our new empirical analysis of unions. Chapters 3–5 focus on what unions do to the level, composition, and distribution of compensation. Chapters 6–10 turn to what unions do to various nonwage outcomes: labor turnover and the attachment of workers to firms, cyclical work force adjustments, work rules, and job satisfaction, and examines the potential spillover of union gains to nonunion workers. Chapters 11–14 analyze what unions do to the "bottom line" economic outcomes of productivity and profitability, and to the "bottom line" social outcomes of internal union affairs and national economic legislation. Chapter 15 examines the ongoing decline in unionism in the United States. Finally, chapter 16 seeks to construct a whole from the preceding parts. It contrasts the voice/response and monopoly effects of unionism to reach an overall quantitative assessment of the benefits and costs of what unions do.

CHAPTER 2

U.S. Industrial Relations: The Figures and the Settings

WHO IS UNIONIZED in the United States? Where do union members work? What kinds of jobs do they hold?

Who are the unions? What are the activities of different levels of union organization? How important are the AFL-CIO, national unions, and local unions in collective bargaining? What are the important management and government organizations in the labor sector?

Before evaluating what unions do, we must understand the structure of the labor movement, the interaction of management with worker organizations, and the involvement of government in private-sector industrial relations.

The Union Members

About one out of every five private-sector wage and salaried workers is unionized. However, as table 2–1 indicates, this fifth does not reflect a random draw from the workforce; some types of workers are highly unionized, while others are scarcely organized at all. In particular, the probability that a worker will be a union member is greater if that worker is male, nonwhite, over twenty-five years old, with no formal schooling beyond high school, living outside the south, and employed

TABLE 2-1
Who Belongs to Unions?

Percentage of private-sector wage and salary employees who belong to a labor union or association similar to a labor union

	All Workers (%)	Blue-Collar Workers[a] (%)	White-Collar Workers[b] (%)
All employees	20	30	9
Sex			
Male	27	37	10
Female	11	17	8
Race			
White	20	30	8
Nonwhite	27	31	17
Age			
Under 25	12	25	7
25–44	23	37	9
45–54	27	42	10
55 or over	22	34	10
Education			
Less than high school graduate	23	25	11
High school graduate, no post–high school education	25	38	11
Some post–high school education	13	29	7
Region			
Northeast	24	38	11
Central	25	38	9
South	13	18	5
West	22	30	11
Industry			
Agriculture, forestry, and fisheries	3	3	2
Mining	34	47	7
Construction	32	36	12
Manufacturing	34	45	10
Transportation, communication, and other public utilities	48	61	33
Wholesale and retail trade	10	14	6
Finance, insurance and real estate	4	17	3
Services	7	9	9

SOURCE: May 1977 Current Population Survey conducted by the Bureau of Labor Statistics (see appendix).
[a]Blue-collar workers include those in the following occupations: craftsmen and kindred workers; operatives; nonfarm laborers; private household workers; all other service workers; and farm laborers and foremen.
[b]White-collar workers include those in these occupations: professional, technical and kindred workers; managers and administrators (except farm); sales workers; clerical and kindred workers; and farmers and farm managers.

in a blue-collar job, in transportation, mining, manufacturing, or construction.

What accounts for these differences?

Male versus Female Workers

The low rate of unionization of women does not seem to be due largely to differences between men and women in their desire for unions. When asked if they would vote for a union if a union representation election were held with secret ballots, female nonunion workers were more likely to state that they would vote for a union than were male nonunion employees (see table 2–2). This fact is consistent with analyses of actual voting behavior in union representation elections, which show that female voters are at least as likely to vote "union" as are their male counterparts.[1]

What, then, explains the low female unionization rate? A key reason is that women tend to be in sectors of the economy—industries, occupations, and firms—where unionization is, for whatever reason, below average. Statistically, if we limit our comparisons to individuals working in the same sized firm in the same industry and occupation, the difference in unionization rates between men and women is reduced by over 60 percent (from 16 to 6 percentage points). If we further control for job tenure, on the assumption that workers whose length of service tends to be below average are less likely to expend time and effort to organize their workplaces, the lower tenure of women explains an additional part of the differential. Finally, because some of the fringe benefits won by unions are less valuable to women than to men—for example, health insurance (because many women already receive their benefits as a result of their husbands' pay package)—another part of the remaining membership differential can be attributed to differences in the relative need for fringes of men and of women. When we compare workers who are similar in all the characteristics already mentioned, and who are covered by retirement and health insurance plans, the initial 16 percentage point differential in membership is reduced to a bare 3 percentage points. In total, over 80 percent of the male-female differential in unionization appears due to differences in the characteristics of the jobs held by men and by women and in the economic interests of each group, rather than to any innately lower desire for union membership by females.[2]

TABLE 2–2

Who Wants Unions?

Percentage of private-sector wage and salary *nonrepresented* employees who answered "For" to the question: "If an election were held with secret ballots, would you vote for or against having a union or employees' association represent you?"

	All Workers (%)	Blue-Collar Workers[a] (%)	White-Collar Workers[a] (%)
All nonrepresented employees	33	39	28
Sex			
Male	27	35	20
Female	41	46	38
Race			
White	29	34	26
Nonwhite	69	70	67
Age			
Under 25	40	45	36
25–44	32	42	26
45–54	26	31	24
55 or over	31	28	33
Region			
Northeast	37	37	38
Central	26	28	24
South	35	46	25
West	32	38	29
Industry			
Agriculture, forestry and fisheries	7	10	0
Mining	16	21	0
Construction	22	24	18
Manufacturing	36	46	21
Transportation, communication, and other public utilities	22	35	12
Wholesale and retail trade	34	44	27
Finance, insurance, and real estate	31	40	30
Services	37	38	37

SOURCE: Quality of Employment Survey, 1977, conducted by the Institute for Social Research, University of Michigan (see appendix). Questions asked only of nonrepresented employees.
[a]See table 2–1 for definitions of blue- and white-collar workers.

Nonwhite versus White Workers

While it is common to portray unionism as a barrier to black economic advancement, nonwhite workers are substantially more likely to be union members than white workers; in 1977, 27 percent of nonwhite workers compared with 20 percent of white workers were in unions. The major reason for this is the disproportionate representation of nonwhites in blue-collar jobs (61 percent of nonwhite workers compared to 46 percent of white workers in 1977). If whites were represented in blue-collar jobs to the same extent as nonwhites but maintained their own unionization rates within blue- and white-collar jobs, half of the nonwhite-white unionization differential would disappear.[3] One reason for the remaining half is that nonwhite white-collar workers are relatively highly unionized (see table 2–1).

Nonwhite workers not only are more likely to be union members than white workers but are more likely to want to be union if they are not. As table 2–2 shows, the percentage of unorganized blue-collar workers saying they would vote "union" was 70 percent for nonwhites versus 34 percent for whites; among white-collar workers, the comparable percentages were 67 versus 26. Moreover, analysis of votes in union representation elections indicates that the probability of a black actually voting "union" is substantially higher than that of a comparable white.[4]

The high proportion of blacks in organized labor suggests that union advances are especially likely to benefit blacks, as has been recognized by some black leaders. Norman Hill, Executive Director of the Philip Randolph Institute, a leading center for black trade union studies, has said that blacks "have long understood trade unionism: they know it pays—and pays handsomely—to have a union card."[5]

Older versus Younger Workers

Like women, young workers are less likely to be union members largely because of the kinds of jobs they hold. First, younger workers often work in temporary jobs in what has come to be called "the secondary labor market," where workers perform relatively low-skill tasks for short periods of time before moving on to other jobs. Nonunion McDonald's is such an employer: behind its golden arches it employs more youths than any other U.S. company. A second factor is that since the mid-1950s the traditionally unionized sectors of the economy have grown less rapidly than the nonunion sectors. Growing sectors generally hire relatively young workers, whereas declining sectors tend to retain relatively old workers. For example, one of the rapidly growing areas of employment from 1960 to 1980 was the weakly unionized business- and repair-service sector, where the average age of male workers was 36.4 in 1970. By contrast, the highly unionized railroad and railway express industry grew slowly from 1960 to 1980; here, the average age of male workers was 47.3 years in 1970.[6] The same pattern is found even in areas of traditional union strength, where newer establishments, which tend to have younger labor forces than older establishments, are more likely to be nonunion.

The low rate of unionization among the young does not, however, mean that younger workers want unions to a lesser extent than do older workers. As table 2–2 shows, young unrepresented workers are somewhat more likely to say they would vote for a union than would older unrepresented workers. Consistent with this finding, analyses of hypothetical and actual representation-election voting indicate that younger workers are *more* likely to be pro-union than their older colleagues, even when other things, including wages, are held constant. Unionization is low among young workers because of the jobs they hold, not because they are averse to unionism.[7]

Non-Southern versus Southern Workers

There is substantial geographic variation in unionization in the United States, with the proportion unionized greatest in the central and northeastern states, and least in the South. The strikingly lower rate of unionization in the South undoubtedly has a wide variety of causes. Most analysts, however, would probably agree with former Secretary of Labor F. Ray Marshall that "the prime reason is employer and community opposition to unions."[8] While there are areas of union strength in the South, and while southern nonunion workers evince as much interest in unionism as other nonunion workers (see table 2–2), the archetypical story of the union organizer being run out of town by the local sheriff is not a myth. Indicative of attitudes in the South is the greater prevalence of "right-to-work" laws in southern states. These laws, which forbid labor and management from agreeing on contracts that require all workers to become dues-paying union members within a specified time period after employment, have been passed in eleven of seventeen southern states, but only four of thirteen western states and five of twelve central states. One result of the laws is that 20 percent of southern workers whose wages and working conditions are set by collective bargaining are not union members, whereas only 6 percent of workers covered by collective contracts outside the South are not members.[9]

Blue-collar versus White-Collar Workers

As table 2–1 indicates, blue-collar workers are much more likely to be union members than are white-collar workers. Much, but not all, of this differential can be explained by the fact that white-collar workers are less inclined to want unionization than are blue-collar workers (see table 2–2). Why is this the case? Part of the reason is that white-collar workers have less need for unions than do blue-collar workers, since they usually receive higher pay, have more freedom on the job, and have more job security. Another reason is that 20 percent of all white-collar workers are managers, officials, or proprietors and hence not covered by the National Labor Relations Act. Finally, a larger percentage of white-collar than of blue-collar workers identify with their profession rather than with their employer and rely on mobility rather than voice to obtain desired conditions.

While white-collar workers are less likely to seek unionization, the recent success of unions in organizing teachers and university professors, largely in the public sector, and the longstanding accomplishment of such unionlike organizations as the American Medical Association, one of the most powerful craft organizations in the United States, show that "white collar" does not mean "unorganizable."

Goods-Producing Workers versus Other Workers

The proportion of workers organized in the United States varies substantially among industries. It is high in most goods-producing industries, such as manufacturing, mining, and construction; it is low in most non-goods-producing industries, such as finance, insurance, real estate, services, and trade, with transportation a notable and important exception. Table 2–3 demonstrates that the degree of unionism is strongly related to certain industrial characteristics. In the economy as a whole, industries with higher-than-average rates of unionization are also industries with larger-than-average companies and work sites. Within manufacturing, the more highly unionized industries are also characterized by greater amounts of capital per worker and are more likely to be dominated by a small number of large firms. The tendency for unionism to proliferate in sectors with certain technological and market characteristics implies that workers' needs for unionism, management's opposition to it, and unions' efforts to extend it are not

TABLE 2–3

The Industrial Characteristics of Highly and Lowly Unionized Industries

	Nonagricultural Private Sector	
	Low-Unionization Industries (0 to 18% covered)	*High-Unionization Industries (18% or more covered)*
Industry Average of:		
Number of employees in company (in 1979)	569	1,118
Number of employees at work site (in 1979)	204	540

	Manufacturing Sector	
	Low-Unionization Industries (0 to 36% covered)	*High-Unionization Industries (36% or more covered)*
Industry Average of:		
Number of employees in company (in 1979)	1,144	1,360
Number of employees at work site (in 1979)	548	761
Value of capital per worker (in 1972)	$16,000	$28,000
Percentage of industry shipments by four largest firms (in 1972)	37	46

SOURCE: Based on figures for all employees in 143 industries generated from the May 1979 *Current Population Survey*, conducted by the Bureau of Labor Statistics (BLS); the *1972 Census of Manufacturers*, conducted by the U.S. Department of Commerce; and BLS's figures on plant and equipment in detailed industries in *Capital Stock Estimates for Input-Output Industries: Methods and Data*, Bulletin #2034 (Washington, D.C.: 1979).

random but rather result from fundamental characteristics of these industries.

A Touch of Unionism

To say that only one of five U.S. workers is a union member does not mean that only one of five is in a company that has dealings with a union. In our economic system, firms have many different "businesses" and dozens of establishments throughout the country. With the exception of a very small number of large companies—for example, IBM or

Texas Instruments—that have essentially no unionized workers, and a small number of large enterprises—such as United States Steel or Ford —in which the production workers at all sites are organized, most large companies have some workers at some locations who are covered by collective bargaining and others who are not.

Our estimates indicate that roughly half of private-sector nonagricultural employment (white-collar workers as well as blue-collar workers) is in establishments where a majority of either the production employees or the nonproduction employees are unionized. An additional fraction of the private-sector nonagricultural labor force is employed at the nonunion sites of companies that have some employees covered by collective bargaining. Thus, while only 20 percent of the U.S. work force has joined a union, more than 50 percent work for companies that deal with unions. Since even large companies that deal with no unions whatsoever are aware of what unions do and are often greatly conditioned in their labor relations by the desire to reduce the attractiveness of unionism to their workers, unionism touches many more workers than a simple unionization rate would imply.[10]

Local and National or International Unions

American trade unions are a diverse set of organizations, ranging from local unions to nationals or internationals (which operate in Canada or elsewhere outside the United States) to which most locals belong, to the American Federation of Labor and Congress of Industrial Organizations (AFL-CIO), with which most internationals are affiliated.

At the base of the U.S. union pyramid are about 65,000 locals, many of which represent the employees in one establishment or company, some of which represent those in a given craft, and some of which represent employees in the same industry working for different employers. The majority of the locals are quite small; fewer than 15 percent had more than 500 members in 1966, and in 1982 the average local had 200 members. While often neglected in the public media, the local union is the heart of American unionism. As Estey (University of Pennsylvania) has aptly put it:

The local union reaches the worker "where he's at." The local union is the individual member's point of direct contact with his or her union; its performance is the basis on which the worker judges not only the local but perhaps the national union and the labor movement as a whole.[11]

Local unions play a significant role in collective bargaining, with many contracts signed between a single local and management or between an amalgamation of the locals of a multi-plant enterprise and representatives from management. In many unions, moreover, full agreement between management and labor requires not only an overall national or master contract between the union and the employer(s) but also local agreements designed to deal with the problems and needs at specific sites.

Equally important is the day-to-day role of the local as the voice vehicle at the work place; it is the local with its shop stewards and committeemen or women, or its business agent, that has the responsibility for monitoring the administration of the collective agreement. In particular, the local operates the grievance machinery by which workers may complain about matters that arise in the course of the business day.

Virtually all local unions are part of international unions. In 1980 there were 168 internationals, each a federation of locals normally in the same industry (Automobile Workers) or trade (Bricklayers, Masons, and Plasterers). Table 2–4 shows the membership in the largest national and international unions in 1980. The biggest union in the United States, the Teamsters, claimed 1,891,000 members. Six internationals had at least a million members, twelve had at least 500,000, and forty-four had more than 100,000. In that year, the six largest unions had 37 percent of the country's total union membership and the ten largest had 50 percent. The number of internationals has been declining since the 1970s, though not at a steady pace, with several important unions merging to form unified groups. In 1953, for example, in the retail food sector there were three sizable internationals: the Packinghouse Workers, the Amalgamated Butchers, and the Retail Clerks International Union; in 1981, as a result of mergers, there was one single large international, the United Food and Commercial Workers International Union.[12]

There appears to be a slow but steady trend toward increased concentration of union membership in the larger internationals. In 1948–50,

TABLE 2–4

The Major National or International Unions in 1980[a]

Union	Membership
Teamsters (Ind.)	1,891,000
United Auto Workers	1,357,000
United Food and Commercial Workers	1,300,000
United Steelworkers	1,238,000
State, County, and Municipal Employees	1,098,000
International Brotherhood of Electrical Workers	1,041,000
United Brotherhood of Carpenters and Joiners	789,000
International Association of Machinists	754,000
Service Employees International	650,000
Laborers' International	650,000
Communications Workers	551,000
American Federation of Teachers	551,000
Association	
National Education Association (Ind.)	1,684,000

SOURCE: Membership data courtesy of George Rubin, Bureau of Labor Statistics (phone interview, 20 April, 1982). The figures will appear in *Directory of National Unions and Employer Associations, 1981* (Washington, D.C.: Department of Labor, Bureau of Labor Statistics, forthcoming).
[a]All organizations not identified as "Ind." are affiliated with the AFL-CIO.

25 percent of all union members in the private sector were in the five largest unions; in 1962, 30 percent of private-sector members were in the five largest unions; and in 1974, 34 percent were. Part of the increased concentration results from the amalgamation of smaller unions into larger unions, but the bulk of the trend reflects a very different and important pattern—the movement of internationals once concentrated in relatively few industries or crafts into diverse parts of the economy, a diversification not unlike that found among companies. As a result, about two-thirds of the members of the United Steelworkers work outside of steel, employed in 1974 in as many as twenty-eight different "3-digit" manufacturing industries (out of a possible 143); the United Automobile Workers had members in twenty industries of the set of 143; the Machinists had members in eighteen, and the Teamsters in eleven.[13] The Teamsters' efforts to organize any and all workers regardless of activities is indicative of the changed views of many (though not all) unions with respect to jurisdiction.

While local unions are the primary voice of organized labor within plants, international unions are often important in collective bargaining and wage determination. When a market is national or international, with output produced in one plant competing with that produced in other plants, independent bargaining by individual locals would lose unions their monopoly power, as locals would compete for jobs through lower wages. Local A might agree to accept a wage cut to increase employment at its plant, but this would force local B to follow suit. The result would be a reduction in wages to more or less competitive levels. Hence international unions seek industry-wide wage agreements, either through bargaining with an employer association, as in steel or coal, or through "pattern bargaining," in which locals in one firm follow a pattern set in other firms. Only in industries where the market is basically local do international unions have little impact on wage-setting.

The existence of several international unions in the same industry permits one to see if different unions do different things in the same setting. That is, it is possible to discern whether or not there is such a thing as a "Teamster" contract or an "Autoworkers" contract or a "Steelworkers" contract that to some extent transcends the industry itself. Evidence suggests that in fact, on some aspects of collective agreements such as their duration, the union signing the contract is more important than the industry. Indeed, industrial relations experts have documented the efforts of the United Autoworkers to extend the auto contract into non-auto, but related, industries, such as agricultural implements; the Rubberworkers' attempts to negotiate tire contracts with the non-tire businesses of the tire companies; and the Steelworkers' negotiating in the basic steel, aluminum, and can industries of contracts that are much more related to each other than economic conditions would predict.[14]

The Federation

At the summit of the U.S. union movement is the AFL-CIO. The Federation is a voluntary association whose 102 international unions represent about 70 percent of the total American union membership. Most of the other 30 percent are members of large and powerful unions that have, at various times, been affiliated with the AFL-CIO, in particular the Teamsters (with 1,891,000 members) and the United Mine Workers (with 308,000), or of the National Education Association, which has never been affiliated.[15]

While much public attention is focused on the AFL-CIO, the Federation is not directly active in the negotiation and administration of collective bargaining contracts. The principal role of the AFL-CIO is to serve as the voice of labor in the political sphere, which it does through political action in elections and through lobbying. While at one time the union movement believed in "voluntarism," eschewing political activity of all sorts, trade unions now make a major effort to influence the political process through the AFL-CIO and also through internationals and organizations of locals at city and state levels. The Federation's Committee on Political Education (COPE) raises money and mobilizes bodies in an effort to elect representatives attuned to labor's interests. The AFL-CIO legislative branch, centered in Washington, D.C., plays an important lobbying role, as do the officials of many internationals.

Overall, the structure of the U.S. labor movement seems to yield the institutional apparatus necessary for unions to have both monopoly wage and voice/response effects. The structure provides members with protection at their workplaces and channels through which information can pass from the workforce to management (locals), bargaining agents able to exploit monopoly power across plants (internationals), and well-situated political spokespersons (the federation).

Management Organizations

The bargaining settings in which management faces unions in the U.S. are diverse, ranging from situations that pit a union against a single employer—in many cases at a single plant—to multi-employer bargaining. As table 2–5 shows, single-employer bargaining units are common in manufacturing. In chemicals, for instance, bargaining for nearly 90 percent of workers covered under major agreements is between a union and an employer at a single plant. In transportation equipment, the predominant relationship is between a union and a single company,

TABLE 2–5

Percentage Distribution of Bargaining Units in Major
Agreements, 1980

	Percentage of Total Agreements	Percentage of Total Workers
Manufacturing	48.4	45.9
Single-employer	41.6	39.1
Single-plant	25.6	15.3
Multi-plant	16.0	23.8
Multi-employer	6.8	6.8
Nonmanufacturing	51.6	54.1
Single-employer	18.0	17.8
Single-plant	4.1	2.1
Multi-plant	13.9	15.7
Multi-employer	33.6	36.3
Total	100.0	100.0
Single-employer	59.6	56.9
Single-plant	29.7	17.4
Multi-plant	29.9	39.5
Multi-employer	40.4	43.1

SOURCE: *Characteristics of Major Collective Bargaining Agreements, January 1, 1980* (Washington, D.C.: Department of Labor, Bureau of Labor Statistics, 1981), 19.

with local supplementary contracts at each of its plants. Since employers and unions bargain with knowledge of the contracts elsewhere in their sector and in the economy as a whole, however, one should not regard single-employer settlements as independent events. In fact, in many instances, agreements are very closely linked to one another through "pattern bargaining"—that is, the explicit copying of one contract by many employers and unions.[16]

Outside of manufacturing, multi-employer bargaining is more common. In a multi-employer situation, a single union (or a group of unions) faces an employer association across the bargaining table. While employer associations have rarely received the press given to unions, they are an important factor in determining what unions do. Associations of employers often form as a countervailing force to strong unions that threaten to "whipsaw" employers into unfavorable agreements. It is no accident that the principal associations in collective bargaining are found in industries such as construction, garment manufacturing, trucking, and coal where large national unions face many

39

small enterprises. Table 2–6 lists some of the major associations involved in collective bargaining and the unions with whom they negotiate.

In the political sphere, there are also numerous employer associations that often oppose the desires of the AFL-CIO and the labor movement in general; these associations raise political campaign funds and lobby. At the national level, the National Association of Manufacturers (NAM) is perhaps the major employer group engaged in political action involving labor relations. The NAM has often opposed unionism throughout this century, most recently with its "Council for a Union-Free Environment." The United States Chamber of Commerce is another national employers' association whose activities include lobbying for business interests. A newer group, composed of the chief executive officers of some of the nation's largest corporations, is the Business

TABLE 2–6

Examples of Major National Employer Associations in Various Sectors

Sector Association	Principal Unions Dealt With
Building Construction	
Associated General Contractors (AGC)	Carpenters, Laborers, Operating Engineers, Teamsters, Ironworkers
Associated Builders and Contractors (ABC)	None: nonunion contracting group
Industrial Construction	
National Constructors Association (NCA)	Pipefitters, Electricians, Ironworkers, Boilermakers, Carpenters, Laborers
Trucking	
Trucking Management, Inc. (TMI)	Teamsters
Coal	
Bituminous Coal Owners Association (BCOA)	United Mine Workers, Operating Engineers
Hospitals	
League of Voluntary Hospitals (New York Group)	District 1199 of the National Union of Hospital and Health Care Employees
Steel	
"Group of Four" (nine firms)	United Steelworkers

SOURCE: Information for all industries but steel is from Gerald G. Somers, ed., *Collective Bargaining: Contemporary American Experience* (Madison, Wis.: Industrial Relations Research Association, 1980), as follows: D. Quinn Mills, "Construction," pp. 64–65; Harold M. Levinson, "Trucking," pp. 103–6; William H. Miernyk, "Coal," p. 2 and pp. 14–16; Richard U. Miller, "Hospitals," pp. 400–403 and pp. 411–13. Information on the steel industry is from D. Quinn Mills, *Labor-Management Relations* (New York: McGraw-Hill, 1982), pp. 465–66.

40

Roundtable. In addition, there are dozens of other employer associations or employer-supported groups in the area of labor relations, such as the National Right to Work Committee, the United States Industrial Council, the Center on National Labor Policy, and the National Labor Management Foundation.[17]

In short, just as workers organize into unions to enhance their power in both economic and political forums, employers organize into associations for the same purposes.

Government Agencies

What unions do cannot be understood without some familiarity with the government agencies charged with upholding the two most important laws regulating unions and unionism, the Taft-Hartley Act of 1947 (which amended the National Labor Relations Act of 1935) and the Landrum-Griffin Act of 1959.

The first, and perhaps most important, governmental regulatory agency is the National Labor Relations Board (NLRB), whose primary responsibilities are to run representation elections, in which workers vote whether or not to be represented by unions, and to investigate noncompliance with the labor law. A second important organization is the Federal Mediation and Conciliation Service (FMCS), which assists managements and unions by mediating labor disputes in order to prevent or settle strikes. Third, there is the Department of Labor (DOL), charged with, among other things, administering the Landrum-Griffin Act, which concerns itself with the issues of democracy and corruption in unions.[18]

The way in which the various federal agencies administer the "rules of the game" depends, of course, on the interpretation of the law by the judiciary. Indeed, one frequently heard complaint about American industrial relations is that NLRB interpretations of the law typically change with political administrations, being more favorable to business when Republicans are in power and more favorable to labor when Democrats are in power. Studies of administration of the laws shows that this complaint is quite valid.[19] Another quite different complaint is that agencies regulating labor-management relations typically try only to rectify the harm caused by an illegal action and rarely penalize the guilty party by imposing costs (in the form of fines or imprisonment) beyond the cost of returning things to what they would have been in the absence of the illegal action. Breaking the labor law does not invoke the same sanctions as does breaking other national laws.

Finally, it should be noted that most states have state labor relations boards, labor departments, and mediation agencies that parallel the federal agencies and play an important role in government activities in labor-management relations.

Summary

In this chapter we have sketched the various figures and settings that are central in U.S. industrial relations. What unions do in a free enterprise economy depends greatly upon how these figures interact in the various settings discussed. The remainder of the book presents the outcomes of these interactions.

CHAPTER 3

The Union Wage Effect

EVERYONE "KNOWS" that unions raise wages. The questions are how much, under what conditions, and with what effects on the overall performance of the economy.

How Much Do Unions Raise Wages?

Studies of the magnitude of union wage effects have a long history.[1] At various times observers have expressed fears that the impact of union monopoly power on wages would be so high as to be "an attack on the competitive system" (Lindblom), "the rock on which our present system is most likely to crack up" (Simons), or "the most important domestic economic problem" (Haberler).[2] However, empirical estimates and historical experience have shown such fears to be groundless.

The early work on union wage gains made extensive use of data on the wages of groups of workers in different industries, occupations, and/or areas. Some studies compared the wage of union workers with the wage of nonunion workers, but most of the early work used a more indirect procedure, estimating the effect of unions on wages by comparing *average* wages for more organized groups of workers with average wages for less organized groups, attributing the difference in wages to the extent of organization. If, for example, all else the same, a sector that was 80 percent organized paid $4.00 in wages while a sector that was 30 percent organized paid $3.50 in wages, the analysis yields an estimate of the effect of unionism of 1 cent per percentage point organized ($4.00 − $3.50)/(80% − 30%). This estimate in turn implies that the difference between the wages of a completely unionized sector and one that was completely nonunion would be $1.00, producing a 33 percent ($1.00/$3.00) "union wage effect." The reason for this procedure was that data on the wages of unionized versus nonunionized individuals or establishments was neither available nor, given the state of technology, readily amenable to statistical analysis.

Much of the early work on union wage gains was summarized in 1963 in an influential book by H. Gregg Lewis, then at the University of Chicago. In capsule form, the early work found a union wage effect of 10–15% on average, with considerable variation over time and among different groups of workers. The union impact appeared to decline during inflationary periods and to rise during recessions. It was high for such workers as airline pilots, coal miners, and skilled construction workers, and low for such workers as unskilled laborers and employees in competitive industries like men's clothing.[3]

As noted in chapter 1, the computerized-data revolution has provided economists with massive bodies of information on thousands of individuals and firms and thus has yielded more sophisticated and detailed analyses of union wage effects. The new data on individuals enables analysts to compare the wages of union and nonunion workers with similar demographic characteristics working in the same industry, occupation and area. The new data on establishments enables analysts to compare the wages of union and nonunion establishments in the same industry and area and with the same number of employees. In addition to the cross-sectional data, moreover, there is now available new data on workers before and after unionization (longitudinal data), which permit researchers to look at what happens to the wages of an individual upon becoming a union member or upon giving up membership.

Neither the modern cross-sectional nor the before/after studies of union wage effects should be taken as the final word on union impacts. Like virtually all social science investigations, both types of studies suffer from potential "nonexperimental data biases" because neither represents the results of controlled laboratory experiments in which the

44

researcher is, in fact, able to vary one factor (unionism) while holding all else constant.

The often raised problem with the cross-sectional studies is that the comparison of different persons may lead one to misinterpret wage differences as differences due to trade unionism, when they are actually due to differences in the skills and abilities of workers. Because employers are charged more per hour of labor in the union sector than in the nonunion sector, they are likely to hire better workers. If the measures of worker skill and ability in the data are inadequate, then the typical cross-sectional calculation will overstate the union wage effect for workers comparable in all respects other than unionism.[4]

Before-and-after comparisons contrast the same person over time, so they do not suffer from this problem and thus represent a way of eliminating "ability bias." However, they have their own difficulties: by limiting analysis to persons who change union status they lead one to infer union effects from a small sample of persons, some of whom may have changed jobs for special reasons that make them unrepresentative of the average worker. Moreover, to the extent that workers voluntarily change jobs in order to improve their earnings, the before/after comparisons are likely to understate the union wage effect, because workers going from union jobs to nonunion jobs are likely to require as large an improvement in wages as those going in the other direction. When wages are higher under unionism, few persons will voluntarily give up jobs in the union sector, but those who do will, according to this line of reasoning, enjoy wage gains comparable to those of persons moving from nonunion to union jobs, even though unions raise wages. Indeed, workers who obtain union jobs are likely to be especially able and thus especially highly paid in nonunion work and are likely to start at the bottom of the union wage ladder, which will further understate the gain that would be obtained by an *average* worker. Finally, the before/after studies suffer from potential problems in the measurement of a worker's union status, which would lead to an underestimate of the true union effect on wages. The measurement problem occurs because some changes in union membership on a computer tape are likely to result from the miscoding of an employee's union status in one of the two periods.[5]

It is for these reasons that neither cross-sectional nor before/after studies of the impact of unions on wages are perfect. The most that one can hope for is that the two types of analyses yield roughly consistent pictures of what unions do to wages.

Table 3–1 presents estimates of the union wage effect from a variety of data sets for individuals and from one data set for enterprises. To isolate the union impact, the calculations control for many wage-determining factors other than unionism, as noted in the table. The table itself shows that, while estimated union wage effects vary among surveys and groups covered, in all cases unionized labor is substantially more highly paid than nonunionized labor. In the 1970s, the archetypical union wage effect was on the order of 20 to 30 percent.

What about the effects of unions on the wage of the same worker, as he or she changes union status over time? Table 3–2 provides a representative set of estimates of union wage effects from before/after data. The table makes three kinds of comparisons between the changes in the wages for workers who switch union status and those for workers

TABLE 3–1

Estimates of the Impact of Unions on Wages, Using Cross-Section Data

Source of Estimates:	Year	Number of Observations	Approximate Percentage Gain in Wages Due to Collective Bargaining
Data on Individuals			
May Current Population Survey, Bureau of Labor Statistics	1979	16,728	21
Panel Study of Income Dynamics, University of Michigan	1970–79	11,445	26
Older Men, National Longitudinal Survey, Ohio State University	1976	1,922	25
Younger Men, National Longitudinal Survey	1976	2,335	32
Mature Women, National Longitudinal Survey	1977	1,724	25
Younger Women, National Longitudinal Survey	1978	2,068	21
Data on Establishments			
Expenditures for Employee Compensation Survey, Bureau of Labor Statistics	1972–76	15,574	27

SOURCE: Tabulated with the specified data set; see appendix for discussion of each set. Approximate percentage gains were calculated as antilogs of estimated union coefficients in semi-log regression models.

TABLE 3-2

Changes in Wages Associated With Changing Union Status

	Approximate Percentage Change in Wages Associated with Changing Union Status (U = Union, N = Nonunion)		
Data Source (Years)	Workers Joining Unions vs. Workers Remaining Nonunion (NU − NN)	Workers Remaining Union vs. Workers Leaving Unions (UU − UN)	Workers Joining Unions vs. Workers Leaving Unions $\frac{NU - UN}{2}$
1. May Current Population Survey (1974–75), BLS	9.2	8.7	9.6
2. Panel Study of Income Dynamics (1970–79), Michigan	8.3	29.7	15.0
3. National Longitudinal Survey of Men Aged 14–24 in 1966 (1971–78), Ohio State	15.7	10.5	20.3
4. Quality of Employment Survey (1973–77), Michigan	27.6	12.8	21.5

SOURCES: (1) Tabulated from May 1974–75 Matched Current Population Survey file for 7,887 workers with 5,626 NNs, 1,776 UUs, 217 NUs and 266 UNs. (2) Tabulated from Panel Study for 635 workers with 254 NNs, 259 UUs, 62 NUs and 60 UNs. (3) Tabulated from National Longitudinal Survey for Younger Men, for 1,733 workers with 1,034 NNs, 307 UUs, 248 NUs and 144 UNs. (4) Tabulated from Quality of Employment Panel Survey, for 566 workers, with 340 NNs, 136 UUs, 57 UNs and 33 NUs. Approximate percentage changes were calculated as antilogs of estimated differences in log units.

who remain union or nonunion over the entire period, to infer the union effect. In the first column, the changes in wages for workers who switch from nonunion jobs to union jobs are compared with the changes in wages of workers who remain nonunion, showing the gain in wages for workers who go union as opposed to remaining nonunion. In the second column, the changes in wages for workers who move from union to nonunion jobs are compared with the changes in wages for workers who stay union, measuring the likely *loss* in wages by a worker who leaves a union job. In the third column, the changes in wages for workers who switch from union jobs to nonunion jobs are compared with those of workers who switch from nonunion jobs to union jobs. If there is, indeed, a union wage effect, one would expect joiners to receive larger increases than leavers, with one half the difference measuring the "union effect." The figures in the table show union wage effects that are sizable, though generally smaller than the cross-sectional estimates of the wage effect from the same bodies of data.[6]

Since neither the cross-sectional nor the before/after "experiments" represent the ideal laboratory experiment, neither should be taken as "the true union wage effect." What each does document is that the effect is not a chimera of union leaders' boasts and management's complaints.

For Whom Do Unions Raise Wages?

Unions do not raise the wages of all workers by the same percentage amounts. "The" union wage effect found in cross-sectional or before/after studies is, in fact, an average. The actual effect differs significantly among workers, depending on their demographic characteristics and the occupation and industry in which they are employed.

The principal factor determining the union wage effect on demographic groups doing similar jobs is the standard rate pay policies of unions. These policies require firms to give "equal pay for equal work" to workers within a firm and across firms, denying management the right to set pay on an individual-by-individual basis (see chapter 6 for more on this policy). By equating pay across workers within a market, standard rate policies raise the pay of otherwise lower-paid workers more than of otherwise higher-paid workers. Accordingly, one expects larger union/nonunion differentials for lower-paid demographic groups.

The estimates of the difference between the hourly wages of otherwise comparable union and nonunion blue-collar workers in figure 3–1 show just such a pattern for most, though not all, groups:[7]

- By age, the union wage effect is largest among the youngest workers, who are the lowest-paid, and least for prime-aged members, who are the highest-paid.[8]
- By tenure, there is a similar pattern, with the union/nonunion wage differ-

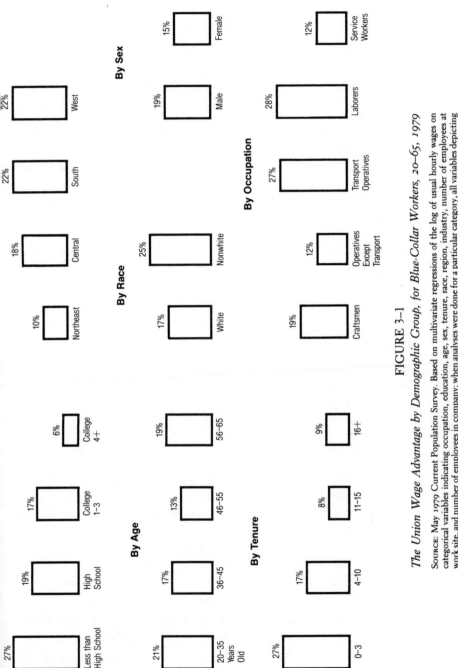

FIGURE 3-1

The Union Wage Advantage by Demographic Group, for Blue-Collar Workers, 20–65, 1979

SOURCE: May 1979 Current Population Survey. Based on multivariate regressions of the log of usual hourly wages on categorical variables indicating occupation, education, age, sex, tenure, race, region, industry, number of employees at work site, and number of employees in company; when analyses were done for a particular category, all variables depicting the other categories were included. The samples used included only private sector nonagricultural workers. The sample size was 6,018. Approximate percentage advantages were calculated as antilogs of estimated union coefficients in semi-log regression models.

ential being largest for those with the lowest service, who are again the lowest-paid.

- By race, the union wage effect is larger for nonwhites than for whites, a pattern that has been found in some but not in all other years. Because of the variation obtained in different studies, we believe the generalization that unions raise the wages of blacks by about as much as they raise the wages of whites is safer than the conclusion implied by figure 3–1.
- By sex also our data show a divergent pattern: despite uniformly higher wages received by men, unions raised male wages somewhat more than female wages in 1979. As with blacks, however, analyses in other years show a diverse pattern of union effects on male and female wages, suggesting that unions raise wages of the two groups by roughly the same amount, although in 1979 they benefited men more than women.[9]

Among occupation, regions and industries, union wage effects also differ greatly, but for different reasons:

- By occupation, unions win much larger gains for blue-collar than for white-collar workers. In our estimates (not reported in the figure), the gain for blue-collar workers is 19 percent, on average, whereas the gain for white-collar workers is a bare 4 percent, on average.[10] Among blue-collar workers, gains are greatest for transport operatives and laborers and least for service workers and operatives outside of transportation.
- By region, unions have large effects in the relatively unorganized South and West and more modest effects in the Northeast and the Central area.
- By industry, there is also substantial variation in the union wage effect. We used the May Current Population Survey for 1973–75 to estimate the union wage effect in sixty-two industries and found very small effects of less than 5 percent in thirteen of the industries surveyed; modest effects of 5 to 15 percent in seventeen of the industries; large effects of 15 to 35 percent in twenty-four of the industries; and enormous effects of 35 percent and above in the remaining eight.[11]

What economic forces underlie the vastly different effect of unions on wages in different industries? The principal factor determining the magnitude of the union wage effect in different industries is the monopoly power held by the union, a power related to the wage sensitivity of the demand for organized labor—that is, to the change in employment induced by a given change in wages. The smaller the response of employment to wages, the greater is the ability of unions to raise wages without incurring significant losses of employment, and thus the greater the likely union wage gains. In areas where employment is relatively unresponsive to changes in wages—for instance, for airline pilots in air transport—one expects sizable union wage gains, whereas in areas where employment is relatively responsive to changes in wages—for instance, for operatives in the shoe industry—one expects modest union wage gains at best.

Analyses of the links between the characteristics of markets that one might expect to influence union monopoly power show that the union wage premium depends strongly on the percentage of workers who are organized. When a union organizes a large proportion of workers in a particular market, it is likely to have a greater impact on wages than when it organizes only a small proportion of workers in that market; with a higher percentage organized, unionized firms can be expected to have less nonunion competition to worry about. Among blue-collar workers in the manufacturing sector, for example, we estimate that a ten-point increase in the percentage of workers organized in the relevant industry raises average union wages by one and one-half percent. By contrast, the wages of nonunion workers do not appear to be influenced by the percentage of workers organized, implying that the union/nonunion wage differential grows with the percentage of the industry that is organized. A similar relationship between the extent of the market organized and the union wage premium also holds for construction workers: the higher the percentage of a state's construction force in unions, the larger is the construction union wage effect.[12]

A second important determinant of a union's monopoly power is the extent to which it bargains for an entire sector rather than for individual plants within a sector. Union wage differentials fall noticeably with plant-level contracts. The reason for this is that workers and managers in a plant, even within a heavily unionized sector, have to worry that wage increases in their plant may shift product demand, and hence jobs, to other plants.[13]

Union wage differentials also fall with the size of a company or work site. In 1979, the differential for blue-collar workers was 35 percent among workers in companies with fewer than 100 employees, compared with an 8 percent differential among companies with 1,000 or more employees; the differential was 25 percent at work sites (establishments) with fewer than 100 employees, compared with a near-zero effect at work sites with 1,000 or more employees.[14] One reason for this pattern is that some large nonunion companies and establishments pay close to union scale to discourage unionization (see chapter 10). Another may be that some large union establishments have the financial wherewithal to "hold the line" in bargaining, whereas smaller union establishments do not.

There has been considerable debate over the relationship between the union wage differential and the product market power of employers. On one side are those who believe that unions are able to win a share of the "monopoly profits" of firms operating in less competitive environments. On the other side are those who argue that firms use their monopoly profits to forestall higher wages by enduring or threatening to endure long strikes. The empirical evidence has not yielded a clear resolution to the debate.[15] Part of the problem reflects the difficulty of measuring market power. To illustrate this problem, consider trucking, where no one firm has a significant market share, but where Teamster wage gains have been sizable, to a large extent because government regulation has worked to both employers' and the union's advantage. Next consider the automobile industry, where the high relative wages won by the United Automobile Workers in the 1970s undoubtedly reflect the fact that in that decade the largest four U.S. auto companies dominated auto sales in this country.

Changes in the Union Wage Advantage Over Time

The union wage advantage is not one of the constants of nature; over time, it varies from what may be called a "normal" level as the economy and economic institutions change. There have been periods in U.S. economic history when the union wage advantage widened greatly— from the 1920s to the 1930s, for example, presumably because unionized workers were better able to fight employer efforts to reduce wages in the Depression than were nonunionized workers. At other times— for example, during World War II, when nonunion worker wages rose

52

due to the tight economy—the wage advantage has declined. As is indicated in figure 3–2, the late 1970s appear to have been a period of substantial increase in the union wage premium. During this period unionized workers maintained or increased their *real* wages while other workers suffered from wage increases below the rate of inflation. For the entire period from 1971 to 1981, the total effective wage rate changes of union workers were 9.4 percent per year compared with an 8.5 percent increase per year for nonunion workers, raising the union/nonunion differential by about 9 percentage points; the annual rate of change of the Consumer Price Index was 8.1 percent over the same period. One factor usually cited as contributing to the pattern is the

**Union/Nonunion
Wage Differential**

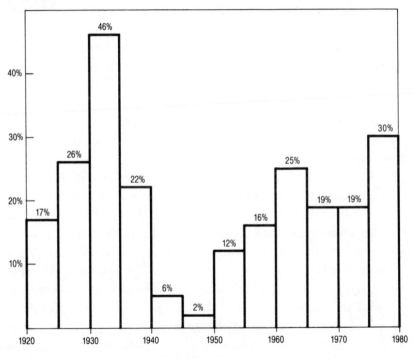

FIGURE 3–2

Union Wage Differential Over Time

SOURCE: George Johnson, "Changes Over Time in the Union/Nonunion Wage Differential in the United States" (University of Michigan, February 1981, mimeographed), table 2. Approximate percentage differentials were calculated as antilogs of estimated union coefficients in semi-log regression models.

existence of cost-of-living-adjustment (COLA) clauses in the union sector; these clauses, which increase wages in response to changes in the consumer price level, were in effect for about 25 percent of all union workers in 1970 and about 60 percent of all union workers in 1979. However, according to our estimates, in manufacturing, COLA provisions contributed only a modest amount to the rising union advantage: union workers without COLA clauses did nearly as well as union workers with such clauses.[16]

A possible reason for the growth in the union wage effect during the late seventies is the sluggish labor market conditions of the period. The wages of union workers tend to be less sensitive to business cycle ups and downs than the wages of nonunion workers; this is true in part because the normal union contract, which is for three years with automatic deferred wage increases, reduces the responsiveness of wages to annual changes in labor demand and in part because unions are less likely to accept real wage reductions in recessions unless the senior employees' jobs are imperiled. By contrast, nonunion firms are more likely to alter wages in the short run, although nonunion wages are also not extremely sensitive to the business cycle. With respect to the inflation of the period, moreover, union bargainers appear to have done a better job of preventing inflation from eroding union wage gains than they did in the past, when the union wage advantage fell with the rate of inflation.[17]

Lest the reader go away with the impression that economists know more than they do, however, it should be noted that inflation and unemployment appear to explain no more than half of the rising union wage advantage in the 1970s.[18] Some of the remaining rise may be due to the timing of major collective agreements in the 1970s, with more workers covered by agreements signed in the relatively good years of 1973, 1976, and 1979 than in the most severe recession years. As yet, however, the contribution of this factor has not been quantified.

Does the seventies growth of the union/nonunion differential represent a movement to historically higher wage advantages to union workers? We believe not. Indeed, we believe that at least in several major sectors the union/nonunion differential reached levels inconsistent with the survival of many union jobs. The extent to which some of the gains were "excessive" can be seen in the publicized pattern of "givebacks" which highlighted collective bargaining in the early 1980s.

The Fabled Givebacks

WASHINGTON—Teamsters union members approved a 37-month national labor agreement that grants major concessions on wages and work rules to the troubled trucking industry. The union maintains that the recession and deregulation of the industry have opened the business to small, nonunion concerns and produced layoffs of about 20 percent of the 300,000 Teamsters members covered by the agreement. . . . Roy Williams, the union's president, said the agreement "protects Teamster jobs while hopefully restoring losses caused by deregulation of the trucking industry."[19]

DETROIT—General Motors Corp. and the United Auto Workers tentatively agreed late last night on a 2 1/2 year contract that offered significant concessions. . . . Under the proposed agreement, GM agreed in return to rescind decisions to close four plants and to apply retroactively an enhanced layoff benefit program to workers idled by the closing of assembly plants in Southgate and Fremont, California. GM further agreed to develop an experimental life-time job security program at four plants. . . .[20]

If the news stories are to be believed, the early 1980s were the period of the giveback. For the first time since the Depression, large numbers of union workers accepted cuts in their normal wages, or postponements in wage gains, in an effort to preserve jobs. According to the Bureau of National Affairs, 427 negotiations in 1982 involved concessionary bargaining, of which nearly half resulted in a concessionary contract in that year, while another quarter were still bargaining at year's end.[21] Many widely publicized collective bargaining sessions focused not on traditional union wage and benefit demands but on employer requests for contract concessions. Some observers saw the contract concessions as representing an entirely new era in American industrial relations.

Yet the union concessions of the early eighties, while unusual, are not unprecedented. In both the distant and the recent past, unions facing particularly adverse labor market and product market conditions have taken wage cuts to save members' jobs: in 1908 the Glass Bottle Blowers accepted a 20 percent wage reduction to reduce incentives for automation; in the 1930s union wage scales fell in construction and printing and in the shoe industry; in the 1950s there were concessions in the apparel and textile industries; in the 1960s wage concessions were given in meat packing and in plastering, among other areas.[22]

What determines union wage concessions?

Because of the political nature of unions, the key factor in a union's decision to make concessions is the extent to which existing wage packages threaten employment of a sizable proportion of the membership. A change in demand for labor that reduces new hires or leads to the layoff of relatively junior employees is unlikely to produce concessions, but potential cutbacks—particularly threatened plant closings—that risk the jobs of senior workers are likely to lead to concessions. Concessions are therefore found only in industries undergoing extreme economic problems. In fact, tabulations from the *Wall Street Journal, Current Wage Developments,* and the *Daily Labor Reporter* show that givebacks have been extensive in seven sectors: meat packing, newspapers, tires, steel, motor vehicles, trucking, and air transport. Bureau of Labor Statistics data show that these industries had substantially greater reduction in employment than did other industries: an unweighted average decline of 14 percent from 1978 to 1982 compared with an overall increase in employment economywide of 2 percent.[23]

Are concessions large or small?

In general wage concessions are very large, as one should expect if they are devised to bail out a company or plant on the verge of closure. The 1980s concessions in the automobile sector were estimated to reduce labor costs per worker below what they otherwise would have been by 7–12 percent; in the airline sector, concessions lowered wages by 10–15 percent. Since inflation was running at 6–10 percent in the period, the *real* wage reductions of these cuts were immense.[24]

Do the givebacks represent a "new era" in industrial relations?

We think not. Certainly the negotiated givebacks are not the rule in labor-management negotiations in recent times. In the first quarter of 1982, when givebacks were in the headlines, the vast majority of collective agreements called for wage increases that were fairly sizable, though smaller than those in earlier years.[25] In light of the rising union wage premium in the 1970s, we view the 1980s concessions as an especially dramatic instance of a return to more normal union-wage premiums in this decade. Such returns to normal differentials after a period of rising premiums have, it should be noted, occurred in the past when union differentials got out of line. Consider, for example, the pattern of wage changes in highly unionized construction. Between 1960 and 1972, average hourly earnings in construction jumped from 1.47 to 1.64 times average hourly earnings in the private sector as a whole and then by 1981 fell to 1.38 times the private sector average. While there were some instances of givebacks in this sector, the reduction in relative wages was due more to modest negotiated increases than to actual negotiated reductions.[26]

How Big Is the Social Cost of Monopoly Wage Gains?

The monopoly wage gains of trade unions cause economic inefficiency. By inducing a firm to use less labor than it did previously and by reducing the size of the union sector, they reduce national output below what would exist if wages were at competitive levels. The workers displaced by the higher wage are forced to seek employment elsewhere, where their contribution to output is lower than it would have been in the union sector. The magnitude of the inefficiency, the extent of the social loss, depends on the difference between the workers' output in the two sectors and the number of workers displaced. A key question in assessing the adverse economic effect of union monopoly wage gains is the size of this loss. Is it large or is it small?

Our analysis, and that of others, shows that the loss of national output due to union monopoly wage effects is quite modest. The primary reason for this is that the social loss depends not on the monopoly increase in wages won by unions for its members but rather on the product of that increase and the number of workers whose employment is lost due to higher wages. Our estimate, based on the standard economic welfare formula for evaluating the social loss due to monopolies, suggests that union monopoly wage gains cost the economy 0.2 to 0.4 percent of gross national product, which in 1980 amounted to about $5 to $10 billion dollars or $20.00 to $40.00 per person. This is of the same magnitude as the 1963 estimate made by

Rees (then at the University of Chicago) and is comparable to estimates of the social cost of product market monopolies.[27]

Are Union Wage Gains a Major Cause of Inflation?

It was once widely believed that union wage increases were a primary cause of cost-push inflation. Until the "stagflation" of the late 1970s and early 1980s, the facts contradicted this belief. Far from outpacing other wages or salaries, union wages increased more slowly in inflationary periods, so that the union wage premium tended to fall. The usual explanation was that by negotiating contracts that set wages over extended periods, typically three years, union wage policies limited responses to rising inflation. Perhaps ensuing union wage gains caused periods of inflation to last longer than they would have otherwise, but one could not reasonably blame unions for initiating cost-push inflation.

The increase in the union wage premium in the highly inflationary late 1970s and early 1980s gives new life to the argument that unions cause inflation. In this period, union cost-of-living-adjustment clauses may have created a new situation in which union wage policies tended to augment rather than to reduce inflationary wage pressures. Just how important might the union wage gains have been to the inflation of the past decade?

If union wage increases have no effect on the wages of other workers, it is relatively easy to demonstrate that unions can be blamed for only a minuscule share of inflation. To see this, we note that

$$
\begin{array}{c}
\text{Contribution of union} \\
\text{wage increases to} \\
\text{percentage change in} \\
\text{unit costs, and, thus,} \\
\text{in prices}
\end{array}
=
\begin{array}{c}
\text{Union labor's} \\
\text{share of costs}
\end{array}
\times
\begin{array}{c}
\text{Percentage} \\
\text{change in union} \\
\text{wage premium}
\end{array}
$$

We estimate that unionized labor accounts for about 25 percent of total cost of national output and that the union wage premium rose

over the entire 1975–81 period by a total of about 9 percentage points.
The result was to add 2.3 percentage points of inflation to the observed
68-point increase in the GNP deflator.[28]

Does this mean that union wages were not an important cause of
inflation?

That union wage gains were not a major direct contributor to the
seventies inflation does not prove that union policies did not contribute
significantly to inflation, for union wage gains could have affected
inflation indirectly by influencing the wages of nonunion workers. It
could be, for instance, that nonunion employers raise the wages of their
workers to match union increases so as to deter their workers from
organizing. If there were significant evidence of such behavior, union
wage policies could have had an important role on the overall inflation
process.

Several macroeconomic time series studies have sought to estimate
the possible transmission of union wage gains to nonunion workers, but
as Mitchell (UCLA) has noted, the answers obtained are ambiguous
and sensitive to the data base used and the period observed.[29] Some
studies find that union wage gains tend to depend on the size of the
union/nonunion differential but that nonunion wages do not depend
on the differential. Other studies yield the opposite results. At present
there is no quantitative evidence confirming the view that union wage
gains are transmitted sufficiently rapidly to nonunion workers to make
unions, even with their COLA clauses, a significant cause of inflation
in past years. This is not to deny, however, the potential importance
that the threat of unionization and the emulation of union wage increases may have on nonunion sector outcomes.

Conclusion

The common-sense view that there is a union wage effect is correct.
Quantitative studies show the general magnitude of that effect to vary
among people, markets, and time periods. Variation in the effect
among people is best understood in terms of union standard-rate policies arising from the voice/response face of unionism. Variation among

markets is best understood in terms of the factors that determine union monopoly power. In the late 1970s, the union wage premium rose substantially, but the givebacks of the early 1980s suggest a return to more normal levels. Union monopoly wage effects have undesirable consequences for resource allocation, but the magnitude of the inefficiency loss seems quite small, from .2 to .4 percent of GNP. There is no evidence that union wage gains were a major factor in the inflation of the 1970s.

CHAPTER 4

Fringe Determination
Under Trade Unionism

PENSIONS, life insurance, major medical benefits, dental insurance, prepaid legal assistance, paid vacation, and payments for holidays—the list of fringe benefits on company account sheets has been growing steadily. In 1951 roughly 17 percent of the compensation of American blue-collar workers consisted of fringe benefits, defined as employer payments to workers beyond money wages. In 1981 that proportion had gone up to 30 percent. In some large firms, over 50 percent of labor costs consists of fringes.[1] Over the same period, thirty-three cents of every dollar of increased labor costs went into fringe benefits, some mandated by law (social security, unemployment compensation, workers' compensation) but most voluntarily decided upon.

How do unions affect the provision of fringe benefits and expenditures on them? Do unions alter fringes via socially deleterious monopoly routes or through potentially desirable voice/response routes? Does the existence of billions of dollars in union pension funds provide unionism with a potentially new source of economic power, as some have suggested?[2]

The Overall Union Effect on Fringes

To determine the impact of unionism on fringe benefits, we have examined two types of data: establishment surveys that report on the expenditures for labor of individual firms (the Bureau of Labor Statistics' Expenditures for Employee Compensation [EEC] survey), and surveys of individuals (The Bureau of the Census' Current Population Survey, Ohio State's National Longitudinal Survey, and the University of Michigan's Panel Study of Income Dynamics and Quality of Employment surveys). The establishment data provide figures on the cost of fringe programs to firms, whereas the individual survey data provide information on whether or not an individual receives a particular benefit and sometimes provide estimates of benefits from such programs. The establishment data permit comparisons of establishments with similar characteristics; the data on individuals provide for comparisons of persons with the same demographic characteristics. Neither set of data is perfect, but together they provide a reasonably definite answer to the question of the union impact on fringe benefits.

Both establishment and individual survey data reveal that unions have a sizable positive impact on the provision of fringe programs and on the dollars spent on fringes, with the percentage increase in fringe spending attributable to unionism exceeding the percentage increase in wages attributable to unionism. Both also show especially pronounced union effects on pensions, vacation pay, and life, accident, and health insurance.

Table 4–1 summarizes the data from the EEC Survey on the fringes paid for union and nonunion production workers in the entire private nonfarm sector and in the manufacturing subsector. The figures reveal a significantly higher proportion of labor costs in the union sector going to fringes. As one would expect, while there is little difference between union and nonunion establishments in the proportion of compensation spent on legally required fringes, there are sizable differences in the proportion going to voluntary fringes, which include vacation pay, holiday pay, pensions, life, accident, and health insurance, shift premiums, sick leave, overtime pay, and several smaller benefits. Overall, 18 percent of the wage bill in unionized establishments was spent on voluntary fringes, compared to 12 percent of the wage bill in nonunion establishments.

If unionized and nonunionized establishments and workers were the same in all characteristics affecting fringe expenditures, the table 4–1 comparisons would suffice to demonstrate that unionism raises fringe expenditures. As we saw in chapter 2, however, there are notable

TABLE 4–1

The Composition of Compensation of Production Workers in Union and Nonunion Plants, 1974–1977

	Union		Nonunion	
	Share of Total Compensation	Percentage with Fringe	Share of Total Compensation	Percentage with Fringe
1. Total Compensation per Hour ($8.58 for Union, $5.37 for Nonunion)	1.00	—	1.00	—
2. Straight-time Pay	.76	—	.82	—
3. Required Fringes	.06	—	.07	—
4. Voluntary Fringes	.18	—	.12	—
Pensions	.04	91	.02	47
Life, Accident	.04	99	.03	79
Vacation	.03	95	.02	88
Holiday	.02	95	.02	82
Sick leave	.01	54	.01	48
Shift Premiums	.01	53	.00	20
Bonuses	.00	20	.01	17
Supplemental Unemployment Insurance	.00	10	.00	—
Severance Pay	.00	10	.00	6
Personal and Sick Leave	.00	70	.00	39
Overtime	.02	95	.02	73
Savings and Thrift	.00	7	.00	5
Vacation funds	.00	9	.00	1

SOURCE: Based on tabulations for 2,699 union plants and 4,633 nonunion plants in the Expenditures for Employee Compensation data file (see appendix). For comparability, each year's figures are deflated by the consumer price index to be in 1977 dollars.

differences between the organized and unorganized sectors, and at least some of these differences may be related to a firm's decisions regarding fringes. To isolate the union impact from that of other highly correlated factors, we need to control for such variables as size of establishment, occupation, industry, region, and demographic characteristics of workers, as well as for union status. Because higher-wage workers generally have greater desires for fringes than do lower-wage workers (both because they are wealthier and thus demand more of all goods and because of the preferential tax treatment given fringes), we also control for the level of wages. Finally, to estimate the effect of unionism on the composition of the compensation package, in other calculations we control for total compensation, that is, wages plus fringes: with total compensation fixed, any increase in fringes due to unionism is counterbalanced by a decrease in wages, so that the union coefficient shows how unionism affects the tradeoff between fringes and wages at a given level of labor cost.

Figure 4–1 presents estimates of the effect of unionism on fringe benefits from a multivariate analysis of the EEC survey of establishments. It shows that, with diverse other factors including wages or total compensation held fixed, unionized establishments pay higher fringes— implying that the table 4–1 differences are indeed the result of unionism and not failure to control for other variables which affect fringe expenditures. In establishments having the same measured characteristics but different levels of wages, the estimated union effect on total fringes is 68 percent. In establishments having the same characteristics and paying the same wages, fringe expenditures are 30 percent higher under unionism. Finally, in establishments having the same characteristics and paying the same *total* compensation (wages plus fringes rather than just wages) the mean effect is 25 percent. The greater fringe expenditure under unionism implies a larger share of fringes in total compensation and a lower share of wages in total compensation.

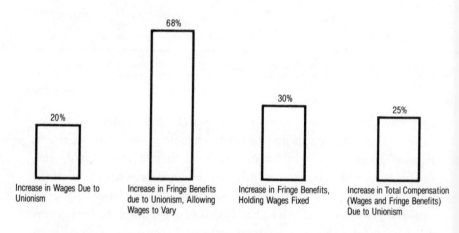

FIGURE 4–1

Estimates of Percentage Impact of Unionism on Wages, Fringe Benefits, and Total Compensation

SOURCE: Based on multivariate regressions with Expenditures for Employee Compensation data, with fifty-three industry dummies, two year dummies, three region dummies, and log of employment in the establishment as a control for size. Approximate percentage increases were calculated as antilogs of estimated union coefficients in semi-log regression models.

Table 4–2 shows the effect of unionism on specific fringes within the compensation package. As one might expect in light of the importance of senior workers in unionized settings, the union effect is large for pensions, life, accident, and health insurance, and vacation and holiday pay. Pensions are more desired by senior than by junior workers because the older workers are closer to retirement age and thus to receipt of pension money. Life, accident, and health insurance are more valuable to senior workers because of those workers' potentially greater health problems. Vacation pay is more valuable to senior than to junior workers because seniority is a prime determinant of vacation time (see chapter 8).

By contrast with the positive union effect on the three main fringes, table 4–2 shows that unionism actually reduces expenditures on bonuses and sick leave. Unions discourage bonus payments because they typically are based on employer discretion, and make compensation sensitive to business conditions; sick leave may be lower because of the tendency for unionized plants to work "by the book," with sick

TABLE 4–2

Estimates of the Impact of Unionism on the Composition of Fringes, Holding Total Compensation Fixed

	Approximate Percentage Change in Fringe Spending	Union Impact on Probability Establishment Has Fringe	Approximate Percentage Change Expenditure on Fringe for Plants with Fringe
All fringes	16	—	11
Pensions	29	.17	−1
Life, Accident, and Health	35	.01	27
Vacation	14	−.04	13
Holiday	12	−.01	11
Bonuses	−100	−.16	−58
Overtime	0	.00	−7
Shift Premiums	15	.09	3
Sick Leave	−11	−.07	−8
Personal and Civic Leaves	0	.06	−10
Severance Pay	−50	−.03	−1
Vacation, Holiday Funds	137	.06	58
Supplemental Unemployment	81	.05	28
Savings and Thrift	−83	−.04	−32

SOURCE: Estimated from Expenditures for Employee Compensation data, 1972–76, using multivariate regressions, as in figure 4–1. The figures in the third column were calculated as antilogs of estimated union coefficients in semi-log regression models.

absences monitored more carefully.[3] Finally, the table decomposes the union effect into an effect on the probability that a firm will have a given fringe program and an effect on the expenditures on that fringe, once it is in place. The union impact on pensions takes the form of a greater likelihood of having a pension plan, whereas the impact on life, accident, and health insurance and on vacation and holiday pay takes the form of increased expenditures among establishments with plans.

In addition to examining fringe expenditures reported by establishments we (and other researchers) have also analyzed the relation between unionism and fringes in surveys of individuals. Because workers rarely know the amounts employers allot to fringes, the standard question asked is whether or not the individual obtains a given fringe from his or her employer. As can be seen in table 4–3, unionized workers are more likely to receive the major fringes, retirement pay (pension benefits) and insurance plans. The Quality of Employment Survey showed that union workers obtain 8 percent more fringes than nonunion workers, but with noticeable differences in the likelihood of specific fringes. Consistent with the table 4–2 results, the figures for sick leave, profit sharing, and several paternalistic fringes such as discounted meals and merchandise and the opportunity for stock options are lower under unionism. Maternity leave, which is especially valuable to pregnant women, does not differ markedly between union and nonunion workers; nonunion employers offer more maternity pay with leave while union employers are more likely to guarantee full reemployment rights after maternity. Overall, the picture given by the data from individuals is quite similar to that given by the data for establishments. Both bodies of data show that unionized employers offer more and better major fringes than nonunion employers.

Finally, while the evidence is limited, existing information on fringe benefits before and after unionism confirms the existence of a positive union effect. In a study of recently unionized white-collar workers, the Conference Board reported that immediately after organization 35 percent of firms improved their pension programs, 35 percent improved their health programs, and 21 percent increased sick leave allowances.[4] Since nonunion white-collar workers generally have some fringes already, it is likely that unionization would have even greater impacts on newly organized blue-collar work groups. Indeed, evidence in the Quality of Employment Survey Panel for 1973–77 from the

TABLE 4-3

Estimates of the Effect of Unions on the Provision of Fringe Benefits, for Individual Blue-Collar Workers with the Same Characteristics and Wages[a]

Data Set (Number of Workers Covered) and Fringe	Probability of Having Fringe in Data Set	Estimated Impact of Unionism on Probability of Having the Fringe
1. May Current Population Survey, 1979 (7,943)		
Retirement Plan	.47	.32
Health Insurance Plan	.65	.18
2. Older Men, National Longitudinal, Survey, 1976 (1,438)		
Retirement Plan	.68	.26
3. Panel Study of Income Dynamics, 1975 (2,075)		
Retirement Plan	.55	.24
4. Quality of Employment Survey, 1977 (varies)[b]		
Retirement Pay	.68	.25
Medical Insurance	.80	.14
Dental Benefits	.33	.25
Eyeglass Benefits	.24	.26
Life Insurance	.66	.10
Paid Vacation	.82	−.10
Thrift Plan	.40	.06
Legal Aid	.09	.00
Maternity Leave with Pay	.28	−.03
Maternity Leave with Full Reemployment Rights	.72	.08
Day Care	.02	.08
Sick Leave	.61	−.12
Profit Sharing	.23	−.16
Stock Options	.21	−.08
Free or Discounted Meals	.16	−.05
Free or Discounted Merchandise	.36	−.07

SOURCES: See appendix for discussion of each data set.
[a]Estimates obtained by multivariate regressions, with controls for wages, industry, occupation, age or experience (age − schooling − 6 years), schooling, tenure, and race, and sex where relevant.
[b]In the Quality of Employment Survey, sample sizes for individual fringes differ, depending on whether question was answered; the minimum sample was 256, for maternity leave with pay, and the maximum sample was 997, for thrift plan.

small number of blue-collar workers changing union status supports such an inference. In this sample, workers who were nonunion in 1973 and union in 1977 went from having 18 percent fewer fringes than the average worker to having 10 percent more fringes than the average in the period in which they changed union status, while workers who began as union members and became nonunion went from having 17 percent more than the average number of fringes to having 7 percent fewer fringes.[5]

The conclusion is inescapable: unionization is a major determinant of the fringe-benefit programs and expenditures that have come to constitute such a large share of U.S. compensation.[6]

Differences in the Nature of Fringe Programs

Benefit programs instituted at the behest of unions differ in their rules and regulations from those set up by management in the absence of unionization. Union-regulated programs tend to reflect the desires of average workers, while management-instituted programs appear more attuned to attracting marginal workers, those on the coming-or-going margin.

A prime example of the difference between union and nonunion fringe programs is in the pension area. First and foremost, union pension plans tend to be defined-benefit plans, which promise workers definite amounts of retirement pay, rather than defined contribution plans, which invest moneys and pay workers the return on the investment. Defined benefit plans are generally favored by senior workers who enjoy the rewards of increased defined benefits without incurring the full costs. In 1977, 89 percent of union private pension plans were of the defined benefit type, compared with 35 percent of nonunion private pension plans.[7] The union preference for defined-benefit plans also reflects the desire of unions and workers to avoid the risk of allowing retirement pay to depend on fluctuations in capital markets.

Rules regulating eligibility and monthly incomes under union and nonunion pension plans also differ. Union plans have less liberal vesting rules than nonunion plans, so that the typical unionized worker is obligated to remain with his employer longer to receive pension income than is the typical nonunionized employee. Why? The likely reason is that nonunion employers offer liberal vesting to attract young marginal workers, whereas union policies are determined by all members and thus are more influenced by the desires of older, more stable workers. Given the choice between higher fringe benefits for persons in the union and liberal vesting for persons when they leave the employer and the union, the union comes down in favor of permanent workers.

With respect to the size of pensions, union defined-benefit pension plans are less likely to have pension benefits rise with last year's earnings, and more likely to have fixed or seniority-related benefits. In a sample of pension plans for blue-collar workers, 52 percent of the union plans paid workers a flat rate unrelated to final earnings, compared with 3 percent of nonunion plans. This is the pension policy equivalent of the wage standardization policies of unions.[8]

There are also significant differences between union and nonunion health and disability insurance plans. The proportion of health insurance premiums paid by employers is 14 percent higher in union settings; many union health plans contain provisions for second opinions and offer diverse other benefits as well. Union disability insurance programs also differ from nonunion disability programs. The ratio of payments to pre-disability earnings is slightly higher for union workers (19.3 percent versus 18.1 percent in 1978), but more importantly the rules for eligibility are strikingly different. In nonunion plans only 47 percent of covered workers with disability plans face age and service tests to receive benefits, whereas in union plans almost 90 percent of the relevant population is affected by age and service requirements, reflecting the tilt of union benefits toward senior workers (see chapter 8).[9]

Variations in the Impact of Unions on Fringes

Just as the union wage effect varies with market conditions, so too does the union fringe effect:

69

- Unions have their greatest effect on fringes in smaller firms. In the EEC survey, fringe benefits in small (fewer than 500 workers) organized establishments exceeded those in small unorganized establishments by 32 percent, whereas in large establishments (more than 500 workers) the difference was only 13 percent.[10]
- Unions have especially great impacts on fringes in industries where workers are more attached to occupations than to employers (construction, for example), and in sectors where firms are relatively small (such as trucking).[11]

An important reason for these variations is that fringe programs with sizable set-up costs and with deferred compensation require a large and permanent market institution to administer and maintain them, and in the above situations unions are the sole such institutions. Multi-employer programs, of the type initiated by unions, make benefits portable across employers and provide the size to reduce average set-up costs. The vast majority of multi-employer pension plans are union run (68 percent in the pension plan file of the Office of Pension and Welfare Benefit Programs, Department of Labor), and while a few have attracted attention for illicit practices (the Teamsters Central States Pension Fund being the most infamous case), most such plans provide workers with benefits otherwise unavailable in their sector.[12]

- Unions' impact on fringes rises with their monopoly power. In chapter 3 we saw that a key determinant of unions' control of the labor market and thus of the union wage effect is the percentage of an industry that is organized. Analysis of fringe expenditures in union and nonunion establishments by Donsimoni (Columbia University) shows similar linkages between indicators of union economic power in the market, including the percentage of workers organized in a sector, and fringe expenditures. In her analysis of manufacturing industries, the union/nonunion differential in total voluntary fringe expenditures rises from 4 percent in sectors where only 20 percent of the workers are organized to about 15 percent in sectors where 80 percent are organized.[13]
- The union fringe effect depends on the age composition of organized workers. Alpert (St. Louis University) has found that the greater the proportion of older workers in an industry, the greater is the union effect on fringes; this is what one would expect if the union responded to the fringe demands of an older membership.[14]

Workers' Evaluations of Fringe Programs

Since unionization raises fringe benefits, one would expect union work- ✓
ers to be more pleased with their fringe programs than nonunion
workers. Indeed, as table 4–4 shows, this is the case; unionized employees are more likely to describe their fringe benefits as good than
are nonunion employees (line 1), and less likely, though only marginally
so, to report not getting fringe benefits that they would like to be
getting (line 2). On the other hand, however, unionized employees are
more vocal in wanting greater increases in current fringe benefits (line
3), indicative of the union voice impact on workers' desires and expectations.

An important issue regarding union fringe programs is whether the
unions do a better job of representing workers' desires for fringes than
does the competitive market. In principle there is good reason to expect
unions to do a better job of eliciting workers' preferences. This is
because the adversarial relation between employers and employees—
the fact that the level as well as the allocation of the compensation
package is at stake in bargaining—argues for circumspection by workers
in providing their employer with information about their preferences.
If employers had complete knowledge of employee preferences, they
would seek to strike a bargain that would leave workers with the minimum they would accept, extracting all of the economic surplus (the
value of the fringes which exceeds the minimum amount for the work-

TABLE 4–4
Workers' Evaluations of Their Fringe Benefits

Statement	Percentage of Responses Indicating "Yes"	
	Union	*Nonunion*
1. "My fringe benefits are good."	75	57
2. "Are there any fringe benefits that you're not getting that you'd like to be getting?"	52	56
3. "Would you like any of the benefits you *get* to be better?"	71	56

SOURCE: Tabulated from data on 1,101 workers in Quality of Employment Survey, 1977.

ers to remain with the firm). Hence nonunion employees have an incentive to withhold information about preferences. As the agent of workers, on the other hand, unions should obtain a more accurate image of preferences through members' bargaining within the union over the demands to be presented to management.

Indeed, there is empirical evidence that this is the case. Lester's 1967 review of surveys of managerial perceptions of worker preferences found "limited data . . . that workers value benefits more highly compared to wages than employers believe their workers do," while by contrast, Lawler and Levin's 1970 study of union leaders concluded that leaders are generally good predictors of the members' preferences for various compensation packages, although union leaders also seem to have understated the desire for fringes. Leigh's analysis of the knowledge workers have of fringe benefits suggests, moreover, that unionism provides greater information about existing fringes. Asked to name the actual value of pensions in their company plan, 52 percent of union workers were able to do so compared with 42 percent of nonunion workers.[15]

One way of measuring the extent to which unions may be better able than the competitive market to represent workers' preferences for fringes as opposed to pay would be to compare the willingness of union and nonunion workers to trade off pay for fringes. If the compensation package were divided between pay and fringes exactly as desired by the average worker, he or she would be indifferent between the two, so that roughly as many workers would be willing to trade off pay for fringes as would be unwilling to do so. One question in the Quality of Employment Survey addresses this issue, asking workers about their preference for more fringe benefits versus more pay. While a majority of both union and nonunion workers answered "yes" to the question "would you prefer more paid vacation days (better retirement, better medical insurance benefits) to a 10 percent pay raise?" the union workers were more evenly divided between the various benefits and pay than the nonunion workers, with one-third of the unionists preferring more pay and two-thirds preferring more benefits, while one-fifth of the nonunionists preferred more pay and four-fifths preferred more benefits.[16] The more nearly equal division between the two responses for union workers implies that the union package is closer to the optimal than the nonunion package. Unfortunately, because the survey instrument failed to specify the precise amounts of the fringes in the trade-off, the responses only suggest that the division of compensation is closer to optimal under unionization.

Asked specifically to evaluate their unions' performances in the fringe area, most unionized workers believe the unions are doing a good job (table 4–5). Older workers are noticeably more likely to rate the unions' performance high than younger workers. In part, this represents a general tendency for older workers to have a more favorable assessment of union performance than younger workers.[17] In part also, however, it represents the greater provision of fringes, particularly those desired by older workers, under unionism. Older union workers are also somewhat more satisfied with the effort their union is putting into fringe benefits (line 2 of table 4–5), though here all union workers are sufficiently satisfied that differences by age are modest.

Another piece of evidence consistent with the notion that unions are more knowledgeable about average worker preferences than are nonunion firms is found in the widely held view (which we examine in chapter 10) that union-negotiated fringes spill over to nonunion firms. Nonunion firms desiring to avoid unionization will imitate union compensation packages only if the union contract offers provisions that are close to those desired by the median nonunion worker. This is because union representation elections are based on majority voting, so that it is the average, not the marginal, worker whose preferences determine election results. If union pay packages did not give a good reading of the desires of the average worker, there would be no reason for nonunion firms to imitate the union package.

TABLE 4–5

Union Members' Evaluation of Their Union's Job in Getting Fringe Benefits

Question	Percentage of Respondents Giving Positive Evaluation of Union	
	Older	Younger
1. "How good a job does it do in getting better fringe benefits?"	81	59
2. "How much effort do you think your union should be putting into fringe benefits?" (percentage satisfied with effort)	95	91

Source: Quality of Employment Survey, 1977. Based on 486 workers, with older workers defined as those over forty years of age and younger workers as those below forty years.

Monopoly and Voice/Response Effects on Fringe Benefits

The union effect on fringes has both a monopoly and a voice/response component. As an institution with monopoly power, unions can be expected to use some of that power to extract more fringes as well as higher wages. Part of the union effect thus represents an additional social cost of union monopoly power. As a voice institution, on the other hand, unions ought to provide management with better information about worker preferences. Part of the union effect represents a social gain: at the same labor cost, unionized workers will have a more desirable set of benefits. In addition, the fact that group purchase of pension, insurance and health plans can save workers from 10 percent to 18 percent of the cost will further benefit them.[18]

How do the monopoly and voice/response impacts on fringes compare quantitatively? The monopoly component of the union fringe impact will be defined as that portion of the increased fringe spending by union firms that raises total compensation per hour. The voice/response component will be defined as that proportion of the increased fringe spending that raises fringe spending without raising total compensation but rather alters the composition of a given total compensation package. Using this dichotomy, the EEC data suggest that the increase in fringe spending under unionism is roughly equally divided between the two effects: fifteen cents (55 percent) of the union-induced increase in fringes comes via reduction in wages and thus reflects union voice, while eleven cents (45 percent) takes the form of higher labor costs and thus reflects monopoly power.

Social Effects of the Use of Union Pension Funds

Ever since Peter Drucker's 1976 book *The Unseen Revolution*, it has become increasingly recognized that pension funds represent a growing source of capital in the United States and thus that union pension funds offer unions a potential tool to influence the economy. Indeed, in 1978 Jeremy Rifkin and Randy Barber published a book calling for unions, particularly public sector unions, to use their pension assets to revitalize the Northeast.[19] Many union leaders have expressed the desire to influence the allocation of pension moneys, at least to discourage investment of union members' funds in non- or anti-union firms. In 1980, the Executive Council of the AFL-CIO declared a Policy Goal: "To exclude from union pension plan portfolios, companies whose policies are hostile to workers' rights." Even *Business Week,* hardly a voice for radical financial change, has expressed support for the investment of pension funds in nontraditional assets and ways.[20]

The success of unions in using pension funds as an economic tool depends on three factors: the magnitude of the pension moneys in the capital market; the legal rights of unions to influence the expenditure of these funds; and the effect of different expenditures on management policies.

That pension funds formed as a result of collective bargaining contain sizable capital assets is apparent from crude statistics. In 1980 the assets held by private pension funds and the estimated assets held by insurance companies as pension reserves amounted to some 240 billion dollars. Over 12 percent of corporate equities and nearly 40 percent of all U.S. government securities and 27 percent of corporate bonds were held by private pension funds, at least half of which were union.[21]

Traditionally these funds have been invested by life insurance companies and banks following conservative financial policies. The Employee Retirement Income Security Act (ERISA) of 1976 places significant constraints on possibilities for targeting private pension fund assets. Under the law, private pension plan management must seek the highest return to funds, subject to definite rules on diversification designed to reduce the risk of catastrophic loss. State and local pensions funds are subject to state rules of a similar kind. One result of the federal and state laws and the fiduciary behavior of pension fund managers is that pension funds have traditionally been invested in conservative ways, which some would even call antiquated.

The new union effort to redirect pension moneys has, however, begun to have an effect, particularly in the construction area. In California, unions have organized a consortium of twenty construction union pension funds, which has invested millions in union construction projects. Similar consortiums have been organized in other states. The new consortiums have, thus far, met with the approval of federal regulatory agencies. In response to the union demands, traditional pension fund managers have developed similar investment policies; for example, Aetna Insurance invests some union pension funds under its control in union-built construction projects. At the national level the Industrial Union Department, AFL-CIO, has begun publishing a series called *Labor and Investments*, covering critical issues in the areas of union voice in investments.

One criticism of the union desire to influence investment of pension moneys is that they will direct funds to lower-return investments, thereby harming beneficiaries. While it is true that pension funds that shun the stocks of major nonunion firms could earn lower returns than other funds, both theory and empirical evidence show that they need not. In theory, with thousands of different stocks and financial instruments available in the capital market, union pension funds ought to be able to earn normal returns, with normal risk, by excluding a moderate number of companies from their portfolios. They should be able to do this even if nonunion firms earn higher profits and have, for whatever reason, better growth potential, because in an efficient market, the stock prices of those firms will be high, reflecting growth and profits potential, so that they will not be a bargain.

In fact, union pension plans appear to have done at least as well as nonunion plans in years past. Analysis of the portfolios of seventy-five union-related pension plans and twenty employer-controlled plans in 1978 shows that, while the union plans put a much smaller part of their portfolios in the stocks of major predominantly nonunion firms (McDonald's, Sears, Texas Instruments), they did not suffer from this in ensuing years. Indeed, from 1977 to 1982, the shares of the nonunion firms did worse than market averages, so that over this period the union plans benefited from avoiding these stocks. Consistent with this, median rates of return on the equity portion of union multi-employer plans and of corporate plans developed by A. G. Becker Company show similar rates of return year by year, over a decade; in some years, the union plans do better, in other years they do worse. The AETNA Insurance Company Union Separate Account also reports no problem in earning normal rates of return.[22]

There is an important difference between shunning the stocks of primarily nonunion firms in the stock market and investing in projects that employ union labor. Since there are millions of investors in the market, directing investment funds away from certain stocks will not permanently influence the value of those shares. Thus, the benefit to unions of excluding "hostile" companies will be largely psychic. (To influence the policies of those companies unions would do better to direct their pension fund savings into those companies and use their ownership to pressure management to drop anti-union activity.) Investing in projects that employ union labor, by contrast, has direct benefit for union labor, helping to preserve the union wage differential, and thus may represent a better long-term strategy.[23]

As a tool in labor's arsenal, union use of pension fund capital to aid the union sector is both ironic and intriguing. It is ironic because it is labor's use of capital to strengthen the labor movement; Marx would turn over in his grave. It is intriguing because it represents one of the few major innovations in industrial relations in the late 1970s–early 1980s with potential for strengthening the labor movement.

Conclusion

The analysis and findings of this chapter show that trade unions are a major determinant of fringe expenditures, with the union fringe effect being considerably greater in percentage terms than the union wage effect. The type of fringes favored in union settings appears consistent with the voice face of the institution. Unionized establishments are especially likely to allot funds to deferred forms of compensation favoring senior workers, such as pensions, insurance, and vacation pay, and to have a large impact on smaller establishments. Roughly half of the union impact on fringe spending can be attributed to the monopoly face of the institution, raising labor costs; half can be attributed to the voice/response face, altering the composition of compensation. Union-negotiated pension funds have become an important asset in capital markets, which appear to offer organized labor a new tool for affecting the economy.

CHAPTER 5

Labor's Elite:
The Effect of Unionism
on Wage Inequality

ONE of the most damaging criticisms of trade unions is the claim that, for all the talk of worker solidarity, unions increase income inequality. As Milton Friedman has argued (see the quotation in chapter 2), union wage increases reduce employment in the union sector, increasing the number of persons seeking jobs in the nonunion sector and depressing wages there.[1] To the extent that unions are strongest among high-wage workers, this monopoly effect increases inequality. Many people champion unions in the belief that they are an egalitarian force, and if in fact unions increase inequality, the case for a positive role of unions in the economy would be greatly weakened.

This chapter shows the claim that unionism increases inequality to be wrong; that, on the contrary, unionism tends to be in general a powerful force for equalization of earnings in the economy. The claim is wrong not because the effect to which it directs attention—raising wages of some workers at the expense of other workers—does not occur. It does. The claim is wrong because the increase in inequality induced by monopoly wage effects is dwarfed by three other trade union effects on wages that reduce inequality: union wage policies lower inequality of wages *within* establishments; union wage policies favor equal pay for equal work *across* establishments; and union wage gains for blue-collar labor reduce inequality between white-collar and blue-collar workers. The bulk of this chapter will analyze these three inequality-decreasing effects of unionism. Then we will compare the inequal-

78

ity-increasing effects of monopoly wage gains with the inequality-decreasing effects to see which dominate the distributional formula.

Union Wage Policies Within Establishments

Consider two possible methods by which management can pay workers with nominally similar skills and job tasks: *individual determination*, in which supervisors decide within wide wage ranges how much to pay each worker on the basis of perceived performance (or favoritism or discrimination); and *single rate*, in which all workers classified in a given job category are paid the same wage. Individual determination attaches wages to workers. Single rate attaches wages to jobs. Given reasonable variation in supervisor's perceptions of workers, and fewer jobs than workers, inequality is likely to be much lower under single-rate pay schemes than under individual determination. In the extreme case of one all-encompassing job category, single rate yields no wage inequality, a result unlikely to occur under individual determination unless supervisors view workers as clones.

Which of these two methods of pay is likely to be favored by a trade union? The voice-response model of unionism suggests three reasons for expecting unions to press for single-rate payment.

First, as a political organization whose policies reflect the preference of average workers, unions can be expected to adopt wage policies benefiting the majority of the work force. In most situations the majority of workers have earnings below the mean level, suggesting that the majority will favor pay policies that accord greater gains to the lower paid. In a simple voting model of union behavior in which union policies are set by the median worker (the member whose vote gives a policy the majority), a pattern of lower median than mean wages is likely to result in a policy of greater gains for the lower paid. In more complex models of intra-union political activity, with differing intensity of preferences among workers, log-rolling, and coalition-formation among groups, it is also likely that the political process will produce a preference for reduction in differentials among members.[2]

Second, unions are likely to favor single-rate policies because they

79

replace managerial discretion and power at the workplace with more objective decision rules. Because the value of a worker's contribution to a firm is extremely difficult to measure and different supervisors may read the same facts in different ways, the union will seek to protect the membership from the uncertainty of arbitrary supervisory decisions by pressing for a one-rate-per-job pay policy.

Third, unions are likely to seek to equalize wages among workers doing similar tasks for reasons of worker solidarity and organizational unity. Considering unionism's ideology of egalitarianism, it is difficult to see how a union would be able to maintain its organizational strength if there were significant personal differences within occupations. Moreover, since all workers presumably obtain higher wages in the presence of the union, there are no losers from the policy, but simply differential gainers.

To see the extent to which unions in fact obtain methods of wage payment that tend to equalize wages and thus reduce inequality within establishments, we have examined actual methods of payment in some 10,000 unionized and nonunionized establishments in nine specific industries. The results of our analysis, summarized in table 5–1, show

TABLE 5–1

Percentage of Workers Paid Under Different Wage Payment Plans, by Union Status of Establishments

	Automatic Progression		Single Rate		Individual Determination	
Industry	Union	Nonunion	Union	Nonunion	Union	Nonunion
Paints & Varnishes	25	17	52	13	4	44
Textile	14	7	74	51	0	18
Chemical	14	19	75	27	0	5
Wood	9	2	28	2	5	8
Plastic	6	4	63	12	2	9
Cotton	2	2	65	62	10	46
Steel	37	19	28	6	4	49
Wool	6	0	61	57	5	24
Foundries	17	6	40	13	5	36
Unweighted Average	14	8	54	27	4	27

SOURCE: Tabulated from Richard B. Freeman, "Union Wage Practices and Wage Dispersion Within Establishments," *Industrial and Labor Relations Review* 36 (October 1982): 10–11.
NOTE: Percentages do not add up to 100 because of additional payment systems not included in the table, such as piece rates.

that the unionized plants are much more likely to choose single-rate or closely related automatic-progression schemes, in which workers within a job grade obtain different amounts according to seniority, as opposed to individual determination or other methods. On average, about two-thirds of union workers compared with about one-third of nonunion workers are paid by single rate or automatic progression, whereas just 4 percent of union workers, compared with 27 percent of nonunion workers, have individually determined wages. Multiple-regression analyses show that while some of the establishment differences in pay practices can be attributed to differences in plant size and other factors that differ between union and nonunion establishments, most differences are attributable to unionism per se.[3] The nine-industry sample appears, moreover, to represent fairly the nature of union policy in the economy as a whole. In the 1970s, whereas just 13 percent of major union contracts allowed for merit progression plans, which set up formal methods of individual determination, 43 percent of all companies had such plans for their blue-collar labor.[4] Labor-management participants report, moreover, that since unionized workers not given merit increases can raise and win grievances, many union merit plans resemble automatic-progression plans.

Granted that union policies produce plant wage practices that reduce inequality in pay on the shop floor, the question becomes: How important is the reduction? Is it a large or a small factor in the distribution of earnings?

To obtain quantitative estimates of the union-induced reduction in inequality within establishments, we have analyzed the wage inequality of about half a million workers in some 4,000 establishments in the nine industries listed in table 5–1. We have chosen one widely used measure of inequality, the standard deviation of log earnings—a measure favored by many economic analysts because of the widespread finding that wages follow lognormal distributions.[5]

Figure 5–1 shows the results of this analysis. It records the average levels of wage inequality for union and nonunion establishments in the nine-industry sample. It reveals large differences in within-establishment inequality, with union establishments averaging one-third less inequality than nonunion establishments. While one may debate the social value of such a reduction in inequality, with the claim that pay for performance motivates workers more, the data makes it clear that

**Level of Inequality
(measured by standard
deviation of log of wages)**

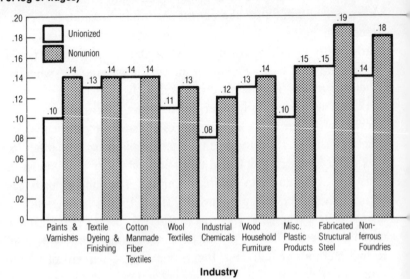

FIGURE 5–1

Comparison of Inequality in Wages Within Establishments

Source: R. B. Freeman, "Union Wage Practices and Wage Dispersion Within Establishments," *Industrial and Labor Relations Review* 36, no. 7 (October 1982): 10–11.
Note: The figures graphed were calculated as the square root of the mean of within-establishment squared errors (other factors held fixed).

unions have a major impact on within-plant inequality, and thus on overall inequality.[6]

Standardization of Rates Across Firms

The second major goal of union wage policies is to equalize pay of similar workers across establishments, thereby "taking labor out of competition." Indeed, according to Slichter, Healy, and Livernash, "wage standardization within an industry or local product market is the most widely heralded union wage policy."[7] Sufficient examples exist of major collective bargaining agreements that achieved standardization of rates to suggest that the goal of uniformity across firms has also influenced the wage structure. The development of the Cooperative Wage Study in steel in 1946–47 appears to have increased uniformity among plants in that industry. Successive steel contracts from 1947 to 1954 eliminated the longstanding southern "Birmingham" geographic differential.[8] The International Ladies Garment Workers Union and Amalgamated Clothing Workers have established uniform piece rates in their contracts in broad geographic areas. The Teamsters reduced regional differentials for over-the-road drivers (those who drive trucks over long distances) in 1964 when the National Master Freight Agreement was signed. In most instances of multi-employer bargaining (which in 1980 was the practice in agreements covering 43 percent of the major contract workforce) or multi-plant bargaining (the practice relevant to an additional 40 percent),[9] uniform or near-uniform rates are fixed across establishments.

The policy of standardization of rates across establishments is not, of course, adhered to blindly. Exceptions are often granted to take account of specific competitive situations, such as the danger of a site closing or a company going bankrupt, as when the United Auto Workers permitted Chrysler to pay workers less than General Motors paid in the 1980s. In addition, the relevant sector or wage "contour" for standardization may change as market conditions change.[10]

The economic rationale and strength of policies aimed at standardizing rates across establishments will depend on market conditions. When firms compete in the same national market, standard rates are likely to be favored by both the management and unions. On the company side, no enterprise wants union contracts that are more expensive than those of its competitors. On the worker side, an inviolable single rate is necessary to prevent intraunion competition. Without a common rate across competing units in the same market, the union wage would come under severe pressure in economic downturns, when some union members might seek to preserve their jobs by undercutting the rates of other workers.

When firms operate in separate markets, so that the union can charge different rates without risking potentially undesirable rate-cutting, standardization of rates will be weaker. And indeed such is the case in construction, where the product market is local. Even here, the need to maintain union solidarity will limit wage differentiation, as sizable differences in pay for workers doing the same job invite division within the organization and loss of certain common advantages, such as joint strike funds and interrelated policies toward major employers. On the employer side, firms in low-wage local markets have often fought standardization of rates on the grounds that standardization causes their unit labor costs (which reflect both wage rates and labor productivity) to be above those of their competitors. Despite some opposition to standard rates from high-wage union locals and low-wage firms, however, the overall pressures appear to operate toward standardizing rates, and the granting of exceptions will be influenced by unusual factors, such as very unfavorable market conditions.

To see the effect of unionism on the dispersion of wages across establishments, we have determined the extent to which the average wage varies from one plant to the next, controlling for other wage-determining factors. In five of the nine industries in table 5–1, inequality is smaller in the union sector; in one there is no discernible difference; in three industries, inequality is larger in the union sector. A large sample of establishments in *all* industries yields more impressive results. As shown in figure 5–2, inequality is 25 percent lower among the

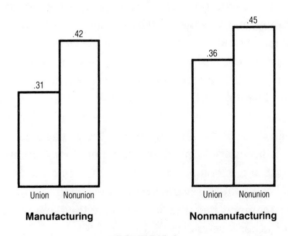

FIGURE 5–2
Inequality in Total Compensation Per Hour for Union and Nonunion Establishments

Source: Tabulated with Expenditures for Employee Compensation data for 4,285 nonunion manufacturing plants, 1,692 union manufacturing plants, 8,468 nonunion nonmanufacturing plants, and 1,489 union non-manufacturing plants.
Note: Inequality is measured by the standard deviation of log compensation.

union establishments than among otherwise comparable nonunion establishments in the manufacturing area; outside of manufacturing, it is 20 percent lower among union than nonunion establishments.

Further analysis showed that within the sixty-one industries for which there was a sufficient number of establishments to compare inequality among union and nonunion establishments, inequality was lower in the union sector of the industry in fifty-six industries, or in 92 percent of the cases.[11]

While there are undoubtedly exceptions, union standard rate policies tend to produce greater similarity in pay across establishments than does an unorganized labor market.

Union versus Nonunion Blue-Collar Workers

The total impact of trade union wage policies on the distribution of hourly earnings for union as opposed to nonunion blue-collar workers is examined in figure 5–3. The figure displays the percentage of workers

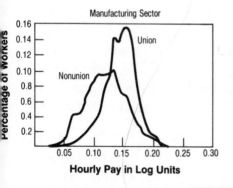
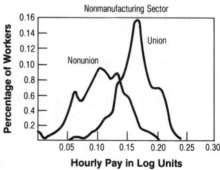

FIGURE 5–3

Comparison of the Distribution of Hourly Pay Among Union and Nonunion Male Blue-Collar Workers by Sector

SOURCE: Calculated with Current Population Survey data for May 1973, 1974, and 1975. The wages were adjusted for inflation using deflators derived from average hourly earnings of workers on private payrolls in *Employment and Training Report of the President* (Washington, D.C.: Department of Labor, BLS, 1977), table C–3.

paid different amounts in manufacturing and nonmanufacturing sectors, as reported by a sample of over 30,000 workers in the Current Population Survey. The more concentrated and peaked the distribution, the greater the earnings equality: perfect equality would be a vertical line, with all workers paid the same amount. The figure shows the union distributions in both sectors to be noticeably more concentrated around the average wage than the nonunion distributions. The fraction of workers paid much below the average is, in particular, noticeably smaller in union settings. In terms of the standard deviation measure of inequality, the distribution in the figure suggests that inequality is 25 percent lower in union manufacturing than in nonunion manufacturing and 20 percent lower in union nonmanufacturing than in nonunion nonmanufacturing. Multivariate statistical analyses suggest that about 20 to 30 percent of the difference in inequality is due not to union wage policies per se, but rather to the fact that union workers are more alike in terms of age, education, and so forth than are nonunion workers. The remainder of the observed difference appears to represent the impact of union wage policies on earnings inequality. Even so, the effect of unionism on the inequality of blue-collar organized workers remains substantial: we estimate that union wage policies reduce inequality by 15 to 20 percent among otherwise comparable workers.[12]

How much of the reduction is attributable to reduced differentials within establishments, as opposed to standardization of rates across establishments?

While we lack sufficient data for the economy as a whole to provide a general answer to this question, the evidence from the table 5–1 nine-industry sample suggests that much of the overall reduction in inequality is attributable to the reduction of inequality within establishments.

Personal Characteristics and Wage Equality

Unions replace wages based on the personal characteristics of workers with wages based on jobs. Our chapter 3 discussion of who gains the most from the union wage effect shows this to be the case. There, we found that the union wage effect was generally larger for lower-paid workers. In the context of inequality this implies that the characteristics of workers that raise wages have a smaller impact in the union sector, and thus that inequality is lower. We estimate that roughly half of the lower dispersion among union workers is due to the fact that such important measured wage-determining characteristics as schooling, age, occupation, and industry, among others, have less pronounced effects on union than on nonunion workers. In the union sector, for example, we find that workers whose schooling differs by four years will have earnings that differ on average by 6 to 8 percent, compared with an 11 to 14 percent difference in the nonunion sector. The smaller impact of personal characteristics on the wages of union than of nonunion workers has been found in nearly all estimates of wage equations. However, even if personal characteristics had about the same effect on the wages of union as on the wages of nonunion workers, there would still be less inequality of earnings in the union sector. Roughly half of the union reduction in inequality takes the form of less pay among workers with observationally identical characteristics (that is, of the same age, sex, race, years of schooling, and working in the same occupation, industry, and region).[13]

Do Unions Reduce Inequality, or Does Equality Favor Unionism?

The findings that (1) unions choose wage policies designed to reduce inequality of wages among organized labor and that (2) inequality is lower among unionized workers would seem to point to but one interpretation: union wage policies reduce inequality of wages among organized blue-collar workers.

Economists enamored of the monopoly view of unions have, however, raised objections to such a reading of the statistical results. Perhaps, they say, dispersion is lower in organized firms not because of union policies but because firms with lower dispersion of earnings are more likely to be organized. For instance, it may be that workers with similar pay are more alike and therefore have more common grounds for collective action than workers with very different rates of pay.

This objection to our interpretation finds no support in fact. Existing institutional and statistical evidence suggests, if anything, that workers in plants with greater dispersion of wages, not those with a narrow dispersion, are more favorably attuned to unionism. Early studies of unionism show that claims of inequities with respect to wages and other factors, such as supervisory favoritism to particular workers, and unequal treatment of workers, were a motivating force for organization in the first place.[14] In the words of one nonunion manager, "favoritism gets you the union the quickest." In a study of actual votes in NLRB representation elections, Farber (MIT) and Saks (then of Michigan State, now of Vanderbilt) found that wage inequality within plants was positively, not negatively, related to the fraction of workers voting for unionization. They also report that individuals with earnings below the average in their firm were significantly more likely to vote for unions than those with earnings above the firm mean, suggesting that "workers at the lower end of the intra-firm earnings distribution . . . expect a larger increase in earnings from unionization," which of course implies that unionism reduces inequality. Our analysis of the earnings of nonunion blue-collar workers in the 1977 Quality of Employment Survey yields somewhat weaker but comparable results. We find no difference in inequality of wages between workers who said they would vote for having a union represent them and workers who said they would vote against a union, but a sizable difference in the level of wages, with pro-union workers paid 16 percent less than anti-union workers.[15]

Finally, we studied inequality of wages among workers who did or did not change union status over a period of time. According to the hypothesis that unionism reduces inequality, wage dispersion should fall among workers moving from nonunion to union status and should rise among workers moving from union to nonunion status. According to the contrary hypothesis that the lower inequality in wages among union workers is due entirely to organization of workers with similar characteristics, inequality should not change as workers change union status. The comparisons of changes in dispersion in table 5–2 show the argument that the unions cause reduction in dispersion to be correct: those joining unions experience a decline in dispersion compared with

TABLE 5–2

Change in Inequality Associated with Changing Union Status

Data Source (Years)	Change in Inequality for Workers Joining Union vs. Change in Inequality for Workers Remaining Nonunion	Change in Inequality for Workers Remaining Union vs. Change in Inequality for Workers Leaving Union	Change in Inequality Among Workers Joining Union vs. Change in Inequality Among Workers Leaving Union
1. May Current Population Survey (1974–75)	–.08	–.05	–.06
2. National Longitudinal Survey of Men Aged 14–24 in 1966 (1970–78)	–.10	–.13	–.09
3. Panel Study of Income Dynamics (1970–79)	–.15	.01	–.03
4. Quality of Employment Survey (1973–77)	–.23	.03	–.07

SOURCE: R. B. Freeman, "Longitudinal Analyses of the Effects of Trade Unionism," *Journal of Labor Economics* 2 (January 1984): table 5.
NOTE: The degree of inequality is measured by the standard deviation of the log of earnings.

those who do not, and those leaving unions experience an increase in dispersion compared with those who stay in unions.

In sum, the evidence supports the argument that unions choose wage policies that reduce dispersion.

The White-Collar/Blue-Collar Differential

The average white-collar worker is higher paid than the average blue-collar worker. Therefore anything that reduces the white-collar/blue-collar differential will necessarily reduce wage inequality. Since union wage gains accrue primarily to blue-collar workers in the United States, the monopoly wage effect that increases inequality between organized and unorganized blue-collar labor also reduces inequality by lowering the white-collar/blue-collar differential in the organized sector.

To determine the quantitative magnitude of this reduction, we have examined the differential in the compensation of white-collar and blue-collar labor in 6,539 establishments in the Expenditures for Employment Compensation survey, which we previously used to analyze fringe benefits. We find that, with many other factors held fixed, unionism reduces the advantage of white-collar over blue-collar workers by about 15 percentage points. In the average nonunion establishment, the white-collar worker earns about one and a half times as much as the blue-collar worker. In the comparable union establishment, the white-collar worker earns about one-third more than the blue-collar worker, a considerably smaller premium. The union monopoly wage effect that is usually cited as a contributor to blue-collar inequality is at the same time a contributor to equality between blue-collar and white-collar labor.

The Inequality-Reducing versus the Inequality-Increasing Effects of Unionism

Thus far we have examined the inequality-related effects of union wage policies in the organized sector and found those effects to be quite substantial. The bottom-line question is: do the inequality-reducing or the inequality-increasing effects of unions predominate?

To answer this question it is necessary to add the *decrease* in inequality due to wage standardization and the *decrease* due to the reduction in the white-collar/blue-collar differential to the *increase* due to the greater wages of blue-collar union workers over other blue-collar workers.

We have performed such calculations using the standard mathematical formula for the decomposition of the variance of the log of earnings, and then transformed the estimates into the standard deviation metric by taking square roots. The formula makes the effects of unionism on inequality a function of the fraction of the work force that is unionized, the fraction that is nonunion white-collar and the fraction that is nonunion blue-collar, the magnitude of the union-induced change in inequality among union members, the union/nonunion wage differen-

TABLE 5–3
The Total Impact of Unions on Earnings Inequality

Due to:	Estimated Change in Inequality as a Percentage of Total Inequality
Reduction in Inequality Among Union Workers	−2
Reduction in White-Collar/Blue-Collar Differential	−2
Union Monopoly Wage Gain	1
Total Effect of Unionism	−3

SOURCE: Our calculations are derived with May 1979 Current Population Survey (CPS) data and various estimates in the text, as follows:

1. Initial variance, taken to be variance of log earnings among all nonunion workers in the May 1979 CPS, .281. The square root of this is the initial standard deviation, .530. We calculate all percentages in the table relative to .530.

2. To estimate the reduction in variance among union blue-collar workers, we take 70 percent of the difference in the variance of wages for union blue-collar (.156) and in wages for nonunion blue-collar workers (.229) on the basis of calculations showing that 20 to 30 percent of differences are due to differences in worker characteristics (Freeman, "Unionism and the Dispersion of Wages," *Industrial and Labor Relations Review* 36 [October 1982]: table 4, lines 1 and 2). This yields −.050; we subtract .050 from .281 to obtain .231 as our estimated variance with unionism. The square root of this is .481, which is 10 percent below .530. Finally, we multiply −10 percent by 0.25 (the union share of nonagricultural private employment) to obtain (properly rounded) −2 percent.

3. To estimate the contribution of changes in the white-collar/blue-collar differential, we used data from the 1972–1976 Expenditures for Employee Compensation Survey to obtain a .43 log differential in the absence of unionism and a .29 differential in the presence of unionism, square each and take the difference to obtain −.101. Multiplying by the white-collar share of employment (.5) and the union share of employment (.25), we obtain −.013, which produces an overall variance of .268, which is .518 in standard deviation units, or 2 percent below .530.

4. To estimate the contribution of the union monopoly effect, we use the estimated .22 impact on the log of total compensation from the EEC. data, square it, and multiply by the union share of the workforce and the nonunion blue-collar share of the workforce, to obtain .003. Adding this to .281 yields .284, or a standard deviation of .533, which is 1 percent higher than .530.

5. To obtain the total effect we add all the estimated union effects on variances weighted by the relevant percentages as follows:

1. effect on blue-collar workers (.25) (−.050)	=	−.03
2. effect on white-collar/blue-collar differentials (.5) (.25) (−.074)	=	−.009
3. effect on blue-collar union/nonunion differential (.25) (.25) (.22)^2	=	.003
Total Effect	=	−.019

The initial variance was .281, so the variance after the union impact is .262. Taking the square root of .262, we obtain .512, which is 3.4 percent below .530.

NOTES: Inequality is measured in standard deviation units, but underlying calculations are based on variances. The sum of the three effects need not add up in standard deviation units, though they do in variance units.

TABLE 5-4
Studies of the Impact of Unionism on Wage Inequality

Study	Nature of Data	Finding
1. Freeman (1980)	May Current Population Survey data on individuals and Expenditures for Employee Compensation data for firms.	Unionized workers have 15 percent lower standard deviation of log earnings than otherwise comparable nonunion workers; unionism reduces white-collar/blue-collar differential by 10 percent. These effects produce a 2–3 percent reduction in inequality among comparable workers.
2. Freeman (1982)	BLS *Industry Wage Survey* data on individuals working in nine industries.	Standard deviation of log (wages) in union sector is on average 22 percent lower than in nonunion sector.
3. Hirsch (1982)	Cross-Sectional Analysis of 1970 Census of Population data on 3–digit industries.	Each percentage point of unionization lowered the variance of log earnings by .015 points.
4. Hyclak (1977)	Cross-Sectional Analysis of 1970 Census data on earnings in SMSAs.	Each percentage point of unionization lowered the gini coefficient .021 points.
5. Hyclak (1979)	Cross-Sectional Analysis of 1970 Census data on male earnings in SMSAs.	Each percentage point of unionization lowered gini coefficient for men by .038 points.
6. Hyclak (1980)	Cross-Sectional Analysis of 1950, 1960, and 1970 Census data on family income in the 48 contiguous states.	Each 1 percent increase in the mean for unionization lowered the mean of the percent of families earning under $3,000 in 1970 by 3.0 percent. Similar findings for 1950 and 1960.
7. Plotnick (1982)	Time series analysis of Current Population Survey data for men.	Each 1 percentage point of unionization lowered variance of log (earnings) by .065 points.

SOURCES: (1) R. B. Freeman, "Unionism and the Dispersion of Wages," *Industrial and Labor Relations Review* 34 (October 1980): 3–23. (2) R. B. Freeman, "Union Wage Practices and Wage Dispersion Within Establishments," *Industrial and Labor Relations Review* 36, no. 7 (October 1982). (3) Barry Hirsch, "The Interindustry Structure of Unionism, Earnings and Earnings Dispersion," *Industrial Labor Relations Review* 36, no. 7 (October 1982). (4) Thomas Hyclak, "Unionization and Urban Differentials in Income Inequality," *The Journal of Economics* 3 (1977): 205–7. (5) Thomas Hyclak, "The Effect of Unions on Earnings Inequality in Local Labor Markets," *Industrial and Labor Relations Review*, October 1979: 77–84. (6) Thomas Hyclack, "Unions and Income Inequality: Some Cross-State Evidence," *Industrial Relations* 19 (Spring 1980): 212–15. (7) Robert D. Plotnick, "Trends in Male Earnings Inequality," *Southern Economic Journal* 48 (January 1982): 724–32. NOTE: Some of these studies used the variance of log earnings; others used the gini coefficient, a related measure of inequality; still others used the standard deviation of earnings. The different inequality measures should yield different reductions in inequality, as they do.

tial among blue-collar workers, and the average wage advantage accruing to blue-collar workers as a result of unionism relative to the average wage of white-collar workers.[16]

Table 5-3 presents the results of our analysis. Line 1 shows our best estimate of the reduction of inequality among union workers due to standard-rate policies. The reduction in inequality is 2 percent of the estimated total inequality in the absence of unions. Line 2 shows that the reduction in the white-collar/blue-collar differential lowers inequality by 2 percent; line 3 shows that the union monopoly effect on inequality among blue-collar workers has the smallest impact: raising inequality by 1 percent. Summing the three effects we find that on balance unionism reduces the dispersion of wages, lowering inequality by about 3 percent—a substantial impact for an organization encompassing a minority of the overall workforce—and a substantial impact compared with estimates of the effect on inequality of changes in education or the age composition of the labor force.

Because of widespread concern about wage inequality, the finding that unions reduce rather than increase wage dispersion has been put to several tests quite different from ours. Hyclak (Lehigh University) has examined the effect of unionization on earnings inequality in SMSAs (Standard Metropolitan Statistical Areas) and in states (other factors held fixed); Hirsch (University of North Carolina) has examined the effect of the fraction organized in an industry (again holding fixed other factors); and Plotnick (Dartmouth) has examined the effect of the fraction organized on inequality over time (again, other factors held fixed).

As documented in table 5-4, all these studies have yielded results comparable to ours: in each case, unions are estimated to reduce wage inequality, by roughly similar and economically sizable magnitudes. While scholarly concordance is no guarantee of truth, the new quantitative analysis of unionism appears to have answered at least one longstanding issue in the debate over what unions do. On the basis of the new empirical research, it appears that trade unionism in the United States reduces wage inequality by around 3 percent. On this front, the voice/response effects of the institution seem to dominate the monopoly wage effects.

The Exit-Voice
Tradeoff

THE MONOPOLY and voice/response faces of unionism lead to the same expectations about labor turnover. On the monopoly side, unionism is expected to reduce labor turnover by raising wages above competitive levels, a socially harmful effect. On the voice/response side, unionism reduces turnover, first by creating desirable work conditions, and second by providing discontented workers with a voice alternative to quitting. This reduction represents the "exit-voice" tradeoff discussed in chapter 1 as one of the key aspects of union voice. It changes the employment relationship from a casual dating game, in which people look elsewhere at the first serious problem, to a more permanent "marriage," in which they seek to resolve disputes through discussion and negotiation. Because permanent employees behave differently from temporary employees, the reduction in exit due to unionism has potentially far-reaching implications for the operation of firms.[1]

Which of the two faces is more important? Are voice-induced reductions in exit large, or small, relative to monopoly-wage-induced reductions? How important is the exit-voice tradeoff in any social evaluation of unionism?

not healthy to stay to have "long term" relationship

The Union Voice Effect on Exit Behavior

To answer these questions, we have examined the exit behavior of union and nonunion workers in several data sets encompassing thousands of workers. Some of our analyses contrast the proportion of union and nonunion workers who report quitting their jobs. Other analyses compare the average quit rate reported by establishments in industries that are heavily unionized with that in industries that are lightly unionized. Still others compare the number of years union and nonunion workers remain with the same firm.[2]

All the studies seek to isolate the effect of union voice on exit from other factors that influence exit by comparing workers with the same personal attributes (age, sex, and so on) and, most important, with the same wage. Controlling for the wage is critical, because union-induced wage increases also reduce quit probabilities, leading to a possible confusion of monopoly and voice effects.

Finally, because quitting is a dichotomous decision (either you do it or you don't), the analyses consider it in a probabilistic framework, examining the effect of unionism and other factors on the *probability* a worker quits or stays with the firm.

As can be seen in tables 6–1 and 6–2, our principal finding is that unionism greatly reduces the exit behavior of workers paid the same wages.[3] With wages and other factors the same, unionized workers are likely to quit much less frequently than nonunion workers (table 6–1) and to accrue more tenure than nonunion workers (table 6–2). In the analysis of all workers, the reduction in quits under unionism is estimated to vary from 31 percent to 65 percent of the average level of quits (table 6–1, lines 1 and 2), while the increase in tenure varies from 23 percent to 32 percent (table 6–2, lines 1 and 2). In the National Longitudinal surveys, which deal separately with older men, young men, mature women, and young women, we also find large reductions in quits and large increases in tenure, which vary across groups.

In addition to reporting the impact of unionism on quits for workers paid the same wages (our "voice effect"), table 6–1 also records the estimated effect of a 20 percent "monopoly wage" increase on quits. By comparing the effect of unionism with that of the 20 percent wage increase, we can see whether or not "union voice" has a greater or lesser impact on exit than union monopoly power.[4] In every case, the voice effect dominates the monopoly wage effect. The reason that unionized workers quit less and accrue more tenure than otherwise comparable nonunion workers has more to do with the fact that unionism transforms working places through "voice" than with the fact that it raises pay. When it comes to mobility, the voice face of unionism dominates the monopoly face.

TABLE 6-1
Estimates of the Effects of Unionism and a Twenty Percent Wage Increase on the Probability of Quitting

	Approximate Percentage by Which Quits Are Reduced by:	
Sample, Data Set, Years, (Number of Persons)	Unionism, for Workers Paid Same Wage (Voice Effect)	20% Wage Increase (Monopoly Effect)
1. All Workers, Panel Study of Income Dynamics, 1971–79 (10,938)	31	8
2. All Workers, May Current Population Survey, 1973–75 (98,593); analysis is of unemployment due to quitting	65	12
3. All Workers, Quality of Employment Survey, 1973–76 (796)	33	2
4. Older Males, National Longitudinal Survey, 1972–74, 1977–79 (3,718)	60	9
5. Younger Male Workers National Longitudinal Survey, 1969–78 (3,845)	21	5
6. Mature Females, National Longitudinal Survey, 1972–74, 1977–79 (3,718)	26	9
7. Younger Females, National Longitudinal Survey, 1970–80 (2,657)	16	8

SOURCES: (1) Based on linear probability analysis of pooled cross section of quits year to year from 1971 to 1979 with controls for industry, occupation, race, education, sex, and experience. Mean level of quits=.08. (2) R. B. Freeman, "The Exit-Voice Tradeoff in the Labor Market: Unionism, Job Tenure, Quits, and Separations," *Quarterly Journal of Economics* 94 (June 1980): table IIII. Mean level of quits=.004. Figure is low because it is limited to quits into unemployment. (3) Based on linear probability analysis with controls for industry, occupation, sex, education, race, tenure, and region. Mean level of quits=.05. (4) Based on linear probability analysis of pooled sample for 1972–74 and 1977–79 with controls for industry, occupation, education, race, and tenure. Mean level of quits=.15. (5) Based on linear probability analysis of pooled sample for periods 1969–71, 1971–73 and 1976–78 with controls for education, race, and tenure. Mean level of quits=.24. (6) Based on linear probability analysis of pooled sample for periods 1972–74, 1977–79 with controls for industry, occupation, experience, and schooling. Mean level of quits=.15. (7) Based on linear probability analysis of pooled sample for periods 1970–72, 1973–75, 1978–80 with controls for industry, occupation, experience, and schooling. Mean level of quits=.25. For discussion of each data set, see appendix.

Differences Among Groups

Does unionism reduce the exit of different types of workers by similar amounts, or do union exit effects differ among workers, as do union wage effects?

Comparisons of the union-caused increase in tenure for different groups of workers shows similarities for some groups and differences for

TABLE 6–2

Estimates of the Effect of Unionism and a Twenty Percent Wage Increase on Tenure of Workers

Sample, Data Set, Year, (Number of Persons)	Approximate Percentage Amount by Which Tenure Is Increased	
	Unionism, for Workers Paid Same Wage (Voice Effect)	20% Wage Increase (Monopoly Effect)
1. All Workers, Panel Study of Income Dynamics, 1979 (2,169)	32	9
2. All Workers, May Current Population Survey, 1979 (12,278)	23	11
3. Older Males, National Longitudinal Survey, 1976 (1,432)	35	2
4. Younger Males, National Longitudinal Survey, 1976[a] (1,882)	11	5
5. Mature Females, National Longitudinal Survey, 1977 (1,852)	32	12
6. Young Females, National Longitudinal Survey, 1978 (2,079)	27	11

SOURCE: Based on regressions of log tenure on union status, with industry, occupation, race, education, experience, and log wage controls. Approximate percentage amounts were calculated as antilogs of established union coefficients in semi-log regression models.
[a] 1976 tenure was calculated by a computer algorithm that estimated the variable by following the employment of young men.

others (see figure 6–1), as do comparisons of union-voice decreases in quits (see table 6–3). Indicative of the difference between what unions do as a wage-increasing monopoly and what they do as a voice institution, the union exit effect is relatively large for some groups of workers for whom the union wage effect is relatively small. More specifically, figure 6–1 and table 6–3 show:

• Unions have a roughly similar impact on the tenure of women and men. Studies of the quit behavior of men and women show a similar pattern (see lines 3 and 4 of table 6–3). Unions raise the tenure of blacks somewhat less than they raise the tenure of whites, but they have a roughly comparable effect on the quit behavior of blacks and whites (see lines 2, 4 of table 6–3). The implication of these union-induced increases in tenure and reductions in quits for women and for blacks is that the union voice improves the workplace for those groups significantly. It does *not*, however, mean that black or female workers are as well off in union settings as white or male workers. Since we are comparing unionized workers with nonunion workers in given demographic groups, all we can infer is that unionism affects all group members similarly.[5]

- Unionism raises the tenure of older workers more than that of younger workers. This is exactly the opposite pattern to that found for union wage effects in chapter 3, where we saw that unionism raises the wages of young workers more than those of older workers. What explains the reversal in differential impact? The major reasons are union seniority rules, which are so important that we devote all of chapter 8 to them; deferred compensation such as pensions, which are desired more by older than by younger workers; and the probably greater reliance on voice among immobile, long-service employees than among mobile new hires.

- Unionism raises the tenure of less educated workers and of less skilled workers more than that of more educated or skilled workers. This finding reflects the fact that under unionism formal work rules cover all employees, so that supervisors cannot treat those with better outside market opportunities more favorably than those with worse outside opportunities. By applying the same standards to all workers, unionism improves workplace conditions more for those at the bottom than for those at the top of the firm hierarchy and has a greater effect on their exit rates.

- Unionism has different effects on tenure by industry. It has large effects among service workers, where nonunion employees are likely to be especially poorly treated, moderate effects in manufacturing, and virtually none in construction. The lack of an exit-voice tradeoff in construction (where unions raise wages greatly) reflects the nature of construction work. In this industry union workers obtain short-term jobs with different contractors at the union hiring hall and are tied to their occupation rather than to their employer. Some of the other industrial differences are, we shall see, linked to specific clauses in collective bargaining contracts in the different sectors.

The question of how unionism affects quits has received considerable attention from other researchers in recent years, with the result that there now exist a large number of studies similar to ours. Because these studies use models, data, and statistical procedures that are somewhat different from ours, they obtain different estimates of the size of the union effect. If these different estimates told a substantially different story from ours, the reader would have a right to be suspicious of our findings, although (barring computer error) ours can be reproduced exactly. In the social sciences, it is not exact duplication of "experiments" that confirms a finding, but rather similarity of findings under different specifications. When reasonable researchers differ in what

Percentage Change in Tenure

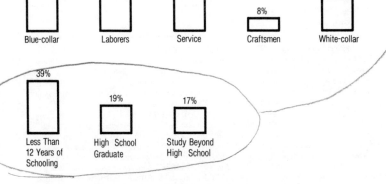

FIGURE 6–1

Whose Tenure Is Increased by Unionism?

Source: Calculated from May 1979 Current Population Survey. Based on regressions of log tenure on union variable and diverse control variables. Approximate percentage effects were calculated as antilogs in semi-log regression models.

TABLE 6–3
Results of Other Studies of Unionism and Exit

Studies of Individuals	Approximate Percentage Change in Quits Due to Unionism (for Workers Paid Same Wage)	Quit Effect Exceeds Effect of 20% Wage Increase
1. Blau and Kahn		
Young Men	−37	yes
Older Men	−92	yes
2. Leigh		
Older White Men	−81	yes
Older Black Men	−94	yes
Younger White Men	−37	yes
Younger Black Men	−1	no
3. Mitchell		
Males	−7	yes
Females	−20	yes
4. Blau and Kahn		
White Young Men	−33	yes
Black Young Men	−44	yes
White Young Women	−43	yes
Black Young Women	−18	yes
5. Long and Link		
Older Male Workers	−15	yes
Studies of Industries		
6. Pencavel, 1959	−49	yes
7. Stoikov and Raimon		
1963	−45	yes
1966	−43	yes
8. Burton and Parker, our revision	−35	yes
9. Brown and Medoff	−27	yes

SOURCES: (1) Francine Blau and Lawrence Kahn, "Unionism, Seniority and Turnover," *Industrial Relations* (forthcoming). (2) Duane E. Leigh, "Unions and Nonwage Racial Discrimination," *Industrial and Labor Relations Review* 33, no. 4 (July 1979): 439–50. Calculated using nonunion means to transform the estimates to percentage terms. (3) Olivia S. Mitchell, "Fringe Benefits and Labor Mobility," *Journal of Human Resources* 17, no. 2 (Spring 1982): 293. (4) Francine Blau and Lawrence Kahn, "Race and Sex Differences in Quits by Young Workers," *Industrial and Labor Relations Review* 34, no. 4 (July 1981): 563–77. (5) J. E. Long and A. N. Link, "The Impact of Market Structure on Wages, Fringe Benefits and Turnover," *Industrial and Labor Relations Review* 36, no. 2 (January 1983). (6) John Pencavel, *An Analysis of the Quit Rate in American Manufacturing* (Princeton, N.J.: Industrial Relations Section, Princeton Univ., 1970), p. 57, equation 1. (7) V. Stoikov and R. Raimon, "Determinants of the Differences in Quit Rates Among Industries," *American Economic Review* 63, no. 5, pt. 1 (December 1968): 1283–98. (8) J. Burton and S. Parker, "Interindustry Variation in Voluntary Labor Mobility," *Industrial Labor Relations Review* 22, no. 2 (January 1969): 199–216, as adjusted in Richard B. Freeman, "Why Do Unions Increase Job Tenure?" (Harvard Institute of Economic Research Discussion Paper 625), table 1. (9) Charles Brown and J. Medoff, "Trade Unions in the Production Process," *Journal of Political Economy* 86, no. 3 (June 1978): 335–78.

they view as the appropriate experiment or specification (that is, whether one includes current tenure in estimating the union impact on quits, whether one examines blue-collar workers separately from white-collar workers, or which of several functional forms one uses to model the probability decision), believability requires that all these different specifications yield qualitatively similar results.

In the case of the union impact on exit, the research has in fact produced such similar findings. Regardless of data set or specification, all the studies confirm the major claim of this chapter: that, independent of raising wages, unionism substantially reduces quits (see table 6–3). Virtually every study of the behavior of individuals finds this result, with the union impact on quits far in excess of the impact of a 20 percent wage increase. Virtually every study of industry turnover also finds that unionism lowers quits, with, however, the estimated effects of wages on quits being substantially larger than in the studies of individuals.[6]

Monopoly

Objections to the Empirical Studies

Numerous studies with different data and models covering thousands of workers produce the same findings. Does that mean the case is closed?

Someone unfamiliar with the problems of empirical social science or with the tenacious views of those who believe in the pure monopoly picture of unionism might regard the preceding evidence as conclusive and expect this chapter to end quickly. When we first presented some of these results, that was our expectation. But because social scientists are unable to control (or even measure) every *possible* determinant of behavior, the evidence is not unassailable. And adherents to the strict monopoly view of unionism have accordingly raised several objections to the empirical findings:

Objection 1: "The findings are marred by a failure to measure the full monetary rewards under unionism and thus the incentive to remain with an employer for reasons of union monopoly power."

The principal monetary reward omitted is fringe benefits, about which most surveys contain only spotty information. Since unions raise fringe benefits and since fringe benefits, like other forms of compensation, should reduce quits, the objection has merit. Omission of fringes will lead to an understatement of the impact of union monopoly power and an overstatement of the effect of union voice on quits. The question is, by how much?

Our answer, based on analyses of three data sets with measures of fringes included and excluded, is that the overstatement of the effect of voice is modest indeed. In one data set, the impact of unionism drops by 15 percent; in others, it barely changes at all.[7] Corroborating our analysis, Mitchell (Cornell) has found a sizable union impact on quits, with inclusion of various fringe benefits, in her analysis summarized in table 6–3, line 3. We conclude that omission of fringes from most studies does not seriously mar the estimated voice effects of unionism.

Objection 2: "The studies of unionism and exit are flawed because they do not measure the wages workers can earn outside the firm."

Since in principle the decision to quit or stay depends on a comparison of current wages and the wages individuals *could* get elsewhere (information that is essentially unobservable in a survey), this objection correctly points out another flaw. While all studies control for differences in personal characteristics (age, education, and so forth) and job characteristics (industry and occupation), persons with the same objective characteristics may have very different earnings in the market, producing a potential bias in the analyses. The question is, by how much and in what direction?

Our answer is that omission of "true" alternative earnings leads to an underestimate of the union impact on exit. This is because union workers have, in general, better opportunities outside the firm than nonunion workers with the same measured characteristics and wage.[8] Since the union workers have better opportunities outside, the pecuniary incentive for them to quit their employer is greater than it is for nonunion workers. By failing to take account of the greater incentive for unionists to quit, our calculations (and those of other researchers) underestimate the true impact of unionization on quits. At the same time, however, lack of information on the wages a worker could get elsewhere leads to an underestimate of the effect of wages on quits, suggesting that we may have overstated the impact of union voice relative to the impact of union monopoly power on exit. We have made statistical adjustments to correct for this problem as well, and we still find that the voice effects of unionism reduce exit by more than does a 20 percent monopoly wage increase.[9]

Objection 3: "Union workers are innately more stable than nonunion workers. After all, it's easier to organize stable workforces than those with high turnover. You have misinterpreted the direction of causality: unions do not increase stability; rather, stable workers choose unions."

The essence of this objection is that because cross-sectional studies of the union exit effect compare the behavior of *different* persons, it is possible (though unlikely) that the observed relation is due to innate differences between those persons rather than to union-induced changes in behavior. There is one empirical way to respond to the objection: to compare the exit behavior of the same worker when he or she is a union member and when he or she is not a union member. If the estimated union-exit relation were due to unions' organizing more stable workers, such a comparison would show *no* difference in behavior. If, by contrast, unions really reduce exit, then the same worker would quit less and accrue more tenure in the unionized setting than in the nonunion setting.

Comparisons of the exit behavior of the same workers over time, summarized in table 6–4, show that the bulk of the estimated impact of unionism on exit is due to changes in behavior. The same person has a lower probability of quitting a union job than a nonunion job, even when the two jobs offer the same wages.[10]

How Union Voice Reduces Exit

What do unions do to a workplace that causes this change in worker behavior? What is special about a unionized work environment that reduces exit? Our analysis points to two specific union innovations:

103

TABLE 6-4

Studies of the Impact of Unionism on Exit Behavior, Based on Comparisons of the Same Person Over Time

Sample, Data Set, Years Covered	Approximate Percentage Reduction in Probability of *Quit* When Worker Is Union	Approximate Percentage Increase in Tenure When Worker Is Union
1. All Workers, Panel Study of Income Dynamics, 1968–72	−21	—
2. Young Men, National Longitudinal Survey, 1972–79	−30	26
3. All Workers, Quality of Employment Survey, 1973–77	—	63
4. National Longitudinal Survey, 1967–69, 1971–73		
Younger men	−13	—
Older men	−11	—
5. All Workers, Panel Study of Income Dynamics, 1968–78	−52	—

Sources: (1) Richard B. Freeman, "The Exit-Voice Tradeoff in the Labor Market: Unionism, Job Tenure, Quits, and Separations," *Quarterly Journal of Economics* 94 (June 1980): 643–74. (2,3) Richard B. Freeman, "Fixed Effects Modes of the Exit-Voice Tradeoff": National Bureau of Economic Research Working Paper (Forthcoming). (4) Calculated from Jacob Mincer, "Union Effects: Wages, Turnover, and Job Training": National Bureau of Economic Research Working Paper No. 808 (1981). We have averaged the difference between quits for workers becoming unionized and those leaving union (table 8) and divided by the average quit rate in the sample (calculated from table 1 and table 7). In Mincer's data there is a large reduction in quits from joining a union but little change from leaving a union. (5) Calculated from Mincer, "Union Effects." We averaged the difference between quits for workers becoming union and those leaving union and divided by the average quit rate in the sample (calculated from table 1 and table 7). Again, the data show a large reduction in quits from joining a union but little change from leaving. Approximate percentage increases in tenure were calculated as antilogs of estimated union coefficients in semi-log regression models.

development of grievance-and-arbitration systems, which enable workers to appeal managerial decisions, and seniority-based personnel policies.

Nearly all unionized work places have grievance-and-arbitration systems, though the scope of issues covered varies widely (table 6–5). These systems provide workers with a judicial-type mechanism to protest and possibly to redress unfair or incorrect decisions of their supervisors. In a typical manufacturing plant, grievance/arbitration generally involves four steps. At the first one, the worker complains to his or her steward, who talks to the worker's supervisor. At the second step, a member of the union's grievance committee meets with a member of the personnel department at the plant. At the third, an officer of the local union meets with the plant's top management. If this step fails

TABLE 6-5

Grievance/Arbitration Provisions in Major Collective Bargaining Agreements

	Percentage of Contracts	Percentage of Workers
All Agreements	100.0	100.0
1. With Grievance Clauses	98.8	98.5
With Grievance Clauses Covering All Disputes	43.2	47.3
With Grievance Clauses Covering Only Some Disputes	55.6	52.0
2. With Arbitration Clauses	96.1	96.5
With Arbitration Clauses Covering All Disputes	67.2	63.0
With Arbitration Clauses Covering Only Some Disputes	28.9	33.5

SOURCE: *Characteristics of Major Collective Bargaining Agreements* (Washington, D.C.; Department of Labor, Bureau of Labor Statistics, Bulletin 1957, 1977), tables 8.1 and 8.2.

to produce agreement, the two sides will call on outside arbitration for a binding decision.

Regardless of who eventually wins the grievance, quits will be lowered by the presence of the appeals system. If the worker wins the protest, the cause of discontent will be removed, keeping the worker at the firm. If the worker loses but feels he or she received a fair hearing, the probability of quitting will be reduced. Finally, even if the worker eventually quits, plant level quits will be lower as a result of the delay while the grievance was being settled.

To examine the effect of grievance-and-arbitration procedures on quits, we have analyzed the impact of unionism on the quits of workers with varying degrees of job satisfaction, on the assumption that those who are dissatisfied are more likely to raise a grievance than those who are satisfied, and thus that the union impact on quits should be greater on those with the greatest dissatisfaction. In fact, figure 6-2 shows this to be the case, with quit rates rising much more modestly among union than among nonunion workers as dissatisfaction rises.[11] In a corroborating study using the 1977 Quality of Employment Survey, Kochan (MIT) and Helfman (Cornell) found that, wages held fixed, "Job dissatisfaction exerts twice as strong an effect on the (subjective) propensity to quit of nonunion workers as of union members. . . ." They go on to note that this finding is "consistent with the voice hypothesis."[12]

An alternative way of testing the effect of grievance and arbitration on exit behavior is to compare unionized workers in sectors of the

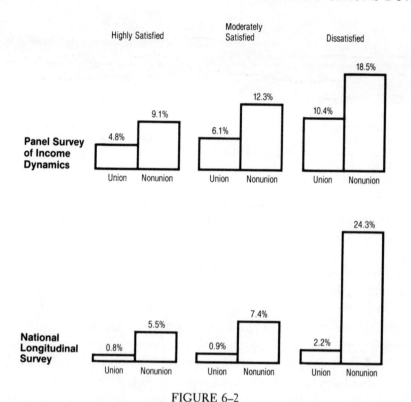

FIGURE 6–2

Quit Rates Among Workers with Different Levels of Expressed Job Dissatisfaction

SOURCE: R. B. Freeman, "The Exit-Voice Tradeoff in the Labor Market: Unionism, Job Tenure, Quits, and Separations," *Quarterly Journal of Economics*, 94, no. 4 (June 1980): table VI.

economy having different types of grievance systems. The stronger or more inclusive the grievance system, the greater should be the reduction in exit. While detailed knowledge of the operation of grievance machinery is needed for a definitive evaluation, the data on collective bargaining clauses from the Bureau of Labor Statistics (table 6–5) provide a rough measure of the scope of grievance systems. The BLS divides grievance clauses into those with "unrestricted" coverage in which "any dispute or complaint could be processed as a grievance" (43 percent of the total) and those with "restrictive" coverage that "limit the grievance process to disputes arising under or relating to specific terms of the contract" (56 percent). Analyses of the relation between the type of grievance system in an industry and the union impact on the tenure of union workers shows greater levels of tenure of union workers in sectors with grievance systems having wider scope.[13]

In sum, one reason for the lower quits under unionism is the dilution of managerial authority over workers by a system of negotiated rules and procedures in which workers have a right to appeal and obtain reversals of management decisions.

Seniority provisions give advantages to senior workers in promotions and protection against layoffs and favor them for other benefits and rights as well. Our analysis suggests that the quit patterns of workers are greatly affected by the existence and strength of seniority rules. First, as we noted in the discussion of figure 6–1, we found that unionism has a greater effect on the exit of older than of younger workers; the logical reason for this is the greater value older workers place on seniority provisions, which benefit them, at the expense of the young. Secondly, we have compared the tenure of union workers in industries with strong seniority layoff clauses with tenure in other industries and found that unionists accrue more tenure where the clauses are strongest. Analysis of quit rates among industries by Block (Michigan State University) yields a similar result, with quits lower where union-negotiated seniority clauses are strongest.[14] We conclude that seniority rules play an important part in the lower turnover under unionism.

Why Don't All Companies Have Grievance-and-Arbitration Systems?

If grievance-and-arbitration and industrial jurisprudence rules reduce turnover, and if such reductions save companies money, the question naturally arises as to why nonunion firms don't mimic union firms and offer workers the benefits of voice as part of a profit-maximizing strategy. One reason they do not is that nonunion firms respond more to the desires of young, mobile workers, who are less likely to want a grievance-and-arbitration system, than to the desire of older, more permanent employees, who presumably have greater desire for such voice mechanisms. The exit-voice tradeoff runs both ways: workers with voice exit less, but at the same time workers who rely on exit have less desire for voice. As long as nonunion firms are attuned to the desires of potentially mobile workers, they are unlikely to see the need for grievance and arbitration.

Studies of the response of firms and workers to union organizing drives, which depend on the desires of the majority rather than the mobile minority of workers, bear this out. In nine of the ten nonunion grievance systems we investigated, managers admitted that their firms introduced the system to prevent unionization. Several companies put the systems in place after a union organizing drive, making the threat of unionism the cause of the grievance system. A study by the Conference Board of white collar unionization drives confirms this finding: 63 percent of firms who turned back a union drive introduced new communication systems immediately thereafter, in several cases including formal grievance systems. Finally, indicative of the desire of the majority of workers for grievance systems, the Conference Board further reports that companies with an appeals system won 79 percent of union representation elections in their sample compared with 51 percent of those with a less formal "open door" policy and 44 percent of those with no such policy. If nonunion firms always responded to majority rule, they would have more formal grievance systems than in fact they do.[15]

A second reason for the absence of grievance and arbitration in the nonunion sector is that, for such systems to work, management must give up power and accept a dual-authority channel within the firm. Such a change in power is difficult to attain in the absence of a genuine independent union or union-like organization. During the 1920s many firms experimented with so-called "employee representation" plans designed to provide a nonunion voice mechanism for workers. Many of these plans ended in failure, despite the best intentions, because workers were unwilling to express their desires for fear of retaliation by management and because they lacked power to affect decisions. Other plans led to the formation of company unions which, in several industries, became the building blocks of independent unionism in the 1930s.[16] Under current law, of course, company unions are illegal. The dilemma is that if management gives up power, it creates the seeds of genuine unions; if it doesn't, employee representation plans may be mere window-dressing.

A study by the Bureau of National Affairs of personnel policies for unorganized workers shows the difficulty of operating an effective grievance system without a union. In the BNA study, which covers firms especially attuned to "good labor relations," 30 percent reported that they had some type of formal grievance system. But few claimed the system worked well. According to company spokesmen, "often the formal procedures are rarely if ever used" either because of "timeliness —it takes too long to get complaints resolved—[or because of] employees' fear of reprisal from their supervisors." Even more striking is the fact that when the procedures are used, "the percentage of the final decisions that upheld the original action by management is very high," with about one-half of the companies supporting the supervisor in *every* case.[17] Less than one in three nonunion grievance systems allowed outside arbitrators, rather than company officials, to make the final decision on a grievance.

The problem is akin to that of operating a democratic parliament in a monarchical or dictatorial regime. As long as the monarch or dictator has the final word, the parliament cannot truly function. This is not to say that no nonunion firm will have a viable grievance system, for some do, but rather that it is exceedingly difficult to institute an effective system in the absence of a union.

The Economic Impact of the Exit-Voice Tradeoff

Granted that, monopoly wage effects aside, unionism substantially lowers quits and increases tenure with a firm. Is the reduction in exit worth a lot to the firm? to the worker? How does the possible gain in social product from lower turnover compare with the monopoly cost of unionism?

To evaluate the economic worth of the exit-voice tradeoff, we have estimated how much the voice-induced reduction in exit is worth to firms and to workers. For firms, we estimate that the lower turnover is equivalent to a 1 percent to 2 percent reduction in cost, or equivalently, to a 1 percent to 2 percent increase in productivity.[18] While not negligible, these savings are dwarfed by the union wage effect, guaranteeing that firms will not invite organization to enjoy the benefits of lower turnover. For workers, we estimate the dollar value of the lower quit behavior as being, conservatively, about equivalent to a 2 percent increase in wages. We obtain this estimate by a two-step procedure. First, we calculate the increase in wages necessary to reduce the nonunion quit rate to the union quit rate: after correcting for the potential underestimate of the reduction in quits due to wages (see objection 3 earlier), we estimate that unionism is equivalent to a 40 percent wage increase. That is, it would take a 40 percent increase in the wages paid nonunion workers to lower nonunion quit rates to the union level. Second, assuming that only the minority of workers whose quits would be reduced by unionism value unions so highly, we multiply the 40 percent figure by .05, the approximate difference between union and nonunion quit rates. This yields our estimate of 2 percent of wages ($=40$ percent $\times$ .05). Given that workers not at the coming-or-going margin also value unionism highly, this 2 percent may understate the extra welfare created by union voice for union workers. Transformed into the equivalent increase in GNP, the increase in welfare is worth 0.2 to 0.3 percent of GNP or $20 to $30 per person in 1980 dollars. This is of comparable magnitude to the social cost of unionism estimated in chapter 3. There is, however, one difference between these two estimates: the benefit of voice accrues to organized workers only, whereas the costs come out of everyone's pocket. Even so, it is striking that the voice benefits, traditionally ignored in quantitative evaluations of unionism, are as large as the monopoly costs.

C H A P T E R 7

Adjustment to Business Cycles

Ford Motor Company said it plans to temporarily close six of its 15 U.S. car assembly plants for periods totalling five to 11 work days next month. . . . Ford said the temporary plant closing scheduled for March will result in the idling of some 17,200 workers. The closings are a continuation of a series of production cutbacks by auto makers, who are trying to hold inventories in check in the face of slumping new car sales.[1]

Last November 27, Frank Georges, a 38-year-old steelworker, arranged for a loan to buy a $56,000 house that was roomier and closer to his job at U.S. Steel Corp.'s Ohio Works here. But on the way home from the bank that day, Mr. Georges got the news over his car radio: U.S. Steel was closing the Ohio Works, the related McDonald Works five miles away, and many other facilities. Some 13,000 steelworkers around the country would lose their jobs.[2]

ONE of the most important personnel decisions made by a firm is how to adjust its employment, wages, and hours to swings in product demand. During a slump, some firms sit back and hope that normal voluntary attrition will reduce unnecessary employment. Other firms attempt to mitigate the effects of falling demand by reducing the level or growth in hourly compensation. Still others try to reduce total hours paid for by reducing average weekly hours. A final group turns to layoffs, which may be temporary or permanent, depending on the severity and duration of the downturn.

A firm's choice among adjustment alternatives determines which of its employees, if any, will bear labor's share of the cost of the downturn. Lowering wages or sharing the work distributes the cost among all employees, from the most senior to the newest hire. Laying off workers by inverse seniority hurts junior employees while protecting the position of senior workers. Closing down a plant obviously harms all, with those whose opportunities elsewhere are relatively worse suffering the most. Because unions are concentrated among blue-collar workers in the most cyclically sensitive sectors of the economy, the policies of unions toward the various adjustment mechanisms are important both to organized workers and to society as a whole.

How does collective bargaining affect labor adjustments to the business cycle? Does a given change in demand affect employment, hours, and wages differently in unionized as opposed to nonunionized firms? Do union adjustment policies create greater unemployment among union workers than is found among otherwise comparable nonunion workers?

Effects of the Business Cycle on Unionized and Nonunionized Industries

Before comparing the adjustments of union and nonunion firms to the business cycle, it is important to recognize that heavily unionized industries face more substantial cyclical swings in demand than do lightly unionized industries. As shown in chapter 2, two of the most heavily unionized sectors of the economy are manufacturing and construction, both of which are cyclically volatile in the extreme. While manufacturing employs only one-fourth of nonagricultural employees, it has been the source of more than half of the economy's cyclical employment variation.[3] From 1950 to 1982, employment in manufacturing dropped significantly seven times. Two sets of downturns were quite severe: the one between 1973 and 1975, when the percentage of unemployed experienced private sector wage and salary workers in manufacturing rose from 4.3 to nearly 11 percent, and the one between 1979 and 1982, when the comparable unemployment rate rose from 5.5 to over 12 percent. Each of the downturns was followed by an upswing; in some cases the upswing brought about large employment gains (in the 1966–69 upturn, employment grew by 5.0 percent), but in other cases, notably in the 1970s, the upturns were modest. Construction activity and employment also vary greatly over time, although the sensitivity of the industry to interest-rate changes often produces a different timing to cyclical swings. Indicative of the sizable swings in employment in construction, during the 1979–82 recession, the number of workers in this sector fell by 10 percent, while total employment remained nearly stable.[4]

Table 7–1 documents the differential cyclical sensitivity of union and nonunion industries in terms of the variation in changes in total hours and employment over business cycles from 1958 to 1981. The greater the reported measure of cyclical sensitivity, the greater is the impact of the business cycle on the sector. The figures show cyclical swings in total hours more than four times larger in high-unionization industries than in low-unionization industries in the private sector as a whole. A large percentage of the difference is due, as noted, to the concentration of union membership in manufacturing, although within manufacturing heavily unionized industries show greater cyclic variability in total hours than lightly unionized industries. The figures on employment variation are somewhat less pronounced, but basically tell the same story.

TABLE 7–1
Cyclical Changes in Hours Worked and Employment

	All Workers, All Industries (34)		All Workers, Manufacturing Industries (20)	
	Lowest Unionization Industries (17)	Highest Unionization Industries (17)	Lowest Unionization Industries (10)	Highest Unionization Industries (10)
Variance of Cyclical Changes in Total Hours (in log units)	.011	.045	.017	.026
Variance of Cyclical Changes in Employment (in log units)	.008	.029	.012	.015

SOURCE: Variances in the log of hours and the log of employment were based on calculations isolating cyclical factors from long-term trends or seasonal variation. These variances were derived with data for 34 2–digit SIC industries for the period 1958–81. Based on research discussed in J. L. Medoff and J. A. Fay, "The Pattern of Cyclical Labor Adjustment in U.S. Manufacturing," National Bureau of Economic Research Working Paper (Forthcoming).

There are two possible causes of the greater cyclical swings in employment in unionized industries: 1) greater cyclical swings in product demand, or 2) greater adjustment of labor to a given change in product demand. Analysis of changes in shipments in union and nonunion sectors and of responses of labor to given changes in shipments suggests that employment fluctuates greatly in unionized industries within the manufacturing sector largely because of product demand fluctuations. Indeed, within the manufacturing sector, we estimate that the variation in shipments over the business cycle is nearly twice as large in the heavily unionized as in the lightly unionized industries. By contrast, we find no noticeable difference in the response of union and nonunion sectors to given changes in shipments. Our estimates suggest that every 10 percent change in shipments generates approximately a 7 percent change in blue-collar hours in both sectors. While union hourly wages are less responsive than nonunion hourly wages to changes in output, the wage responses in both sectors are too modest to be a major component of the overall adjustment pattern.[5]

Responses to Cyclical and Permanent Change

The amount of cyclical labor adjustment is similar in union and nonunion firms within an industry, but the mechanism by which the firms respond to the business cycle differs greatly. In particular, when demand for output declines, unionized establishments are more likely to reduce labor costs by placing workers on temporary layoffs than by cutting wage growth or weekly hours. Temporary layoffs typically last less than a month and generally end with the recall of the laid-off workers.[6] Because workers are generally recalled or rehired, temporary layoffs are not as serious as permanent layoffs, which occur as a result of such permanent economic changes as the shutting down of an entire plant.

Table 7–2 shows the differential rate of layoffs in unionized and nonunionized firms and the extent to which union and nonunion workers are unemployed because of temporary layoffs. The differences

TABLE 7–2

Layoffs in Manufacturing

Unit of Observation	Union	Nonunion
Average Monthly Percentage of Layoffs for All Workers		
1. State by Broad Industry Cells, 1965–69	2.3	.5
2. Detailed Industries, 1958–71	2.2	1.0
Average Monthly Percentage of Blue-collar Workers Unemployed Due to "Temporary Layoffs"		
3. Broad Industries, May 1973, 1974, and 1975	3.9	2.5
4. Detailed Industries, May 1973, 1974, and 1975	4.0	2.6

Source: J. L. Medoff, "Layoffs and Alternatives Under Trade Unions in United States Manufacturing," *American Economic Review* 69, no. 3 (June 1979): 380–95. The units of observation for the first two rows were: (1) States within 2–digit SIC Manufacturing Industries; (2) 3–digit SIC Manufacturing Industries. In both cases figures are derived from regressions that have controls for the nature of each industry's technology, product market, and workforce; figures are calculated with cross-industry mean values. The units for the third and fourth rows were: (3) 2–digit Census (of Population) industries; (4) 3–digit Census industries. The figures in each row are weighted averages, with the size of each industry's workforce as its weight. The industry proportions were derived from Current Population Survey data.

are substantial: layoff rates are two to four times higher in the union than in the nonunion sector, and union workers are 50 to 60 percent more likely to be on temporary-layoff unemployment as a result.

Why do unionized workers and firms choose temporary layoffs rather than reductions in wages or hours? Perhaps the most important reason is that temporary layoffs usually mean laying off junior workers, not the senior employees who have a greater influence on union policies than they would have on the policies of a nonunion firm. Faced with the choice of reduced earnings through fewer hours or lower wages or the unemployment of a junior worker, the senior worker will select the policy that is personally most beneficial. Except in cases where mass layoffs are threatened, this will lead him or her to prefer layoffs to the other forms of adjustment.

A second reason is that part of the cost of temporary layoffs can be shifted onto other firms through the unemployment insurance (UI) system. Under this system employers put money into a fund that goes to workers in the form of UI benefits when they are unemployed. The system operates in such a way that firms and workers with above-average layoffs are subsidized at the expense of firms and workers with below-average layoffs. The UI tax to the firms has an upper limit, so that the cost of UI benefits going to laid-off workers beyond that amount is not borne by the firm. The benefits received by the worker are not taxed unless the worker has a significant income (for example, in Massachusetts, $12,000 or more for a single worker and $18,000 or more for one who is married), so the worker gets a tax break. Because of the UI subsidy to the unemployed, both unions and firms may prefer layoffs to other forms of labor adjustments. We estimate that the average annual union/nonunion differential in per-employee (not per-laid-off employee) UI subsidy represents from .4 to .6 percent of the average annual after-tax earnings of a fully employed manufacturing worker with three dependents. Comparing this with the wages union workers lose as a result of greater layoffs, which we estimate ranges from 1.2 to 2.0 percent of after-tax earnings,[7] unemployment insurance repays about one-third of the lost wages of the temporarily laid-off worker.

The union preference for temporary layoffs over worksharing appears to have increased in recent years. Slichter, Healy, and Livernash report that prior to the Second World War, " . . . a substantial number of unions insisted on reasonable work-sharing before layoffs could be made, whereas today the trend of union preference is more and more toward the restriction of work-sharing arrangements." Indeed, they note that after the Second World War, "In some cases the union asked that layoffs be used exclusively without any work-sharing."[8] Comparison of contracts that contain worksharing (hours reduction) provisions in 1954–55 and in 1970–71 support this conclusion. In 1954–55, 5 percent of the major contracts covered by hour-reduction provisions stated that layoff proceedings would begin when hours worked were below normal for four weeks or less. By 1970–71, that figure had risen to 43 percent. Moreover, the union role in the decision to lay off workers as opposed to sharing work through hours reduction has increased. In 1970–71, 72 percent of the workers covered by reduction-in-hours provisions had a guarantee of union participation in the choice between reduced hours and immediate layoffs, compared with just 31 percent in 1954–55. The Bureau of Labor Statistics wrote in 1970–71 that one of the main reasons why a union wants a meaningful voice in decisions involving work sharing is that "if . . . it is known that man-power needs will be curtailed for a lengthy period, the union may prefer to bypass the reduced hour provisions and initiate layoffs immediately."[9]

Just as union and nonunion firms respond differently to cyclical downswings, so do they respond differently to upswings. Since unionized firms make greater use of layoffs in recessions and are as likely as nonunion firms to recall laid-off workers when demand grows, they increase employment more by rehiring laid-off workers relative to hiring new employees than do nonunion firms. The magnitude of the difference between rehiring laid-off workers and hiring new workers is substantial; our calculations show a ratio of rehires to new hires that is two to three times greater in the unionized sector.[10]

It is one thing to be laid off temporarily, knowing you will be recalled to your job in a few weeks. It is another matter entirely to face the danger of extended joblessness because of an event such as a plant closing or bankruptcy. In a temporary layoff, the senior worker is protected by inverse seniority layoff rules; when a shutdown threatens, all workers' jobs are seriously endangered. As a result, union policies with respect to shutdowns differ from their policies with respect to temporary layoffs. Threatened with shutdowns, unions frequently accept the alternatives to layoffs, including—as we saw in chapter 3—substantial wage concessions.

The result of these policies is that, in sharp contrast to the higher rate of temporary layoffs and temporary layoff unemployment found among union than among nonunion workers, the rate of permanent layoffs is roughly the same between the groups (see figure 7–1). Moreover, the rate of unemployment due to permanent job loss turns out to be less among union workers than nonunion workers, as we shall soon see.

Unions, Unemployment, and Employment

Do union adjustment policies raise unemployment and lower employment? There are two ways to analyze this important question. First, we can compare the impact of union cyclical adjustment policies on the level of unemployment of the organized sector relative to the level in the unorganized sector of industries. Second, taking a more global perspective, we can analyze the full impact of unionism on unemploy-

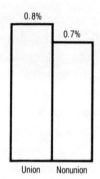

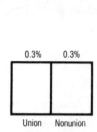

Union	Nonunion	Union	Nonunion
Percentage of Workers		**Percentage of Workers**	
Permanently Laid Off		**Permanently Laid Off**	
per Month 1958–71		**per Month 1981**	

FIGURE 7–1

*Monthly Rates of Permanent Job Loss Among Comparable Union and Nonunion
Manufacturing Workers*

Source: 1958–71 estimates obtained from data for 3-digit SIC industries as described in table 7–2; the permanent layoff rate was defined to equal the total layoff rate minus the difference between the accession rate and new hires rate, which approximates the recall or rehires rate. The 1981 permanent layoff rate was estimated as the total layoff rate minus the recall rate in the last six months of 1981 (the only months for which recall rates were available).

ment and employment in the economy as a whole, including the possible increased unemployment among workers displaced by union monopoly wage gains.

The first approach yields a definite and somewhat surprising answer. As figure 7–2 shows, unemployment rates for experienced blue-collar union and nonunion workers in the same manufacturing industry turn out to be quite similar, despite the greater use of temporary layoffs under unionism. In some years the union blue-collar workers have slightly greater levels of unemployment; in other years they have slightly lower levels than otherwise comparable nonunion workers. We find the same result when we compare unemployment rates for experienced blue-collar workers in non-manufacturing industries.

If unionized workers are more likely to be laid off and, as seen in table 7–1, are more likely to be unemployed due to layoffs, how can the unemployment experiences of unionized and nonunion workers in the same industry be virtually identical? The reason for similarity in unemployment rates is found in the smaller flow into unemployment of

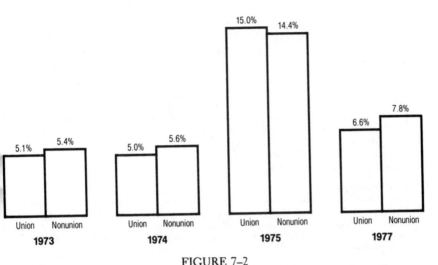

FIGURE 7–2

Unemployment Rates Among Union and Nonunion Experienced Blue-Collar
Workers from the Same Manufacturing Industry

Source: Based on May Current Population Survey data. To obtain these figures we calculated the rates of unemployment of union and nonunion workers for each 3-digit manufacturing industry and then aggregated these rates to all-manufacturing figures by taking weighted averages, using as weights total employment in each industry.

Note: The year 1976 is missing because in that year the Bureau of the Census did not ask unemployed workers whether they were or were not union members (as they have not from 1978 to the present).

workers who quit or who are permanently laid off under unionism. As table 7–3 indicates, there are three ways in which an experienced worker can become unemployed: by being temporarily laid off and failing to obtain another job while awaiting recall; by being permanently laid off and failing to find another job; and by quitting work without having another job lined up. Unions raise unemployment by increasing temporary layoffs but reduce unemployment by lowering quits and, in the period covered, also by lowering the flow of permanently laid off workers into unemployment.

While adjustments to the business cycle under unionism do not produce excessive unemployment in the organized sector, unionism could still lower employment and raise unemployment by reducing the jobs available in the economy. If workers who are displaced or not hired because of high union wages cannot find employment elsewhere, the total level of unemployment will be raised. How important is this indirect effect of union monopoly power?

To answer this question, we have examined unemployment and

119

TABLE 7-3

Unemployment Percentages for Blue–Collar Workers in Same Manufacturing Industry

	1973–75		1977	
	Union	Nonunion	Union	Nonunion
Unemployment Due to Involuntary Permanent Job Loss	2.3	3.1	2.3	3.4
Unemployment Due to Temporary Layoff	4.0	2.6	2.0	1.4
Unemployment Due to Quitting Job	1.8	2.7	2.3	3.0
Total Unemployment	8.1	8.5	6.6	7.8

SOURCE: To obtain these figures, we calculated the rates of unemployment for blue-collar union and nonunion workers, using Current Population Survey microdata for workers in each 2–digit industry category. We then aggregated these figures to get all-manufacturing estimates by taking weighted averages, using as weights total employment in each industry.

employment from 1970 to 1978 among geographic areas of the country, comparing the percentage of the labor force unemployed and the percentage of the population employed in high and low unionization areas. As figure 7–3 shows, our results suggest that there is, indeed, higher unemployment in unionized areas. It is not clear, however, whether this fact results from unionism or simply reflects union concentration in older industrial parts of the economy. We estimate that in areas where unionization is relatively high, unemployment rates are about 1.0 point higher than in areas where unionization is relatively low. It is important to note, however, that the magnitude of the differences vary across data sets and time periods, suggesting that the union effect is not well specified.[11]

When we look at the percentage of the population of working age that is employed, by contrast, we find no evidence that unionism has adverse effects on employment. As figure 7–3 makes clear, unionism appears to be unrelated to the percentage of the population employed. One possible explanation of the differential impact of unionism on unemployment and employment among areas is that unions raise unemployment for the most part not by reducing employment but by increasing the labor force. High union wages, after all, ought to attract more persons into the job market. In short, the evidence on the effect of unions on employment and unemployment in an area presents a mixed picture.

Percentage of the Labor Force Unemployed

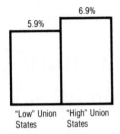

Percentage of the Population Aged 16 and Above that is Employed

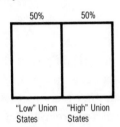

FIGURE 7–3

Unemployment and Employment in "Low" and "High" Union States, 1970–1978

SOURCE: The state employment and unemployment rates are from the May Current Population Survey for each year. The state union percentages are from R. B. Freeman and J. L. Medoff, "New Estimates of Private Sector Unionism in the United States," *Industrial and Labor Relations Review* 32 (January 1979): 143–74. NOTE: "Low" union states are those whose level of unionization is one standard deviation or more below the mean; "high" union states are those whose level of unionization is one standard deviation or more above the mean. The percentages presented are based on the results of a pooled cross-section/time-series regression.

Conclusion

While unions affect neither the total amount of labor adjustment to the business cycle nor the aggregate level of unemployment, they alter the firm's choice between layoffs and both wage and hours adjustment. In the union sector this choice is dictated by the preferences of senior workers, who are protected against being temporarily laid off by inverse seniority rules but are not protected against the job loss resulting from a plant closing or bankruptcy. The choice reflects the web of union policies designed to favor senior members, to which we turn next.

CHAPTER 8

"Respect Your Elders": The Role of Seniority

SENIORITY, defined as length of service in an employment unit, governs numerous personnel decisions in modern firms. The seniority of one worker relative to another ("competitive status seniority") frequently determines who gets temporarily laid off, terminated, or promoted. The absolute amount of seniority entitles workers to various fringe benefits or levels of benefits, such as vacation time ("benefit seniority"). In the union sector, seniority operates through explicit clauses in collective agreements, such as the following on layoffs, promotions, and vacations:

When fitness and ability are equal, bargaining unit seniority will determine the order of layoff in the event of a decrease in the working force due to curtailed operations, any reduction of personnel within a job classification, or because of any other reason.[1]

Management will select the senior employee, provided the qualifications, such as ability, aptitude and attendance of the individuals considered meet the job classification requirements and are judged by Management to be reasonably equal.[2]

Employees will be entitled to two weeks' vacation with pay after completing one year of continuous service. Employees will be entitled to three weeks' vacation with pay after completing five years' continuous service. Employees will be entitled to four weeks' vacation with pay after completing fifteen years' continuous service. Employees will be entitled to five weeks' vacation with pay after completing twenty years' continuous service. Employees will be entitled to six weeks' vacation with pay after completing thirty years' continuous service.[3]

In the nonunion sector, management often takes account of seniority but can ignore it when it chooses. Since unions tend to be more responsive to the desires of senior workers and since explicit contracts are more binding (and legally enforceable) than either unwritten or written nonunion management policies, seniority should be more important in the operation of union than of nonunion firms.

How much more important? Which personnel practices are most affected by seniority rules? How much does the greater role of seniority under unionism benefit older union members at the expense of younger members? Are union seniority rules socially desirable or undesirable?

To answer these questions we have analyzed data from collective bargaining contracts, from surveys of union and nonunion workers, and from specially designed questionnaires concerning the employment practices of managers of union and nonunion work groups. The questionnaires were developed to quantify actual practices in nonunion settings, where the role of seniority is otherwise difficult to assess, and to provide comparative data from union environments.

The Importance of Seniority in Layoffs

Sales fall. The company reduces output. It must lay off some workers. Will the company choose to lay off a senior worker, whose compensation exceeds the compensation of a junior worker, or will the company choose to lay off a junior worker under a last-in-first-out layoff policy?

Table 8–1 shows that a majority of both union and nonunion hourly or blue-collar workers are covered by seniority policies with respect to layoffs, but that the actual degree of protection given senior workers is much greater under unionism. Indeed, among a sizable fraction of the unionized workforce there is such strong job protection for those with long service that a senior worker is "never" terminated before a junior co-worker.

Even when a union contract lacks a written seniority-layoff provision, moreover, the union will pressure management at the shop floor to institute defacto layoffs by seniority. Among the managers surveyed for table 8–1, 59 percent of those in union firms who did not have a written

TABLE 8-1

The Role of Seniority in Deciding Whom to Lay Off

	Written Policy or Collective Agreement		Practice		
	Have Written Policy or Collective Agreement that Deals with Permanent Layoffs (%)	Seniority Stipulated to Be Most Important Factor in Permanent Layoffs (%)	Senior Never Let Go in Place of Junior (%)	Senior Let Go if Junior Believed to Be Worth Significantly More on Net (%)	Senior Let Go if Junior Believed to Be Worth More on Net (%)
BNA Review of Union Contracts, 1983					
All	89	78	—	—	—
Manufacturing	98	89	—	—	—
Nonmanufacturing	74	63	—	—	—
Medoff-Abraham Survey (Results for Hourly Employees), 1982					
All Union Firms	92	84	84	14	3
All Nonunion Firms	36	68	42	44	14
Large Union Firms	96	83	87	13	0
Large Nonunion Firms	51	69	42	45	13
Small Union Firms	87	86	78	15	7
Small Nonunion Firms	21	67	42	42	15

SOURCES: Bureau of National Affairs, Daily Labor Report, 9 March, 1983, pp. E1–E2; Katharine G. Abraham and J. L. Medoff, "Length of Service, Terminations, and the Nature of the Employment Relation": National Bureau of Economic Research Working Paper No. 1086 (1983). See appendix for discussion of the Medoff-Abraham Layoff/Promotion data set.

NOTE: For this table, "large" means at least 200 employees and "small" means fewer than 200.

agreement about seniority in layoffs said they would never lay off a senior worker before a junior worker. By contrast, only 36 percent of those in nonunion firms without a written policy said their practice was always to layoff junior workers first. Unions improve the security of senior versus junior workers through their day-to-day actions as well as through the contracts they negotiate.

An older worker has a smaller chance of job loss relative to a younger worker under unionism, but that does not mean that in a downturn the older union worker is less likely to be laid off than the older nonunion worker. After all, as we saw in the preceding chapter, layoffs are more common under unionism. Seniority could lead to lower layoff rates for older (senior) union workers than for comparable nonunion workers, or it could simply offset the higher overall rate of layoffs among unionists.

Actual layoff rates of union and nonunion workers by seniority for the 1969–71 and 1974–75 downturns show that in those years the seniority advantage to older union members did indeed give them greater security with respect to permanent job loss than that held by older nonunion workers (see table 8–2). Whereas younger union workers had much higher chances of being laid off permanently or temporarily than their nonunion peers, older union workers had a higher chance of being temporarily laid off, but a much lower chance of being permanently laid off.

Consistent with the weight given seniority in layoffs under unionism, the percentage of union workers who regard their job security as "good" rises steadily as length of service increases, whereas among nonunion workers, the percentage regarding job security as good rises early in the work life but falls later on (figure 8–1). As a result 55 percent of union workers with twenty or more years of seniority compared to 33 percent of nonunion workers with twenty or more years of seniority report good job security.

Finally, as further evidence of the importance of seniority in union layoff decisions, about one-quarter of the major collective bargaining contracts have clauses under which senior employees have the right to be laid off *ahead* of their junior compatriots. By giving the senior workers the option to be laid off first, these provisions allow the senior worker to take "layoff vacations" for short periods of time. This right is usually exercised if the layoff is temporary and if a large fraction of

TABLE 8–2

The Effect of Seniority or Age on the Chance of Being Laid Off Among Blue-Collar Workers

	Young Men (19–24)		Mature Men (35–54)	
	Union	Nonunion	Union	Nonunion
1. Young and Mature Men, National Longitudinal Survey, 1969–71				
Percentage Experiencing a Temporary Job Loss	9	2	4	2
Percentage Experiencing a Permanent Job Loss	13	14	4	6

	Junior Hourly Employees		Senior Hourly Employees	
	Union	Nonunion	Union	Nonunion
2. Medoff-Abraham Survey, 1982				
Percentage Experiencing Permanent Job Loss	8	3	1	3

Sources: (1) Francine D. Blau and Lawrence M. Kahn, "Union Coverage, Seniority, and Layoffs" (University of Illinois at Urbana, 1980, mimeographed). (2) K. G. Abraham and J. L. Medoff, "Length of Service, Terminations, and the Nature of the Employment Relation" (National Bureau of Economic Research Working Paper No. 1086, 1983). See appendix for discussion of the Medoff-Abraham Layoff/Promotion data set.

an employee's earnings would be replaced by private supplemental unemployment benefits and Unemployment Insurance benefits.

The Importance of Seniority in Promotions

Sales rise. The company increases output. It expands the workforce and decides to promote some workers. Will the company choose to promote a senior worker or a junior worker?

Seniority can enter promotion decisions in several ways:

- Seniority can dominate the decisions, with the most senior person, regardless of ability, receiving the promotion.
- Seniority can be of primary importance, with the most senior of all employees *minimally able* to perform the job being promoted.

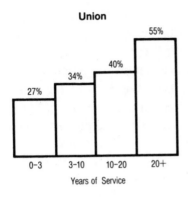

FIGURE 8–1

Proportion of Blue-Collar Workers Who Say Their Job Security Is Good

SOURCE: The figures are based on the responses of blue-collar private sector wage and salaried workers to the 1977 Quality of Employment Survey. These figures give the percentage answering "very true" as opposed to "not at all true," "not too true," or "somewhat true," to the following statement about their job: "The job security is good."

- Seniority and ability can be used with equal weight as two determining factors.
- Seniority can determine promotions only when the ability of the senior person is approximately equal to other applicants.
- Seniority can be ignored completely in decisions, or even be a negative factor, reducing one's chances of a promotion.

To see how unionism affects the weight placed upon seniority in promotions, we have compared the seniority provisions in major collective bargaining agreements with the practices of companies in the Bureau of National Affairs' Personnel Policy Forum. As the Forum companies include both union and nonunion companies, who are not differentiated in the published data, our comparison is likely to under-estimate differences in the weight placed on seniority in union and nonunion settings. In the contracts, we find more than 70 percent specifying seniority as a "factor" in promotions, with 45 percent of all collective contracts stipulating it to be the most important factor in promotions. By contrast, in the BNA survey just 53 percent of compa-nies specify seniority as a factor and only 12 percent view it as a "major factor" in promotions.[4]

Corroborating the inference of a greater role of seniority in promo-tion under unionism, the Medoff-Abraham survey of managers found that 33 percent of the managers of unionized workers, compared with 12 percent of managers of nonunion workers stated that in actual practice they would never promote a junior over a senior worker, even if the junior employee were a much better candidate for the job. While seniority is evidently weighed more heavily in promotion deci-sions among organized employees, it is important to note that 43 percent of the managers of union employees stated that they promote junior workers if they are *"significantly* better" than senior workers, and nearly one-quarter of those supervising union members said they might promote junior workers if they were simply "better."[5] Hence, these figures show that in contrast to relatively rigid first-in-last-out layoff rules, there is a wide divergence in promotion rules under col-lective bargaining. Some unionized managements are rigidly con-strained by seniority, and others are relatively free to promote the "better" worker.

The way in which seniority practices affect the actual career paths of individuals in union and nonunion settings has been analyzed by Olson (SUNY at Buffalo) and Berger (Purdue). In a study of about 1,000 union and nonunion workers, in which they controlled for a variety of other factors, including sex, race, education, occupation, and industry, Olson and Berger found that seniority significantly raised the probability of being promoted for union workers but had no such effect for nonunion workers.[6] Detailed analysis of promotions within six com-panies studied by Abraham (MIT) and Medoff has yielded similar results: seniority *per se* appears to be very important among unionized hourly workers, less important among nonunion hourlies, and unimpor-tant among those paid salaries, in particular among managers and professionals.[7]

The Importance of Seniority in Benefits

Most fringe benefits tend to be more highly valued by senior than by junior workers. Some benefits, such as paid vacation time, rise with seniority; other benefits, such as life, accident, and health insurance, which are equally available to all workers, are more likely to be used by older (that is, senior) workers; still others, notably pensions, are more valuable to seniors because they are nearer retirement.

Unions can influence the extent to which the benefit package favors senior workers in two ways: by affecting the presence of, and expenditures on, fringes favorable to them and by affecting the degree to which benefits rise with seniority (the "tilt" of the benefit schedules). Our analysis of the three fringe benefits whose value differs greatly between junior and senior workers—vacation pay; life, accident, and health insurance; and pensions—suggests that unions raise the benefits of senior workers relative to junior workers both by inducing firms to introduce fringes beneficial to seniors and by tilting benefits toward older workers.

With respect to vacation pay, unionized firms give their employees more paid vacation days than do nonunion firms, particularly when the workers have accrued considerable seniority. In terms of paid vacation days the average union blue-collar worker with a year or less of service receives six days compared with five days for the average nonunion blue-collar worker; the unionist with one to ten years of service receives eleven days compared with eight for the nonunionist, while the unionist with ten or more years receives seventeen days compared with twelve days for the nonunionist.[8] For the purposes of comparing these differences with differences in wages, we divide them by 260, which is the potential number of nonweekend working days in the year. By this measure the union vacation days "raise" the wages of the least senior worker by 2 percent, those of the worker with one to ten years seniority by 4 percent, and those of the most senior by 7 percent. The nonunion vacation days are equivalent to wage increases of 2 percent, 3 percent, and 5 percent, respectively.[9] These figures imply that the total compensation (wages plus benefits) of the most senior workers relative to their junior co-workers is raised by roughly two percentage points more under unionism.

With respect to life, accident, and health insurance, unionized firms are more likely to offer such benefits and spend more on them. Since seniors are more likely to get sick, the expenditures on such plans benefit them more than they benefit juniors. To obtain a crude notion of the differential benefit accruing to younger and older workers from life, accident, and health insurance, we have examined the cost to workers of different ages of obtaining such insurance from insurance companies. The costs rise sharply with age, as one might expect.[10] Translating the cost differences into wage equivalences for comparison with wages and other benefits, we estimate that for a worker in his twenties, a representative life insurance program is roughly equal to a 1.0 percent wage increase; for a worker in his forties, it is equal to a 3 percent increase; for a worker in his sixties, it is roughly equal to a 7 percent wage increase.[11] The greater expenditures by union firms on such programs will accordingly tilt the proportion of benefits further in favor of senior workers in the union sector.

The third major fringe which benefits seniors more than juniors is defined benefit pension plans. Unlike defined contribution pension plans, in which each worker's payments ultimately go for his own pension, defined benefit plans promise a worker a given amount for which all workers may be viewed as paying. The extent to which senior workers benefit more than junior workers from a defined benefit plan depends on the rate at which future earnings are discounted, the probability that workers will ultimately receive the pensions (dependent on mobility, vesting rules, and life expectancy), and the rate at which the defined benefits rise over time. For a worker in his twenties, we estimate that the value of pensions rises annually by the equivalent of a 3 percent wage increase; for a worker in his forties, the value rises annually by the equivalent of a 5 percent wage increase; for a worker in his early sixties, the value rises annually by the equivalent of 10 percent wage increase. If we translate the pension into annual wages, we see that it improves the position of older relative to younger workers by as much as a 7 percent wage increase for older workers[12] (10 percent less 3 percent). Once again the tilt toward the senior worker is greater under unionism, because, as we saw in chapter 4, union workers were 20 to 25 percent more likely to have a pension plan than otherwise comparable nonunion workers, and because the union plans are more likely to be of the defined benefit type.

Table 8–3 presents our estimates of the wage equivalence (value as a percentage of wages) of the three benefits by the age of the worker. According to the figures, whereas young union and nonunion workers obtain benefits having a roughly similar wage equivalence, older union workers get fringes with a considerably higher equivalence than do older nonunion workers. By providing more deferred compensation, unions do more for older union workers than nonunion firms do for older nonunion workers. The magnitudes in the table are large enough to suggest that the standard comparison of wages by age substantially understates the economic rewards to older workers in the union sector.

Explaining the Age-Wage Anomaly

One of the most puzzling findings of union wage studies is that age and seniority have smaller positive impacts on union than on nonunion wages, implying that older workers benefit less from unionism than younger workers. Because this result runs counter to many theories of unionism (our own included), which stress the tendency for unions to be especially attuned to the desires of senior workers, it is disturbing.

Our analysis of seniority offers a resolution to the anomaly. We find that, while wages do not rise as rapidly with age or seniority for union workers as for nonunion workers, nonwage benefits rise more rapidly with age under unionism, and by more than enough to offset the slower increase in wages with age. When we examine the full spectrum of economic rewards—fringe benefits and inverse seniority layoff rates as well as wages—we find that unions do indeed benefit older workers to a greater extent than younger workers.

Figure 8–2 shows this result. The first graph shows the age-wage paradox: the decrease in the union wage advantage with age. The second graph shows that, after allowance for the wage value of fringes, the union differential is highest for the oldest group of workers but is still greater for the youngest group than for middle-aged workers. Finally, adjusting for the greater job loss rates of younger than of older union workers reduces the relative well-being of younger union members, as members who lose their jobs lose *all* of the union compensation

TABLE 8–3
Value of Major Fringe Benefits as Percentage of Wages, by Age and Union Status

Age of Worker	Union Workers				Nonunion Workers			
	Vacation Pay %	Life and Medical Insurance %	Pensions %	Total %	Vacation Pay %	Life and Medical Insurance %	Pensions %	Total %
20	2	1	2	5	2	1	1	4
30	4	2	3	9	2	1	2	5
40	5	3	5	13	3	2	3	8
50	6	5	7	18	4	3	4	11
60	7	7	9	23	5	5	5	15

SOURCE: Calculated as described in text. See R. B. Freeman and J. L. Medoff, "The Return to Seniority Under Unionism," National Bureau of Economic Research Working Paper (Forthcoming).

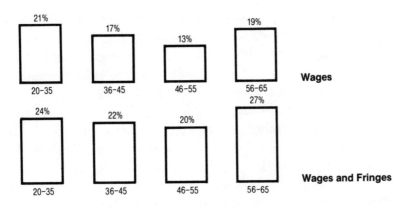

FIGURE 8–2

The Approximate Effect of Unionism on Compensation, by Age Group

SOURCES: Wages, figure 3–1; Wages and fringes, derived with data from table 8–3. See R. B. Freeman and J. L. Medoff, "The Return to Seniority Under Unionism," National Bureau of Economic Research Working Paper (Forthcoming).

differential. This reinforces the point of figure 8–2: the full effect of unionism on economic well-being (as opposed to just wages) rises with the age of workers.

In judging the economic effects of unionism on workers with different ages, one must look beyond simple wage comparisons.

Union Seniority Rules: Good or Bad?

Granting that unions tilt the economic rewards in favor of senior workers, should we view this as socially desirable or undesirable? Our present knowledge does not permit a scientific answer to this question. There are obvious costs of seniority, such as possible reductions in efficiency as workers find merit to be less well rewarded, but obvious benefits as well, such as replacement of the uncertainty of managerial discretion by rules, and protection for vulnerable older workers. If union seniority rules reduced efficiency greatly, we would probably judge them socially deleterious. If nonunion management made blatantly unfair layoff and promotion decisions, we would probably judge union seniority rules socially beneficial. But neither theory nor evidence

133

supports either extreme view. In theory, the competitive market may fail to produce socially efficient labor contracts because it places too little weight on the interests of workers whose mobility costs are high (usually senior workers) and is generally unable to enforce contracts with deferred benefits that may improve productivity. On the other hand, while unions take account of the desires of senior as well as junior workers, they ignore the interests of workers who may be hired in the future and thus may overvalue seniority benefits. Kuhn (Western Ontario) has analyzed the likely net effect of union seniority rules on economic well-being and has shown that the rules' impact depends on the type of market in which the union operates.[13] Union seniority rules are likely to be socially advantageous when the costs of mobility are high and the productivity of senior workers considerably lower in jobs other than their current jobs and when there are gains to be had from workers staying with firms for long periods. Under other circumstances the effect of the rules is ambiguous. At present our best guess is that the rules are, on net, socially beneficial, but we lack the quantitative studies of the various circumstances to reach a clear conclusion.

Even if union seniority rules create a better labor contract than that found in nonunion companies, some readers may object to the rules because of their alleged negative impact on the progress of minority workers. After all, isn't seniority a major deterrent to affirmative action efforts to improve the position of minorities? The NAACP, among others, has taken this point of view in the past. At its 1976 annual convention it adopted the following resolution:

We call upon EEOC, . . . the courts and Congress to act to insure that blacks, other minorities, and women who have received employment or promotion as a result of affirmative action or other EEO programs, not be deprived of the benefits of that employment under the 'last hired, first fired' theory.[14]

Herbert Hill, then NAACP National Labor Director, went further in stating the NAACP opposition to seniority provisions in collective bargaining agreements, promising a continued "program of litigation and other activities against last-in-first-out" layoff and seniority promotion rules. Not all civil rights activists, however, agree with the NAACP view. For instance, Bayard Rustin, the organizer of the 1964 March on Washington for the Civil Rights Act, has repeatedly come out in favor of seniority. Indeed, if blacks and whites had the same seniority one might argue that strict seniority rules provide the greatest protection against discrimination possible, as they remove any possibility for biased employer treatment of workers.

Our tabulations of 1979 Current Population Survey data show that while among male union blue-collar workers blacks have an average of a year less seniority than whites, implying some disadvantage, black women have nearly a year more seniority than white women, implying some advantage.[15] The differences in either case are sufficiently modest to support the Rustin rather than the Herbert Hill position on the impact of seniority on black economic well-being. The charge that seniority is injurious to minority economic interests is wrong, because large numbers of minority workers have accrued sufficient seniority to be its beneficiaries. While specific cases exist where layoffs by inverse seniority will harm efforts to increase minority representation, in general seniority is not inimical to the economic interests of blacks.

Conclusion

One of the major differences between union and nonunion work settings is the greater importance of seniority under unionism. Union seniority clauses protect older union workers from the danger of layoffs and give them greater chances of promotion compared with otherwise similar older nonunion workers. The economic benefits accruing to senior union workers in terms of fringes and layoff protection are sufficiently large to reverse the finding of union wage studies that junior workers gain more than senior workers from unionism. When the full spectrum of seniority-related benefits is considered, we find unionism benefits senior workers roughly as much or more than junior workers. Because minority workers have considerable seniority in many areas of the economy, seniority is less of a barrier to their progress and more of a protection against discrimination than is often realized.

CHAPTER 9

Are They Satisfied?

WORKERS covered by collective bargaining have higher wages, better fringes, better seniority protection, better grievance systems, and greater voice in determining the conditions of their employment than do other workers. They quit less frequently than other workers. Therefore they should express greater satisfaction with their jobs than otherwise comparable nonunion workers. Right?

Wrong. In survey after survey of job satisfaction, unionized workers express paradoxical feelings toward their jobs. While on the one hand they are less willing than similarly paid nonunion workers to change jobs and are more convinced that it is hard to find jobs as good as their current jobs, union workers also report themselves less satisfied with most facets of their work, notably overall job conditions and supervisory treatment.

What explains the paradox? If unions "deliver the goods" to the workers, why are the members dissatisfied? What facets of employment are particularly unsatisfactory to union workers? To what extent are they dissatisfied with the performance of their union? As for dissatisfied nonunion workers, do they see unionization as a means of resolving workplace problems, or do they rely largely on the exit option of dealing with employer problems?

Measures of Worker Satisfaction

"How do you feel about the job you have now? Do you like it very much, like it fairly well, dislike it somewhat, or dislike it very much?"

136

"Taking everything into consideration, how likely is it that you will make a genuine effort to find a new job within the next year?"

Questions like these are often asked on surveys of individuals to assess attitudes toward work and toward labor mobility. While many economists are leery of the answers to such questions, because they relate to the subjective views of workers rather than to objective behavior, the answers are closely linked to objective behavior, so they are important in understanding or predicting that behavior. Whether a worker is satisfied or dissatisfied with his or her job is, for example, one of the most important determinants of whether or not that worker will quit in the future and also of whether he or she is likely to support unionization. Despite the problems inherent in subjective variables like reported job satisfaction, these variables provide insight into economic behavior and what unions do to that behavior.[1]

The Anomaly of Dissatisfied Union Workers

Most workers respond to questions about satisfaction and future mobility by stating that they like their jobs very much or fairly well and are not interested in changing. *A priori,* one expects a certain consistency in the answers to satisfaction and related "mobility" questions. Workers who report themselves satisfied should not be seriously looking for a new job. Workers who report themselves dissatisfied, by contrast, ought to be especially likely to be looking for new positions and planning to quit in the near future.

In general, this is the case, with groups of workers who report greater job satisfaction (all other factors, including wages, held fixed) also reporting themselves as having less intention to look for other jobs and a smaller probability of quitting in the next few years (see table 9–1). There is, however, one notable exception to the general pattern: union workers. As the last line of table 9–1 shows, union workers report themselves as being less well satisfied than otherwise comparable nonunion workers, while at the same time showing less interest in finding new employers. Perhaps most importantly, the inconsistency between the reported satisfaction and intention to quit is mirrored in

TABLE 9–1

Effect of Selected Worker Characteristics on Job Satisfaction and on Intentions to Seek New Jobs

Characteristics of Workers	Expressed Job Satisfaction	Reported Behavior of Seeking a New Job	Consistent?
Age	Older workers more satisfied with their jobs	Older workers less desirous of changing jobs	yes
Education	More educated workers less satisfied with their jobs	More educated workers more likely to seek new jobs	yes
Wage	Higher paid workers more satisfied with their jobs	Higher paid workers less likely to seek new jobs	yes
Race	Nonwhite workers less satisfied with their jobs	Nonwhite workers more likely to seek new jobs	yes
Unionism	Union workers less satisfied with their jobs	Union workers less likely to seek new jobs	no

SOURCE: These findings are obtained by analyses of expressed job satisfaction and reported likelihood of seeking a new job with the 1977 Quality of Employment Survey. The analyses are based on 1,023 workers with controls for major industry, occupation, log wage, age, race, sex, tenure, tenure squared, and unionism. The indexing calculations used a z-score measure to deal with the categorical variables. Similar results were obtained with other surveys.

an inconsistency between the satisfaction responses and the actual quit behavior of union workers. In general, groups who are dissatisfied with their jobs quit, but (as we saw in chapter 6) union workers are much more likely to stay with an employer than nonunion workers.

This result—lower reported job satisfaction coupled with lower intended or actual mobility among union workers—is found in virtually all large surveys that question workers about satisfaction (see table 9–2) and in most studies on the subject.[2] Union workers complain about their work but neither intend to, nor do, leave.

What accounts for this seeming contradiction?

If it were simply the case that union workers reported less job satisfaction than nonunion workers, the monopoly model of unionism might explain dissatisfaction. One likely response of employers to high union wages is to save money by toughening up work standards and letting nonpecuniary conditions of work deteriorate, thus reducing worker satisfaction. In the extreme case, unionized workers would be no better off than nonunion workers: they would be making more at a cost of less pleasant work. But if this explanation were correct and union workers were truly less satisfied or no more satisfied with

TABLE 9–2

The Conflict Between Expressed Satisfaction and Actual Exit Behavior Among Union Workers

	Estimated Effect of Unionism on		
Data Set, Dates	Job Satisfaction	Intended Quit Rate[a]	Actual Quit Rate
1. Panel Study of Income Dynamics, 1972–73	lower	lower	lower
2. Older Men, National Longitudinal Survey, 1969–71	lower	lower	lower
3. Younger Men, National Longitudinal Survey, 1969–71	lower	lower	lower
4. Quality of Employment Survey, 1973	no effect	lower	lower
5. Quality of Employment Survey, 1977	lower	lower	—

SOURCES: (1), (2), (3) R. B. Freeman, "Job Satisfaction as an Economic Variable," *American Economic Review* 68 (May 1978): 135–41. (4) James Hughes, "An Exit-Voice Model of the Labor Union: Some Implications for the Individual Worker," (Honors Thesis, Harvard College, 1976). (5) Analysis as reported in table 9–1. Also, David Mandelbaum, "Responses to Job Satisfaction Questions as Insights Into Why Workers Change Employers" (Honors Thesis, Harvard College, 1980).
[a]The questions about intentions to quit differ between surveys but this does not appear to influence results.

their work places than nonunion workers, they would also be seeking new jobs at the same rate as nonunion workers, and they are not. The paradox is not that unionists are less well satisfied than others, but that their expressed dissatisfaction is inconsistent with their exit behavior.

The exit-voice analysis offers an intriguing explanation for the paradox, which highlights the role of unions as a voice institution. It differentiates between "true" dissatisfaction, which leads workers to leave their jobs, and "reported" or "voiced" dissatisfaction, which results from critical attitudes toward the workplace and a willingness to complain about problems. The difference between "true" and "voiced" dissatisfaction reflects the nature of the voice institution. As Borjas (University of California at Santa Barbara) has aptly stated the argument,

. . . one of the by-products of union (voice) is the politicization of the firm's workforce, and union members can be expected to express less job satisfaction than nonunion workers. That is, the exit-voice model states that in order for firms to hear the workers effectively, the firm's workforce must express itself "loudly." Note, however, that this dissatisfaction is not genuine in the sense that it leads to quits, but is instead a device through which the union can tell the firm that its workers are unhappy and are demanding more.[3]

A useful analogy can be drawn with the differences in the willingness of citizens to complain about governmental activities in a democracy and in a dictatorship. In a democracy people are vocal about their government, whereas in a dictatorship they are silent. Democratic politics thrives on individuals expressing themselves loudly and dictatorial regimes suppress voice; the difference in the expressed complaints has little if anything to do with actual objective circumstances.

Testing the Exit-Voice Explanation

To test the voice explanation of the dissatisfaction paradox, it is necessary to compare the effect of unionism on specific aspects of the conditions of work with the effect of unions on expressed satisfaction with those conditions. If the explanation is correct, unionized workers should have better (or no worse) work conditions than nonunion workers but should express less satisfaction with those conditions than nonunion workers do. Because most surveys obtain information on workplace conditions from workers rather than from objective sources, however, such contrasts of worker perceptions and reality are few, indeed. The limited work that has been done, however, supports the voice explanation. In one study, Kochan (MIT) and Helfman (Cornell) examined the relationship between unionism and worker perceptions of job hazards and between unionism and actual occupational injuries. Kochan and Helfman found union workers to express greater perception of occupational injuries despite experiencing rates of injury similar to those of other workers. "Union members report more problems with job hazards than comparable nonunion workers . . . even after controlling for the average injury rate in the industry."[4] If we take actual injuries as indicating workplace realities, then there is only one possible interpretation of the reported greater job hazards: that union voice makes workers more aware of hazards and the problems posed by the hazards.

Another study, by Berger (Purdue), Olson (SUNY at Buffalo), and Boudreau (Cornell), found that virtually all union worker dissatisfaction is attributed primarily to workers' negative perceptions of their supervisors and their tasks.[5] If these perceptions reflected reality, rather than union voice, we would find union workers who expressed them to be much more likely to quit than union workers with more favorable assessments. In fact, there is no difference between the proportion of union workers with unfavorable perceptions who quit and the proportion with favorable perceptions who quit. For instance, 21 percent of union workers who regarded their supervisors as competent or only moderately competent quit their job in the next four years, compared with 21 percent of those who regarded their supervisors as somewhat competent and 24 percent of those who regarded them as incompetent.[6]

The observed tendency of even dissatisfied union workers to remain with their employers suggests that the exit-voice tradeoff may itself reduce the level of satisfaction among unionists. If dissatisfied workers who stay with their employer in one year are more likely to be dissatisfied in ensuing years than other workers, the lower quit rate of the dissatisfied under unionism will produce greater dissatisfaction in union workplaces. Indeed, our analysis of data from the Quality of Employment 1973–77 panel survey suggests that the greater tendency for dissatisfied unionists to remain with their employer may raise the percentage of unionists who are dissatisfied by as much as 6 percentage points relative to the percentage who would be dissatisfied if unionism did not reduce quit rates.[7]

What Are They Dissatisfied With?

The degree of unionized workers' dissatisfaction with their workplaces varies greatly with different aspects of their jobs. Since unions take credit for obtaining wages and fringes for workers, one might expect union workers to be more satisfied with those aspects of work, except during periods of contract negotiation, and less satisfied with nonwage aspects of employment. In fact, our analysis of nearly one hundred questions on worker perceptions of their jobs finds this to be the case. Controlling for wages, union workers are as satisfied with their level of pay and with their fringe benefits as nonunion workers. By contrast, as shown in table 9–3, union workers have very poor perceptions of supervisors and of their own relationship with supervisors; they also have somewhat more critical views of physical conditions of work and job hazards. When one looks at the specific questions on supervisory performance, one striking difference is that union workers claim that their supervisors do not encourage or help them to contribute to improving the production process. Union workers were less likely to state that "My supervisor offers new ideas for solving job-related problems"; "My supervisor pays attention to what you're saying"; or "My supervisor encourages those he/she supervises to exchange opinions and ideas." While we lack independent information to determine the extent to which those perceptions reflect reality as opposed to voice-induced complaining, it is likely that at least some of the critical attitude of the union workers is due to their greater awareness of problems and willingness to speak out.

With respect to physical conditions of work, the surveys show a more modest union impact: while union workers report worse workplace conditions in many respects, they also report better workplaces in other respects. Most of the differences are too modest to merit extended attention.

Apparently the voice impact is greatest on the personal relationship between workers and supervisors—a fact that highlights the impor-

TABLE 9–3

Union Versus Nonunion Perceptions of Diverse Characteristics of Jobs, 1969, 1977

	Number of Instances Where Union Members Perceive Job Characteristics as Worse/Better than Nonunion Members			
	1969		*1977*	
Characteristic	*Worse*	*Better*	*Worse*	*Better*
Supervisory Relations	33	4	24	1
Physical Conditions	38	20	17	5
Hazards	14	2	11	1

Source: Tabulated from Quality of Employment Survey, 1969 and 1977. Based on regressions of attitudes toward work conditions on unionism and various controls, including age, sex, race, occupation, and rate of pay. The table counts only those findings where the difference between union and nonunion workers was at least as large as the estimated standard error of the union effect. In most cases, the differences were statistically significant by the usual criterion.

tance of the union in an adversarial relation with management on shop floors. Finally, like Kochan and Helfman, we find union workers reporting more work hazards, despite reporting no difference in actual injuries —a result explicable by the voice effect.

Satisfaction with the Union

Surveys also ask workers about the performance of their union. Are most workers satisfied with their union? Who is dissatisfied, and in what areas do they believe their union is falling down on the job?

The numbers in parentheses in table 9–4 show that about three-fourths of all unionists are very or somewhat satisfied with their union, a proportion noticeably below the proportion of unionists very or somewhat satisfied with the job itself (89 percent, as shown in last row). The cross-tabulation of satisfaction with one's union and with one's job presented in the table indicates further that the two run hand-in-hand. About three-quarters of the workers very satisfied with their union are very satisfied with their jobs, whereas just twenty-four percent of workers not too or not at all satisfied with their union are very satisfied with their jobs. While the direction of causality of the

TABLE 9–4

Satisfaction with One's Union and with One's Job

	Satisfaction with Job		
Satisfaction with Union	Very Satisfied %	Somewhat Satisfied %	Not Too or Not At All Satisfied %
Very Satisfied (25%)	73	23	5
Somewhat Satisfied (49%)	35	57	8
Not Too or Not At All Satisfied (26%)	24	55	21
All Union Workers (100%)	41	48	11

Source: Tabulated from a sample of 319 union workers in Quality of Working Conditions Survey, 1977. Numbers in parentheses are the percentage of all workers reporting the levels of satisfaction with union.
Note: Rows may not add up to 100 percent because of rounding.

relationship—whether workers' dissatisfaction with employers colors their views of their union or whether a poorly functioning union reduces job satisfaction—cannot be determined. It is apparent that most workers are either satisfied with both union and job or dissatisfied with both.[8]

When we study the workers surveyed according to different groups, we find further that older workers are much more satisfied with both than younger workers, that whites are more satisfied than blacks, and that lower-paid workers are less well satisfied than higher-paid workers.[9]

Survey questions have also asked union members for their evaluations of union performance on specific issues relating to wages, fringes, job security, grievances, and the like. As table 9–5 shows, members seemed to be quite satisfied with union performance regarding wages and fringes, in giving them "feedback" on what the union is doing, and in handling grievances. They are less satisfied with how unions affect their say on the job or in the company and what unions do to make their jobs interesting, aspects that may underlie workers' expressed dissatisfaction with their supervisors. Interestingly, while many workers

TABLE 9–5

Members' Views of How Satisfied They Are with Various Aspects of Their Jobs

	Percentage of Workers Viewing Union's Performance as:			
	Very Good	*Somewhat Good*	*Not Too Good*	*Not Good At All*
Aspect				
Wages	36	44	18	4
Fringes	28	43	21	7
Feedback from Union	30	37	23	10
Handling Grievances	36	39	17	8
Job Security	22	52	19	6
Safety/Health	21	50	22	7
Say on Job	7	41	36	15
Interesting Job	6	29	42	23
Say in Union	19	38	27	15
Say in Business	6	30	38	26

SOURCE: Tabulated from the responses of 384 union workers in 1977 Quality of Employment Survey. The figures in the table exclude workers who did not answer particular questions and thus are based on somewhat smaller numbers than the full 384.

are very satisfied with their say in the union, a large number are not satisfied at all. Further analysis shows that those satisfied with their say in the union tend to be older workers or those with more tenure, while the dissatisfied are the younger, less tenured workers.[10]

Member and Nonmember Views of Unions

On average, union members appear to be reasonably pleased with unions as institutions. What about nonmembers? Do their views of union performance differ from those of members and, if so, how? Chacko (Iowa State University) and Green (Oklahoma State University) have analyzed this question. They find striking differences between members and nonmembers in perceptions of what unions do and of union power. Members express more confidence in union leaders and are much more likely to believe that unions protect workers against the unfair actions of employers, improve job security, wages and working conditions, and give the membership its money's worth for the dues it pays. Members are much *less* likely to believe that unions have a lot of influence over what laws are passed, have a lot to say in how the country is run, and "are more powerful than employers." In short, members view their unions as primarily "business union" organizations that deliver the goods at the local level via collective bargaining, while nonmembers tend to view unions as Big Labor. Differences in attitudes or perceptions of what unions do are significant not only between members and nonmembers but also between blue-collar and white-collar workers and between nonwhite and white workers. Blue-collar workers and nonwhite workers have more favorable attitudes toward unions.[11]

There are two possible explanations for these differences in views: members could have a more accurate picture of what unions do, or unions could attract only workers with more favorable views. The research in this book suggests that the former is the more weighty explanation; many nonmembers appear to have an incorrect perception of what unions do.

Dissatisfied Nonunion Workers—
Exit or Voice?

An employee's motivation to organize a union is based on dissatisfaction with the employer's failure to fulfill his part of the psychological contract. . . . He can threaten to quit but such a threat will not be particularly powerful if he is easily replaceable.[12]

*or speak
for them
selves .*

    Consider now the dissatisfied nonunion worker. According to the exit-voice analysis, he or she has two possible ways of trying to remedy an undesirable situation: to quit the job or to invoke the union voice option and form a union at the workplace. While many dissatisfied nonunion workers quit, many also seek unionization. Either they have too much at stake to quit, or they find themselves in poor job markets, or they believe that unionism is a more effective instrument than a job change for improving conditions.

    The relationship between worker dissatisfaction and the desire for unionism has been the subject of numerous studies by industrial psychologists. As table 9–6 shows, the results of the studies are unequivocal across very different samples. For example, in studies of over 87,000 workers from 250 units of a single large employer and of a small number of production workers in a NLRB election, one finds that increased desire for unionization (expressed in union activity or votes for unions) is, indeed, a likely outcome of worker dissatisfaction.

    That the dissatisfied look upon unionization as a means of altering their condition will come as no surprise to management. Indeed, one of the major purposes of satisfaction surveys of work forces is to alert management to dissatisfaction before it leads to an organizing drive.

    From the perspective of the voice/response analysis, however, what is important is not simply that dissatisfaction increases the desire for unionism but that there is a tradeoff between the desire of dissatisfied workers for unions and their desire to quit the firm. As figure 9–1 shows, the vast majority of nonunion workers do, indeed, see these two responses as clear-cut alternatives. Among the more satisfied workers, there is very little overlap between wanting to vote for a union and wanting to quit. Workers want to do one or the other but not both. Among the least satisfied, two-thirds of those who want to change their

TABLE 9-6

Relationship Between Dissatisfaction and Desire for Unionization by Nonunion Workers

Study, Sample	Result
1. Hamner and Smith, 87,740 salaried employees from 250 units of large employer	Units having greater dissatisfaction, especially with supervisors, have more union organizing activity.
2. Getman, Goldberg, and Herman, 1,239 employees in 31 different union elections	Dissatisfied workers more likely to vote for union, with dissatisfaction with economic issues most important.
3. Schriesheim, 59 production workers in NLRB election	Dissatisfied workers more likely to vote for union, with economic issues best predictor.
4. Muczyk, Hise, and Gannon, 130 faculty members in Penn State system	Dissatisfied workers favor union, with dissatisfaction over compensation and administration especially important.
5. Herman, 110 workers: retail clerks and steelworkers	Dissatisfied workers more likely to vote for union.
6. Kochan, 804 workers	Dissatisfaction with economic issues and work conditions raises likelihood of voting union; blue-collar worker dissatisfaction with supervision raises their likelihood of voting union.
7. DeCotiis and LeLouarn, 95 workers	Stress at work and role ambiguity, job satisfaction, view of fairness, and communication affect vote.
8. Hamner and Berman, 112 faculty members in private college	Economic dissatisfaction, contract dissatisfaction, and lack of trust in administration correlate with vote for union.
9. Brotslaw, 78 retail store employees	Overall job satisfaction significantly reduces chance worker will vote for union.

SOURCES: (1) W. Clay Hamner and F.J. Smith, "Work Attitudes as Predictors of Unionization Activity," *Journal of Applied Psychology* 63 (August 1978): 415–21. (2) Julius G. Getman, Stephen B. Goldberg, and Jeanne B. Herman, *Union Representation Elections: Law and Reality* (New York: Russell Sage Foundation, 1976). (3) Chester A. Schriesheim, "Job Satisfaction," *Journal of Applied Psychology* 63 (October 1978): 548–52. (4) J.P. Muczyk, R.T. Hise, and M.J. Gannon, "Faculty Attitudes and the Election of a Bargaining Agent in the Pennsylvania State College System," *Journal of Collective Negotiations* 4, no. 2 (1975): 175–89. (5) Jeanne B. Herman, "Are Structural Contingencies Altering the Job Attitude–Job Performance Relationship?" *Organizational Behavior and Human Performance* 10 (October 1973): 208–24. (6) Thomas A. Kochan, "How American Workers View Labor Unions," *Monthly Labor Review*, 102, no. 4 (April 1979): 23–31. (7) Thomas A. DeCotiis and Jean-Yves LeLouarn, "A Predictive Study of Voting Behavior in a Representation Election Using Union Instrumentality and Work Perceptions," *Organizational Behavior and Human Performance* 27, no. 1 (February 1981): 103–18. (8) Tove Helland Hammer and Michael Berman, "The Role of Noneconomic Factors in Faculty Union Voting," *Journal of Applied Psychology* 66, no. 4 (August 1981): 415–21. (9) Irving Brotslaw, "Attitudes of Retail Workers Toward Union Organization," *Labor Law Journal* 18, no. 3 (March 1967): 149–71.

Workers' Satisfaction with Job

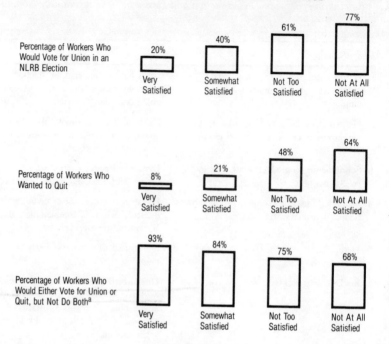

FIGURE 9–1

Relationship Between Job Satisfaction and the Desire for Unionization and for Job Changes

SOURCE: Tabulated from sample of 277 nonunion workers in Quality of Working Conditions Survey, 1977.
[a]Calculated as one minus the ratio of the number who answer "yes, would vote for union" and "yes, want to quit" to the sum of the yes's to those two responses.

situation by unionizing or quitting see the choice as one or the other but not both. In short, either one goes the route of union voice or one seeks to quit.

Conclusion

Subjective reports of job satisfaction are tricky to interpret. According to the analysis in this chapter, the surprising dissatisfaction which union workers express about their jobs appears explicable by the distinctive aspect of voice as a social mechanism compared to exit: whereas exit removes an individual from the undesired condition, voice operates by fanning discontent. Dissatisfaction is also an important factor in workers' desire for unions. And, whether satisfied or not, nonunion workers seeking a better situation see unionism and quits as exclusive alternatives, indicative of the exit-voice tradeoff even in the unorganized sector.

CHAPTER 10

What Unionism Does to Nonorganized Labor

Unions are doing much good for many people who do not pay them any dues.[1]

Unionized firms ordinarily serve as pacesetters in compensation . . . in establishing new benefits and in increasing their levels.[2]

THE DEBATE over the economic effects of unions rages not only over what unions do for organized workers but also over what they do for unorganized labor. Adherents to the monopoly perspective often cite the potential harm unions cause unorganized workers by displacing labor from organized worksites. The displaced workers are forced into lower-wage jobs in the nonunion sector, creating pressures for reductions in wages there, or they end up unemployed. On the other side, industrial relations experts often cite the positive "emulation" of union benefits by nonunion firms, while "many management spokesmen concede that the threat of unionization may have about as much impact as unionization itself."[3]

Whether unionism in one part of the economy benefits or harms the economic well-being of workers in other parts is important not only for assessing what unions do to the overall economy but also for interpreting nearly all studies of union effects. If the presence of unionism improves the economic well-being of nonunion workers, studies that infer what unions do by comparing union and nonunion workers understate the true gains from unionism to unionists. If, contrarily, unions reduce the economic well-being of nonunion workers, standard studies would overstate the increase in well-being to the group of workers who were organized.[4]

What unions do to unorganized labor is important also in assessing the voice face of the institution. If, as claimed, unionism represents the preferences of the majority of workers better than the market can, one would expect nonunion firms to imitate union practices. If unions represent worker preferences poorly, the nonunion firm can safely ignore what unions do.

What are the facts? Is unionism beneficial or harmful to nonunion workers? The answer seems to depend on which workers, which firms, and which sectors are studied.

The Effect of Unionism on Large Nonunion Employers

It is no secret that some of the best employers in the country—firms offering the highest wages and benefits, job security and desirable work conditions—are large nonunion or primarily nonunion firms. IBM is the example most often cited. While not all large employers seek to match union labor contracts, and while some seek to be leaders in the job market for reasons other than the threat of unionization, enough large nonunion companies appear to offer desirable employment packages for the purpose of deterring unionism to suggest that the nonunion blue-collar employees of these companies are among the greatest beneficiaries of unionism.

There are two distinct ways in which nonunion workers in these firms benefit from unionism. First, when some of the workers in the firm are organized, compensation gains won by those workers are passed on to their nonunion peers. According to a Bureau of National Affairs survey, while most firms do not have a definite policy of granting nonunion employees the same gains as union employees, nearly all review their pay scales for "equitable treatment" between union and nonunion employees. About a fifth automatically pass on the same increases (see table 10–1). Others admit privately that they change the pay of their nonunion workers at different times to dis-

TABLE 10–1

*Dependence of Pay Increases for
Unorganized Employees on Pay Increases for
Organized Employees*

Practice: When a General Pay Increase Is Negotiated With a Union, Nonunion Employees Are:	Percentage of All Companies
Granted the Same Increase	20
Granted a Higher Increase	2
Granted a Lower Increase	0
No Standard Policy	69
(No Response)	9

SOURCE: Data are from "Policies for Unorganized Employees," *Personnel Policies Forum Survey No. 125* (Washington, D.C.: Bureau of National Affairs, April 1979), 13.

guise the union influence. Because of the sensitivity of management to wage differentials that might lead its workers to unionize, even a single organized plant can affect the wage policy of a corporation. At Burlington Mills, for example, only a miniscule percentage of the firm's employees are organized, but overall company labor policy depends critically on what the organized percentage achieves in bargaining.[5]

Second, the gains won by union workers in other firms also affect wage-setting in large nonunion firms. Companies make extensive use of wage surveys in their industries or localities as guides to setting wages; 96 percent of manufacturing firms in one BNA survey reported that they relied on such surveys.[6] Union-negotiated wage increases raise the rate of pay on the surveys, producing a gain for nonunion workers whose firms desire to maintain their position in the industry or area wage structure.

Foulkes' (Boston University) study of the large nonunion firm provides numerous examples of such firms copying union wages. In the words of the executives interviewed by Foulkes:

"The company pays a slight premium in its nonunion plants over the wages paid in the general geographic area for similar work at union plants."

"Because we are such a union target, we find that we have to get our start rate at or about at the union rate."

"Cost-of-living clauses are not uncommon in our industry, though the uncapped nature of ours does distinguish us. But you also have to remember that in our area, the United Auto Workers, which have cost-of-living, are strong."

"Our people are treated well. We have what the unions want. That is our goal."[7]

Additional evidence of the positive effect of unionism on nonunion workers is found in the advice of some "labor-management consultants" (experts in keeping work-places nonunion) that their clients "try to do what the union does for its employees, but do it better"[8] and by evidence that in many unionization drives "a reason for the union having lost (is) the fact that what the union was offering or promising was no better than what the employees were already getting."[9]

Firms that follow a strategy of "positive labor relations" to avoid unionism will pay higher wages, offer more benefits, and provide better work conditions than otherwise similar nonunion firms. Since it is primarily large firms that adopt such personnel policies, one result is that union wage and benefit differentials vary inversely with size. Our analysis shows just such variation, with a union wage differential of 5 percent for workers in firms with more than 1,000 workers compared with 22 percent for workers in firms with fewer than 100 workers. A similar pattern is found for fringe benefits. For example, unionism raises expenditures on pensions by 60 percent in small plants (fewer than 500 workers) compared with a bare 6 percent increase in pension expenditures in large plants (more than 500 workers). Overall, our estimates show that unionism raises total fringe expenditures by 25 percent in the small plants, compared with a 9 percent increase in the large plants.[10]

If we assume that collective bargaining raises wages as much among large as among small unionized firms and if there is no spillover of union wages to small nonunion firms, the differential effect of unionism on large as opposed to small firms measures the spillover gains to nonunion large firms workers from unionism. Interpreted this way, the statistics suggest that unionism raises the wages of workers in large nonunion firms by a substantial 10–20 percent, and improves benefits as well.[11]

Finally, there is evidence that union work rules and procedures governing labor relations also spill over to large nonunion firms. Foulkes' study of pay and promotion policies found that "the rules under which some large nonunion companies operate encourage managers to act as if the company had a union." He noted in particular that the erosion of merit pay and of promotion based exclusively on ability made "some of the large nonunion companies . . . resemble the unionized company."[12] Consistent with this finding, the chapter 8 survey data on seniority practices found that some nonunion firms place as much weight on seniority in layoffs as do union firms: in that survey 42 percent of the supervisors of *nonunion* work groups said that they would "never permanently lay off a senior employee in place of a junior employee." While this figure is small relative to the 84 percent reported for organized units, it still suggests that a large number of nonunion firms operate by strict seniority in layoffs. Even grievance systems—the hallmark of the union voice at the shop floor—have been adopted by some large nonunion companies, though with less success.

While large unorganized firms would undoubtedly make some use of seniority rules, automatic pay increases, and grievance procedures in the absence of unionism, the evidence suggests that many firms have adopted these work conditions as a result of pressure from unions outside the company. In the case of grievance procedures, of the ten nonunion firms with this voice mechanism interviewed in one study, nine explicitly said that adoption of the procedure was a response to union pressures, with several stating that their appeals system was introduced after a union organizing campaign. These findings highlight the recognition by companies of the importance of voice in attracting workers to unions.[13]

The Effect of an Organizing Drive

Company X is the target of a union organizing drive. If the union wins, it will improve wages and work conditions. What happens if the union loses the drive? Will wages or work conditions improve or deteriorate? If the threat of unionization raises the economic position of nonunion workers, one would expect companies "under the gun" to offer their workers a better deal than other companies. How else can they avoid eventual organization?

A 1970 Conference Board study of firms before and after organizing drives provides strong evidence for such sizable positive spillovers. In this study, focused on white-collar units, firms were asked what effect union organization drives had on their employment policies. Table 10–2 shows their responses to a union organizing effort: 92 percent reported that they altered policies to offer some benefits; 52 percent raised wages; 23 percent raised fringes; 63 percent made changes in communications, ranging from meetings with employees to instituting formal grievance systems; and from 4 to 8 percent responded with more specific changes in employment practices.

While it is important to recognize that companies defeating union organizing campaigns are less likely to improve their employment practices than companies that go union, enough companies that defeat unions make changes to suggest a sizable payoff to workers from the threat of unionism. Indeed, in one major company cited by Foulkes, the nonunion workers invited union organizers into the plant regularly, though they had no serious intention of going union. The purpose: to frighten management into giving higher wages and benefits.[14]

How many nonunion workers might be the beneficiaries of union

TABLE 10–2

Percentage of Firms Altering Policy After Union Organizing Drive

Specified Change	Percentage of Firms Improving Policy Toward Workers
1. Some Benefits to Workers	92
2. Compensation	52
3. Fringes	23
4. Communications (Regular Meetings, Formal Grievance, and so on)	63
5. Installed Job Posting and Bidding System	8
6. Supervisory Practices	4
7. Work Conditions	7
8. Other Changes	4

SOURCE: E. R. Curtin, *White-Collar Unionization* (New York: National Industrial Conference Board, 1970), 67.

organizing drives? In 1979 about 580,000 workers were eligible to vote in work groups that held NLRB elections; about 370,000 workers were in work groups that remained nonunion after the election. If we extrapolate the Conference Board estimates in table 10–2 to the work force as a whole, roughly 340,000 nonunion workers obtained some benefits from the organizing drive, of whom 192,000 received higher compensation. Whether these numbers are to be viewed as large or small depends on the permanence of the gains: if the nonunion workers whose position improved as a result of an organizing drive maintain these gains, 192,000 to 340,000 per year cumulates to sizable numbers; if the gains are transitory, the numbers are small in an economy with a work force of 100 million.[15]

The Effect of Blue-Collar Unionism on White-Collar Workers

In a typical organized company, the production workers are organized but the nonproduction, white-collar workers are not. Do the white-collar workers benefit from the unionization of blue-collar labor?

To answer this question we have analyzed the wages and fringes of nonproduction workers in organized and nonorganized plants in 1967–72 and 1974–78. The results of our analysis, summarized in table 10–3, suggest that blue-collar unionism has little or no effect on the

TABLE 10–3

Estimated Percentage Change in White-Collar Wages and Fringes Resulting from Unionism of Blue-Collar Workers in the Same Plant, 1968–1978

Data Set, Year	White-Collar Wages	White-Collar Fringes
1. Expenditures for Employee Compensation, 1974–78	4	13
2. Expenditures for Employee Compensation, 1968–72	0	14

SOURCES: (1) Estimated by regression of log wages or log fringes on whether or not the majority of blue-collar workers are organized in the establishment; and controls for size of plant, unionization of white-collar workers and industry. (2) Fringe data from R. B. Freeman, "The Effect of Trade Unionism on Fringe Benefits," *Industrial Labor Relations Review* 34, no. 4 (July 1981): 489–509; white-collar wage estimate calculated for this book using the same model and data as in the article.

straight-time pay of white-collar workers but has some effect on fringe spending and thus a modest positive effect on total white-collar compensation. This finding is consistent with the observation of Slichter, Healy, and Livernash that, for some benefits, "union plant workers have become pattern setters for office groups," with organized companies extending to all workers programs begun under union impetus.[16] One likely reason for this tendency is the visibility of specific fringes within a company. Another may be that union voice provides management with a guide to the compensation desires of white-collar as well as of blue-collar workers.

Other studies of the "spillover" effect of unions to white-collar nonunion workers support our findings. In an analysis of differences in compensation between white-collar workers employed in union plants and those employed in nonunion plants in twenty-three industries, Solnick (Center for Forensic Economic Studies) found that white-collar workers in organized plants had higher wages than white-collar workers in unorganized plants in only six industries but had higher fringe benefits in twenty-three industries.[17] Mitchell (UCLA) has analyzed time series data on rates of change in clerical pay in twenty-four highly unionized cities and has come to a similar conclusion regarding the spillover of unionism on the pay of those white-collar workers: "the overall results suggest that employers did not feel compelled to keep clerical pay apace with union pay. . . . During the period covered union pay gains were generally larger than nonunion pay increases, and employers were apparently willing to let this difference be reflected in their internal pay structures as well."[18] Mitchell argues that only unionization of the clerical workers would have kept their wages in line with those of the plant workers.

While in general white-collar compensation is only slightly affected by plant unionism, there are specific situations in which firms have altered white-collar pay because of the organization of blue-collar workers. A case in point is the General Motors compensation policy of 1982. Following negotiated wage concessions by unionized blue-collar workers, GM announced bonuses for some of its executives. The ensuing uproar and potential loss of morale among plant workers forced the company to rescind the proposed bonuses.[19] In this case, there was a negative spillover, at least with respect to the timing of changes in pay.

Overall, however, the existing evidence suggests only slight impacts of blue-collar unionism on white-collar wages, with emulation concentrated on fringe benefits.

The Effect of Percentage Organized

Consider two nonunion workers. One is employed in a firm in a primarily unionized industry or city. The other is employed in a primarily nonunion industry or city. Holding all other economic factors constant, which worker is likely to do better in the job market?

If the monopoly view of the effect of unionism on nonunion labor is correct, the nonunion worker should fare more poorly in the highly organized environment. If the industrial relations threat and emulation views are correct, the nonunion worker would do better in the organized environment. In the former case, the loss of jobs in the union sector will increase the supply of labor to nonunion firms, driving down wages and possibly reducing the chances of finding a job. In the latter case, nonunion firms in the organized environment will pay higher wages to avoid unionization or discontent that reduces productivity.

To evaluate the effect of working nonunion in a highly unionized versus a lightly unionized setting, we have estimated the relationship between the percentage of blue-collar workers who are unionized in a labor market and the wages of nonunion workers, holding other potential determinants fixed. The results of our analyses for 1973–78 summarized in figure 10–1 show that nonunion workers earn more in highly organized SMSAs than in less organized SMSAs. Roughly, a 10 percentage-point increase in the fraction organized in an SMSA is associated with higher nonunion worker wages of about 5 percent. At the same time, however, some nonunion workers may suffer from unemployment in a highly unionized area: in chapter 7, we found unemployment rates to be higher in more highly unionized states, although we could find no association between unionism and the proportion of the population of working age actually employed.

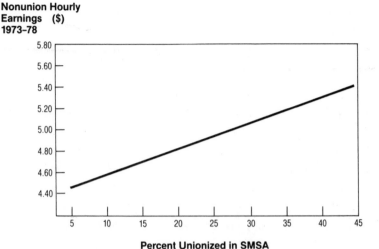

FIGURE 10–1

Relationship Between Nonunion Wages and Area Unionization

SOURCE: This figure was generated from the results of a weighted regression estimated with a Standard Metropolitan Statistical Area (SMSA) data set based on the May Current Population Survey. The regression was of average nonunion hourly earnings in the SMSA on the proportion of the SMSA's population with below-poverty line income, industry dummies, demographic characteristics (mean years of schooling, and sex, race, and age group percentages), year dummies, and the percentage of the SMSA's workers who are in unions. The sample size was 98 SMSAs from 1973–76 and 44 in 1977 and 1978.

Detailed investigations of the characteristics of workers who gain and lose from working in a highly unionized area have been made by Holzer (Michigan State) and Kahn (University of Illinois).[20] In separate studies they have found that some nonunion workers benefit and others lose from unionism. Holzer's analysis shows that in highly unionized SMSAs the wages and employment of young nonunion blacks are lower than they are in otherwise comparable less unionized cities; he also finds the proportion of young whites who are employed is also negatively related to the percentage organized, but that their wages are positively affected by the SMSA's unionization. Kahn finds that nonunion women and nonwhite men suffer from working in a highly organized SMSA while nonunion white men benefit.

Thus, the impact of unionism on nonunion workers appears to differ greatly across groups. As a rough generalization, working nonunion in a union environment seems to benefit relatively permanent employees who can reasonably be expected to seek unionism if they are paid much below union rates and to harm workers in what is commonly called the secondary labor force.

Unionism and the Overall Labor Market

Thus far, we have examined how unionism affects the economic well-being of nonunion workers by comparing nonunion workers in more or less unionized environments. But does not unionism affect the entire operation of the labor market and thus all workers, even those in the least unionized settings? Haven't we understated, possibly seriously, the spillover effects of unionism?

The answer to these questions is "yes." Unionism may have much more pervasive effects on the economy than indicated by our estimates. It is possible that workers in the least unionized sectors of the economy benefit from unionism. It is also possible they lose from unionism. Economic theorists have specified conditions under which one result will occur and conditions under which the other will occur. In an economy with little foreign trade, workers in the nonunion sector would be expected to gain if the union sector were more heavily capital intensive. Then the contraction of the union sector could free capital for the nonunion sector more than it freed labor, raising the amount of capital used per worker in that sector, and most likely raising wages. Contrarily, if the union sector were labor-intensive, the contraction of employment would send more workers than capital to the nonunion sector, reducing the wages of nonunion workers. In an economy with considerable foreign trade, gains or losses depend on whether the union sector produces goods that are traded or goods that are not and the extent to which capital is mobile across countries, as well.[21]

Conclusion

The results of this chapter may surprise readers who believe that union wage gains come at the expense of nonunion workers—a position espoused in years past by such notable economists as Henry Simons and Milton Friedman. The evidence does not support this simplistic view but rather presents a more mixed picture. Some nonunion workers gain from unionism, notably those in large nonunion firms and in firms threatened by organization that choose to combat unionism with "positive labor relations." Other nonunion workers, notably less skilled "secondary" workers, appear to lose from unionism. The net effect on the entire nonunion workforce is unclear.

CHAPTER 11

Unionism: Good or Bad for Productivity?

Firemen on diesel locomotives for which the firing function does not exist. Painters using brushes instead of spray guns. Standby orchestras at radio stations broadcasting recorded music. "Bogus" copy replicating ready-made plates in newspaper printing. Jurisdictional rules that forbid workers other than electricians from replacing a light bulb.

Isn't it obvious that unionism reduces productivity?

More stringent production standards. Greater monitoring of worker performance. Lower labor turnover costs. More experienced and skilled workers. New and better channels of labor and management communication. Systematic and rational personnel policies and practices. Cost pressures to improve efficiency.

Isn't it obvious that unionized workplaces are more productive?

THE IMPACT of trade unionism on productivity has long been one of the major bones of contention among analysts of unionism. As Bok and Dunlop wrote in 1970: "For more than a century and a half, economists have debated the effects of 'combinations of workmen,' or collective bargaining, on the efficiency of business enterprises. The literature is replete with conflicting appraisals of the impact of work stoppages, work rules, regulation of machinery, apprenticeship, and training on employee efficiency and managerial decisions."[1]

Modern quantitative analysis of productivity in organized and unorganized establishments and sectors offers striking new evidence on what unions do to productivity. The new work suggests that in general productivity is higher in the presence of unionism than in its absence. For persons schooled in neoclassical economic analysis this is not a surprising result: after all, since unions raise wages, one should expect management to respond by raising capital per worker and hiring better workers to raise productivity. The surprise is not that productivity is higher under unionism but that it is higher for "voice/response" reasons, ranging from reductions in exit to changed managerial practices, as well as for the reasons stressed by the monopoly model.

Monopoly and Voice/Response Effects on Productivity

The monopoly and voice/response faces of unionism suggest that unions will move a firm's productivity in the same direction. While each allows for unionism to lower productivity in rare cases, both predict that, in general, unionism will raise productivity. The routes by which unionism affects productivity differ, however (see figure 11–1). Accord-

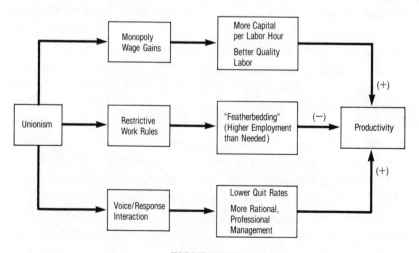

FIGURE 11–1
Unionism and Productivity

ing to the monopoly view, firms respond to unionism by altering capital (and other inputs) per worker and improving the quality of labor until the contribution of the last unit of labor just equals the union wage rate. While under some circumstances unions may use their monopoly power to lower productivity through restrictive work practices, competition in product markets is unlikely to permit such practices for very long except in markets sheltered from competition. An employer who pays a higher cost of labor and gets less rather than more productivity out of his workforce will go out of business in a competitive product market.

While the monopoly model predicts that unionized firms will have higher productivity than otherwise comparable nonunion firms, it is important to realize that the monopoly-wage increase in productivity is socially harmful. In the absence of other interferences with perfect competition, the wage effect causes labor and capital to be allocated in such a way that their contribution to national output is not as high as it would be if competitive market prices determined where these factors were being utilized. Workers who would have been employed in the union sector are forced to take lower productivity jobs in the nonunion sector. Machines that would have been employed in nonunion enterprises are now used in the union sector to raise the productivity of unionized labor. And the size of the union sector is smaller than it would have been in the absence of union monopoly wages. Our chapter 3 estimate of the social cost of union monopoly wage gains can be interpreted as an estimate of the lost productivity due to the increased wages associated with the monopoly face of unionism.

The voice/response routes by which unionism raises productivity are, by contrast, potentially socially desirable, since they result not from inefficient allocation of resources but from improved efficiency within firms. For example, reductions in turnover due to unionism raise productivity by lowering costs of training and recruitment.[2] In industries like construction, productivity gains result from unionized apprenticeship programs that produce better workers. Managerial responses to unionism that take the form of more rational personnel policies and more careful monitoring of work raise productivity by reducing organizational slack. The voluminous case studies by Slichter, Healy, and Livernash (Harvard Business School) and by other researchers have shown the effectiveness of the managerial response to unionism to be perhaps the most important determinant of what unions do to productivity. Some managements will adjust to the union and turn unionism into a positive force at the workplace; others will not. Over the long run, those that respond positively will prosper while those that do not will suffer in the market.[3]

Just as the monopoly analysis allows for the possibility that restrictive workrules reduce productivity, the voice/response analysis allows for the possibility that some work rules, such as seniority or rules restricting managerial flexibility, can reduce productivity. Perhaps most importantly, the voice/response analysis points to the "state of industrial relations" in a sector as a key factor in either raising or reducing productivity. If industrial relations are good, with management and unions working together to produce a bigger "pie" as well as fighting over the size of their slices, productivity is likely to be higher under unionism. If industrial relations are poor, with management and labor ignoring common goals to battle one another, productivity is likely to be lower under unionism.

The empirical question is whether productivity-augmenting or productivity-reducing behavior dominates.

Production Function Analysis

The tool used to study the impact of unionism on productivity is the production function, which traditionally makes output per worker depend on capital per worker, other inputs used per worker, and indicators of the quality of the workers (as reflected in their level of schooling, for instance). To determine the effects of unionism on productivity, one adds to the traditional variables a variable giving the fraction of the workforce that is unionized. In statistical analyses the estimated effect of the fraction unionized reflects what unions do to productivity above and beyond changes in the amount of physical inputs used per worker. To isolate the union effect in this framework, one must have good measures of output, capital, and the quality of labor, and one must specify properly the nature of the production relation itself.

Table 11–1 summarizes the results of studies using the production

TABLE 11-1
Production Function Estimates of the Union Productivity Effect

Studies Using Value Added or Shipments (Sector, Unit of Comparison, Year)	Approximate Percentage Difference in Productivity (with Amount of Capital per Worker and Other Factors Held Fixed) Between Union and Nonunion Units
1. Manufacturing Industries, States	
1972A	20 to 25; 10 to 15
1972B	10
1977	31
Changes between 1972 and 1977	9
2. Wooden Household Furniture, Plants, 1975–1976	15
3. Construction (Revenue Deflated by Area Price Index), States, 1972–1975	21 to 28
4. Office Building Construction (Revenue Deflated by Area Price Index), General Contractors, 1974	39
5. Manufacturing, Individual Businesses, 1980	−2

Studies Using Physical Units of Output (Sector, Unit of Comparison, Year)	
6. Cement (Tons), Plants, 1974	6 to 8
7. Cement (changes in tons), Plants that Went from Nonunion to Union, 1953–1976	6
8. Underground Bituminous Coal (tons), Mines	
1965	33 to 38
1970	−4 to 8
1975	−20 to −17
1980	−18 to −14
9. Construction (Square Feet), Projects, 1974	36

Sources: (1) 1972A: C. Brown and J. Medoff, "Trade Unions in the Production Process," *Journal of Political Economy* 86, no. 3 (June 1978): 355–78; 1972B and 1977: Estimated with Jonathan Leonard from data based on Census of Manufacturers. (2) J. Frantz, "The Impact of Trade Unions on Productivity in the Wood Household Furniture Industry" (Undergraduate thesis, Harvard University, 1976). (3) S. Allen, "Unionized Construction Workers Are More Productive," (North Carolina State University, 1981, mimeographed). (4) and (9) S. Allen, "Unionization and Productivity in Office Building and School Construction" (North Carolina State University, 1983, mimeographed), 27–30. (5) K. Clark, "Unionization and Firm Performance: The Impact on Profits, Growth, and Productivity," Harvard Business School HBS 83–16 (1983). (6) and (7) K. Clark, "The Impact of Unionization on Productivity: A Case Study," *Industrial and Labor Relations Review* 34 (July 1980): 466. (8) M. Connerton, R. B. Freeman, and J. L. Medoff, "Industrial Relations and Productivity: A Study of the U.S. Bituminous Coal Industry" (Harvard University, 1983 revision, mimeographed). Approximate percentage differences were calculated as antilogs of estimated union coefficients in semi-log regression models.

function technique on the relation between unionism and productivity. As the table shows, the studies differ in their measures of labor productivity, with some measuring it in dollar units (value added by the firm or the value of shipments) per worker, and others measuring it in physical units (tons, square feet) per worker. The dollar measures of output (price times quantity) have the advantage of including the full spectrum of goods produced by a firm, valued at their market prices. They also have a disadvantage, however: unless the prices charged by union and nonunion firms are the same, any finding of higher value added (shipments) per worker in the organized establishments could reflect not the higher physical output per worker but rather a higher price per unit of output. In industries where markets are truly competitive, with a single price for each output, and where unionized and nonunionized firms are equally likely to specialize in high-priced or in low-priced outputs, the possible confusion of price with quantity is small. For industries where these conditions do not hold, one must take great care in estimating a union productivity effect. Physical measures of output alleviate the problem of confusing price differences for output differences, but at the cost of being limited to the few distinct goods that can be so measured. Most modern firms produce a wide variety of products with too many dimensions to be captured by a single physical measure. Because neither measure is perfect, researchers have analyzed both dollar and physical measures of labor productivity.

The first study, by Brown (University of Maryland) and Medoff, compared value added per labor hour across states in the same industry and found that, with other factors (including capital per hour) the same, productivity was 20 to 25 percent higher in the more heavily unionized states. They also found, however, that unionized firms used more capital than predicted by the production model estimated. Because the estimated union effect depends critically on how capital affects output, their results are consistent with a 10 to 15 percent productivity effect under alternative assumptions regarding the productivity of capital. Follow-up work for manufacturing done with Leonard (University of California, Berkeley), has produced a smaller positive union productivity effect for 1972, using a different measure of capital, but a larger effect for 1977. Analysis of a single manufacturing industry, wooden household furniture, yielded an estimate of 15 percent higher productivity in union than in nonunion plants. In construction, Allen

(North Carolina State University) has estimated union-nonunion productivity differences in value added (deflated by an area price index, to deal with the danger that in this sector the higher value added reflects higher prices of union-built buildings) ranging from 21 percent to 28 percent. Not all value added studies have, however, obtained positive union productivity effects. In a study of productivity in "businesses," defined as parts of certain large firms that can be considered separate, Clark (Harvard Business School) found a slight negative union impact. Clark's findings make it clear that the production function technique can yield negative as well as positive union impacts and that the union effect is likely to differ across different parts of the economy—a point to which we will return later.

Analyses of measures of productivity in physical units, summarized in the bottom half of the table, have in two cases found positive union effects and in one case found an effect that went from positive to negative over time. Clark estimated that productivity in cement was 6 to 8 percent higher in organized than in nonorganized plants in 1974. For construction, Allen obtained data from the U.S. Department of Labor on eighty-three office-building projects and found that, measured by square feet constructed per worker, the union projects had 36 percent higher productivity. Consistent with Allen's finding of higher productivity in union construction, two studies that examined labor usage in the bids of union and nonunion contractors for identical buildings found that union contractors estimated a need for 20 to 25 percent less labor for the project than was estimated by nonunion contractors.[4] Finally, our analysis of the underground bituminous coal sector (done with Marguerite Connerton of the U.S. Department of Labor), in which the productivity measure was tons of coal per worker day, yielded quite different results in different time periods: positive union productivity effects in 1965, small positive to small negative effects in 1970, sizable negative effects in 1975, and slightly smaller negative effects in 1980. The dramatic switch in the union effect from positive to negative shows that the union productivity effect can move sharply over time, dependent on labor and management policies and relations, which can change radically.

Two of the studies in table 11–1 used a before-after method of analysis, examining the relation between changes in productivity and changes in unionism. Both found productivity increasing with the

168

advent of unionism. In analysis of 1972–77 changes in manufacturing productivity, we and Leonard obtained a positive but statistically insignificant union effect, which showed that productivity growth was better in areas with above-average union growth, but not by a well-defined magnitude. Clark compared productivity in six cement plants before and after they became unionized (in the 1960s) and found an increase in productivity of 6 percent.

In sum, most studies of productivity find that unionized establishments are more productive than otherwise comparable nonunion establishments. Because unionized labor costs are also higher, however, one should not infer from this that firms should be eager to be organized; as we shall see in chapter 12, the productivity increases generally fall short of the cost increases. Higher productivity does not mean higher profits.

Unionism and Productivity growth

All right, productivity is generally higher under unionism, but that isn't what really matters. What's important is how unions affect the growth of productivity. Don't unions reduce growth by opposing technological change?—*An archetypical critic of unionism*

Historically, some unions have opposed technological change. "The Window-Glass Workers, with a strong craft tradition, tried to prevent the use of glassworking machines when they were introduced in 1908. . . . In time, however, the new processes displaced the old, since they were much more efficient, and the window-glass union had to be formally disbanded in 1928."[5] Other unions have endorsed practices such as rigid piece rates which reduce the economic benefits of technological change to employers by keeping labor costs per unit of output fixed despite higher labor productivity.[6]

Because unions that succeed in blocking technological change go out of business, the general union attitude toward new technology is a far cry from the myth promulgated by the self-proclaimed critic. While not all unions encourage technological advance to the extent that John

L. Lewis's Mine Workers did in the 1950s and 1960s (when the UMW favored rapid mechanization of the mines, high productivity, and high wages, at the expense of employment), many unions view change favorably—as long as they can offer protection to displaced members and play a role in determining work procedures under the new technology. In the 1980s, as well as earlier, indeed, some unions have pressed management to modernize their plants with new investments, as they realize that failure to do so means ultimate loss of jobs.[7]

Union policies toward technological change, whether pro or con, however, are not the sole determinant of the impact of organization on productivity growth. Union wage increases may themselves speed up the rate of "technological advance" by inducing management to substitute new machinery for labor or by inducing management to pay for the development and introduction of new technologies. On the other hand, however, high wages reduce profitability of the union sector, discouraging further investments in the area.

To see if unionism is positively or negatively related to the growth of productivity, as opposed to the level of productivity, we have analyzed the impact of the proportion of workers unionized on the rate of growth of value added or value of shipments in three data sets. The results of our analysis, which are summarized in table 11–2, suggest that while unionized industries have, indeed, had somewhat slower growth of productivity than nonunion sectors, the observed relation is too weak statistically to support the claim that unionism reduces dynamic efficiency. Some unionized industries have rapid productivity growth while others have less rapid growth. Because unionized sectors tend to be "older" industries, one expects some negative relation between productivity and unionism because of the life cycle of industries (a growing new industry typically enjoys more rapid productivity growth than an older established industry), even if unionism did nothing harmful to the rate of industrial progress. Consistent with our results, analysis of the relationship between productivity growth and research-and-development spending that includes unionism as a "control variable" shows no clear pattern, with negative relationships between fractions organized and growth of productivity in some periods and positive relationships in other periods.[8] In sum, current empirical evidence offers little support for the assertion that unionization is associated with lower (or higher) productivity advance.

TABLE 11–2

Unionism and Growth of Productivity in Manufacturing

Measure of Productivity, Years Worked	Estimated Effect of Unionism on Growth of Productivity per Worker per Year
1. Value Added per Worker in 176 Industries, 1958–76	Insignificant Negative Union Effect of −.4 Percentage Points with Average Growth of 2.0 Percentage Points
2. Value of Shipments in 450 Industries, per Unit of Labor and Capital, 1958–78	Insignificant Negative Union Effect of −.3 Percentage Points with Average Growth of 0.7 Percentage Points
3. Value Added per Production Worker Hour, State by Industry Cells, 1972–77	Insignificant Negative Union Effect of −.3 Percentage Points with Average Growth of 1.2 Percentage Points

SOURCES: (1) Calculations use the *Annual Survey of Manufactues,* conducted by the U.S. Census Bureau, as described in R. B. Freeman, "Unionism, Price-Cost Margins and the Return to Capital": National Bureau of Economic Research Working Paper No. 1164 (1983). (2) Calculated with Wayne Gray, using shipments data from various volumes of the *Annual Survey of Manufactures* and the *Census of Manufactures,* conducted by the U.S. Census Bureau. (For discussion of both of these data sources, see appendix). (3) Calculated from 1972 and 1977 *Census of Manufactures* data. Value added deflated with GNP deflator.

But productivity is growing very slowly in the United States, whereas it grew rapidly before unions became important. The slowdown in productivity growth is due to union interference and union-governmental interference with the competitive market.—*An archetypical critic*[9]

The claim that productivity has grown more rapidly in periods of lower organization of the workforce is simply false. The U.S. economy has enjoyed rapid growth of productivity in periods of relatively weak unionization (the 1900s, for example) and rapid growth in periods of strong unionization, notably the decades immediately following World War II. While so much changes over time that it would be foolhardy to read any causality into historical associations, the fact is that in both the post-war period and over a longer period stretching back to 1900 (war years and the Great Depression years excluded), there is essentially no connection between productivity growth in the United States and unionization. In some years when unionization has been above average, rates of growth of productivity have been above average, while in other years when unionization has been below average, so too have been rates of growth of productivity (see table 11–3). While it is still possible that union-induced changes in the overall economy are inimical to rapid productivity growth, the historical data do not show such a pattern.

TABLE 11-3

*Number of Years with High/Low Unionization and High/Low
Productivity Growth*

	1950–80	
	Rate of Change in Output per Worker Above Median	*Rate of Change in Output per Worker Below Median*
Unionization Above Median	8	8
Unionization Below Median	7	8
	1900–80 *(excluding war years and Depression)*	
	Rate of Change in Output per Worker Above Median	*Rate of Change in Output per Worker Below Median*
Unionization Above Median	14	15
Unionization Below Median	15	15

SOURCE: Calculated by computing median levels of unionization and rate of change in output per worker in each period, and comparing on a yearly basis unionization and rate of change in output per worker to medians. Unionization figures are from U.S. Department of Labor, *Handbook of Labor Statistics* (Washington, D.C.: Bureau of Labor Statistics Bulletin 2070, 1980) with updates from BLS, and from U.S. Department of Commerce, *Historical Statistics of the United States* (Washington, D.C.: Government Printing Office, 1957). Output per worker figures are from U.S. Department of Labor, *Monthly Labor Review*, various editions, and *Historical Statistics of the United States*. The years excluded were 1914–19 and 1930–45.

Reduced Managerial Flexibility

But dammit, unions don't let me run my plant the way I want to. Union work rules reduce my flexibility.—*An archetypical plant manager of an organized plant*

That unions reduce managerial flexibility is one of the most frequent charges brought against unions by managers. Jurisdictional limitations on what workers can and cannot do; restrictions on the activity of foremen and other nonunion workers to perform the work of members in the bargaining unit; restrictions on contracting work out; insistence on operating by the rules even when it may be more efficient to break them—are all different ways in which unions impair managerial flexibility.

To evaluate the impact of unionism on the flexibility of operations, we have examined the degree to which union and nonunion managements substitute nonproduction labor and capital for production labor when the relative costs of the latter change. If unionism reduces flexibility, the extent of such cost-minimizing substitution is likely to be less in unionized settings. Our analyses of substitutability between production and nonproduction labor across industries and across plants within industries show that unionism is associated with somewhat less substitutability between production and nonproduction workers, but not with less substitutability between production workers and capital. We estimate that a 10 percent increase in the wage of production workers relative to the wage of nonproduction workers causes a 1.9 percent substitution of nonproduction for production labor in a union setting, compared with a 2.8 percent substitution in a nonunion setting.[10]

It should be noted that even substantial reductions in flexibility are unlikely to have a great effect on productivity. When production lines are machine-run, flexibility is simply not important. When operations are more amenable to managerial decisions, the good manager can substitute better advanced planning for flexibility. Perhaps most importantly, flexibility—defined in terms of the substitutability among inputs in a production function—is a second-order rather than first-order factor in affecting the level of productivity.[11] In the construction industry, where complaints about restrictive union work rules are commonplace, experts in the economics of the industry almost uniformly agree that the rules' effect on productivity has been vastly exaggerated:

Although no reliable quantitative estimate can be made of those rules on efficiency, their total impact would appear to be very small.[12]

There is no question that at various times and places, various locals of the building trades unions have resisted technological innovation in tools or materials and have established unduly restrictive work rules or practices. Yet, the results of our survey, as of other field research, do not support the contention that this has been a widespread or consistent policy.[13]

All told, reductions in flexibility, while irritating to management, have only modest effects on productivity.

Explaining the Union Impact on Productivity

Why is productivity often higher under unionism? In what ways does unionism raise productivity? How important are lower turnover of the workforce, changes in managerial techniques, and the other routes hypothesized in figure 11–1?

These are extremely difficult questions to answer, for they require knowledge not only of differences in the characteristics of organized and unorganized plants but also of the actual ways in which the plants operate. Our current knowledge suggests that several factors underlie the union-productivity linkage. In manufacturing, the exit-voice trade-off appears to explain some of the productivity differences in terms of the impact of lower turnover cost. Brown and Medoff estimated that one-fifth of the union productivity effect found in their study was attributable to lower quit rates in the unionized parts of industries. In construction, Allen attributed 10 percent of the union productivity advantage to the reduced need for supervision in union construction and 8 percent to the greater use of standardized components by union contractors.[14] In the cement industry, Clark found some changes in worker behavior likely to raise productivity (lower turnover in half of the plants studied, but no change in two and increased turnover in one; and according to the union, improved morale in three of the plants), but he found the most important changes in managerial performance (table 11–4). In every plant that became unionized, top management replaced the plant manager and many foremen and introduced more professional managers. As a result, previously authoritarian or paternalistic managerial practices were weeded out. Supervisors, "tightened the ship," "kept a close eye on things," and introduced new modes of operation likely to raise productivity. This finding gains credence from the fact that it is similar to the central conclusion of Slichter, Healy, and Livernash in *The Impact of Collective Bargaining on Management*: "The challenge that unions present management has, if viewed broadly, created superior and better balanced management, even though some exceptions must be recognized."[15]

In some industries productivity is advanced by explicit labor-management cooperative ventures. In the men's tailored clothing industry, for

TABLE 11–4

Responses to Unionism in Six Cement Plants

	Number of Plants with Changes in Behavior
Worker Responses	
Turnover	In three plants, turnover down. In two plants, no change in turnover. In one plant, turnover rises.
Absenteeism	In two plants, absenteeism increases.
Discipline problems	In one plant, discipline problems increase. In one plant, discipline problems decrease.
Morale	Union reports improvement in three plants; management reports improvement in one, no change in one, worse in one.
Management Responses	
Plant Manager	Six plants replace plant manager.
Supervisors	Six plants replace supervisors.
Management Practices	
Before Union	One plant rated management practices "professional." Three plants rated as "authoritarian." One plant rated as "authoritarian" or "paternalistic." One plant rated as "paternalistic."
After Union	Three plants report major improvements in methods of management: productivity targeting; performance review meetings; periodic meetings with workers; introduction of standards; new reporting and accounting systems; better supervisor/worker relations. Two plants report minor improvements: more formalized contract procedures; changes in way supervisors deal with people; gradual changes in system of monitoring performance. One plant reports little change: only difference is better supervisor/worker relations.

SOURCE: K. Clark, "The Impact of Unionization on Productivity: A Case Study," *Industrial and Labor Relations Review* 34 (July 1980): 451–68.

example, labor and management established a committee to develop and introduce automatic sewing machines to enable U.S. workers and firms to compete with low-wage foreign competitors, hiring Draper Laboratories, formerly a part of the Massachusetts Institute of Technology, to do the technical work. According to Dunlop,

the program has several distinct features. The Department of Commerce is contributing financially, although no more than the private-sector contributions from labor and management. The managements and the union in the clothing industry have been joined by two leading textile manufacturers and a leading synthetic yarn company to constitute a broad sectoral group to improve coordination and productivity. These joint responses of labor and management are beyond those that could be achieved at the workplace.[16]

While joint efforts are relatively uncommon, increased pressures from foreign competitors may induce other industries and unions to engage in similar cooperative activities in the future.

The Role of the Industrial Relations Climate

An important implication of the voice-response model is that productivity is likely to depend on the state of labor-management relations in shops. When those relations are poor, management is likely to have trouble getting high productivity. When they are good, workers and management may pull together for the benefit of the firm. Three studies have examined the link between productivity and the state of industrial relations at plants, and all three have found strong support for this proposition. In an analysis of productivity at eighteen General Motors plants, Katz and Kochan (MIT) and Gobeille (General Motors) found higher productivity where plant managers rated the industrial relations climate as good or where the rate of grievances filed by workers was low (suggesting that workers viewed the state of labor-management relations as good). In a detailed study of paper mills, Ichniowski (National Bureau of Economic Research) obtained similar results: a plant with a low rate of grievances filed in a given period had notably better productivity than the same plant when it had a high rate of grievances filed (see figure 11–2). In addition, he has estimated that because of the better productivity, low grievance plants have correspondingly higher profits, by as much as a third compared with high-grievance plants. In the third study, Schuster (Syracuse University) examined productivity at nine manufacturing plants over a period of five years during which a cooperative union management program was introduced. He found an increase in productivity in six of the eight plants for which productivity could be measured.[17]

Unionism: Good or Bad for Productivity?

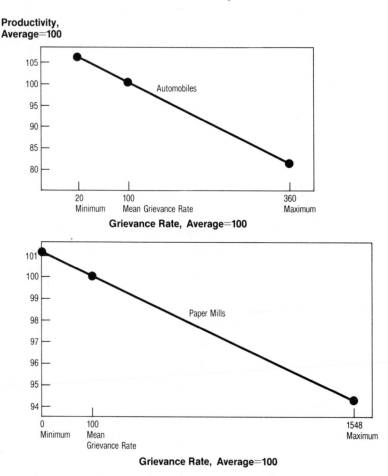

FIGURE 11-2

Grievance and Productivity at Organized Plants

Source: Automobiles graph drawn with data found in Harry Katz, Thomas Kochan, and Kenneth Gobeille, "Industrial Relations Performance, Economic Performance and the Effects of Quality of Working Life Efforts: An Inter-Plant Analysis" (MIT, Sloan School Working Paper 1329–82, July 1982).
Paper mills graph drawn with data found in Bernard Ichniowski, "How Do Labor Relations Matter? A Study of Productivity in Eleven Paper Mills" (National Bureau of Economic Research, Summer Workshop Paper, August 1983), table 8–2 and from his computer printouts.

While all three of these studies were limited to organized plants, the implication is that the impact of unionism on productivity depends not only on what unions and management do separately but on their relationship with one another. Where that relationship is good, productivity is higher than where it is bad. The table 11–1 finding that

177

unionism is generally associated with higher productivity implies that in most organized plants in the United States labor and management have developed amicable working relations.

The striking change in the union effect in underground coal mining from positive in the 1960s to negative in the 1970s, shown in figure 11–3, appears to be at least partially due to a deterioration in the state of industrial relations in the sector. In the 1950s, when John L. Lewis ran the United Mine Workers of America (UMW), the union was a strong, centralized organization (dictatorial, in many respects) whose policy was to favor mechanization, rapid technological change, and rising wages at the expense of employment. The result, as can be seen in figure 11–3, was extremely rapid productivity growth. After the retirement of Lewis in 1960, the union confronted more and more internal dissent, as evidenced by changes in union leadership and workers resorting to wildcat strikes to voice their complaints about work conditions. One union president, Tony Boyle, was convicted of hiring gunmen to murder an insurgent leader. His successor, Arnold Miller, was widely criticized as ineffective, and the next leader, Sam Church, was turned out of office for failing to represent member's desires. Instability in underground coal mining reached such a state that in 1976 there were 1,383 work stoppages—over ten times the number

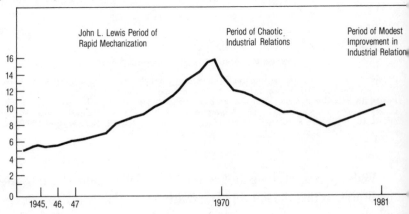

FIGURE 11–3

Industrial Relations and Productivity Growth in Underground Bituminous Coal

SOURCE: The figure was based on information in Peter Navarro, "Union Bargaining Power in the Coal Industry, 1945–1981" *Industrial and Labor Relations Review* 36, no. 2 (January 1983): 228.

fifteen years earlier—and 3.5 percent of total working time was lost because of wildcat strikes—over fifteen times as much as in 1961. Sensing the weakness of the union, some coal managements sought to take advantage of the situation, delaying settlement of grievances and giving the union as much trouble as they could.[18] While other factors, such as the Mine Safety and Health Act of 1972, contributed to the reduction of productivity, the deterioration in industrial relations in the sector is, in our view and that of many industry participants, a major cause of the observed decline. Indeed, as the union began to stabilize in the 1980s, productivity began to rise once more. The lesson is that *unionism per se is neither a plus nor a minus to productivity. What matters is how unions and management interact at the workplace.*

The Importance of Competition

If industrial relations in coal could deteriorate to such an extent that unionized mines became markedly less productive than nonunion mines, what prevents conditions from deteriorating elsewhere in the organized part of the economy, with commensurate adverse effects on productivity? Why does coal in the 1970s appear to be the exception, rather than the rule?

We believe the answer lies with the extent of competition found in the product market for the output produced by unionized labor. Like everyone else, unions, management of organized plants, and workers are more likely to devote effort to productivity-augmenting activities when they face the gun of competition. Indeed, in a competitive sector, only the unions and management that are able to raise productivity to offset union wage gains will survive in the long run. Sectors sheltered from competition, by contrast, may or may not adopt productivity-improving activities. From this perspective the collapse of productivity in unionized coal is understandable. Coal is a natural resource that can be produced only in certain areas, so that the entry of competitors is limited. In the 1970s, the price of coal soared because of the shift in demand from oil to coal, allowing the organized mines to earn reasonable returns and stay in business despite their higher labor costs per unit of output. In 1975, when the estimated union productivity effect was very sizably negative, and when average productivity in underground mining was 40 percent lower than in the 1969 peak year, the rate of return on investment in the entire industry was over four times what it had been in 1969. Of course, the unionized producers suffered a serious loss of market share, from about 70 percent of production in the late 1960s to 44 percent of production in 1980. But they still remained in business.[19]

Conclusion

What unions do to productivity is one of the key factors in assessing the overall economic impact of unions. The new quantitative studies indicate that productivity is generally higher in unionized establishments than in otherwise comparable establishments that are nonunion, but that the relationship is far from immutable and has notable exceptions. Higher productivity appears to run hand in hand with good industrial relations and to be spurred by competition in the product market, while lower productivity under unionism appears to exist under the opposite circumstances.

This "answer" to the debate over what unions do to productivity is probably the most controversial and least widely accepted result in this book. Some cavil at the finding because of a strong prior belief that the higher productivity of unionized sectors is, in fact, the result of the substitution of capital for labor or the hiring of "better" workers, which have not been correctly taken into account in the union productivity studies. Others criticize because they believe that higher productivity implies lower costs in the union setting (which it does not), making managerial opposition to unionism difficult to understand. Yet others find the result troubling because of counter examples known to them personally. While the new work deals with these problems, at least in part, the controversy is unlikely to disappear. Age-old debates do not often end with a bang, even with computerized evidence.

CHAPTER 12

But Unionism Lowers Profits

I'm willing to believe unions raise the well-being of workers and may even spur management to get more out of their workforce. But you don't mean to tell me they're good for my company. Unions lower profits.—*An archetypical employer*

A company faced with the prospect of unionization does not ask, "Is unionism good for workers?" or "Is unionism good for the overall economy?" but rather "Is unionism good for company profits?"

Is it? Does the higher productivity of unionized labor offset increased costs of compensation, so that profits are as high or higher under unionism? Or is the archetypical employer view expressed above correct, at least in most situations?

While the impact of unionism on profitability has not received the same attention from economists as the impact of unionism on the labor market, the existing evidence provides an answer to these questions. Our analysis and those of other researchers show that the view cited above is essentially correct. Though exceptions can be found, unionization is more often than not associated with lower profitability.

Measuring the Union Effect on Profitability

Profitability is one of the most difficult economic variables to measure. The profits reported on company balance sheets generally differ from "true economic profits." They may differ in treatment of interest charges, in depreciation, in valuation of inventories, or in estimation of the cost of pension fund liabilities. For tax reasons, companies often seek to report lower profits than in fact they actually earn. There are also problems in measuring the capital investment with which profits are compared. Valuing machines of different vintages is difficult; the book value reported by accountants differs from the "true value" of assets. Estimates rarely exist of important but nebulous forms of capital, such as "good will" or "reputation."[1]

Studies of industry or company profitability treat two measures of profits: the "quasi-rent" return on capital, defined as business receipts less variable (usually labor) costs divided by some measure of the value of capital, such as the replacement cost of plant and equipment or the gross book value of total assets; and the "price-cost margin," defined as the excess of prices over variable costs. The quasi-rent/capital measure has the advantage of relating returns directly to capital, but the disadvantage of requiring valid measures of capital. The price-cost margin is widely used in industrial organization to measure the potential effect of market concentration on prices: a sector with monopoly prices will charge an above-normal margin and thus earn higher profits on its investment. As neither of the variables comes from a conceptually correct expected present value analysis, each has been criticized in studies of profitability. Some experts in industrial organization favor the quasi-rent/capital measure; others favor the price-cost margin.[2] Because both contain some information about profitability, we have examined the effect of unionism on both, on the principle that when one cannot measure the theoretically correct concept, one does better to look at several indicators, rather than to debate over which imperfect indicator is "best."

Table 12–1 presents the results of our investigation of the impact of unionism on profitability in three industry data sets and the results of an analysis by Clark (Harvard Business School) of the impact of unionism on profitability in a sample of individual businesses. The table records the estimated percentage change in profitability due to unionism in statistical analyses that control for diverse other factors that could be expected to influence profits. The industry analyses infer the effect of unionism on profitability by comparing profits in industries that are heavily unionized with those with less unionization, in much the same manner as early studies of union wage effects inferred how

TABLE 12–1

Estimates of the Effect of Unionism on Profitability

	Approximate Percentage Difference in Profitability Due to Unionism	
	---	---
Sample	Price-Cost Margin	Quasi-Rents Divided by Capital
Industries		
1. 139 Manufacturing Industries, 1958–76	−17	−12
2. 168 Internal Revenue Service Major Industries, 1965–76	−37	−32
3. State by Industry,		
1972, 400 observations	4[a]	−27
1977, 360 observations	−14	−9
Companies		
4. 902 Individual Businesses, 1970–80	−16	−19

SOURCES: (1) and (2): R. B. Freeman, "Unionism, Price-Cost Margins, and the Return to Capital": National Bureau of Economic Research Working Paper No. 1164 (1983). (3): Calculated in conjunction with Jonathan Leonard from 2-digit Standard Industrial Classification by state data. (4): Kim B. Clark, "Unionization and Firm Performance: The Impact on Profits, Growth, and Productivity," Harvard Business School HBS 83–16 (1983). Approximate percentage differences were calculated as antilogs of estimated union coefficients in semi-log regression models.
[a]Not statistically significant.

unionism influenced wages by comparing wages in heavily and lightly unionized industries and localities (see chapter 3). The company or business studies are more akin to studies of union wage effects based on establishment data, in which one compares organized with unorganized plants.

The calculations show clear negative union impacts on both the price-cost-margin and the return-to-capital measures of profitability. On the basis of these results, managements of unorganized firms have good reason, in general, to oppose unionization: organization will penalize them on the bottom line.

The magnitude of the reduction in profitability reported in table 12–1 may strike some readers as suspect, given the estimates of union wage and productivity effects in preceding chapters. If unionism raises wages by 20 percent and if unions raise productivity by 10 to 15 percent, should not one expect (assuming no other variable costs) smaller reductions in profits, on the order of 5 to 10 percent? Is our analysis of profitability consistent with our earlier estimates of union wage and productivity effects?

The figures are consistent. The reason for the large estimated percent of reduction in profitability is that profits are a relatively small component of an industry's income flows, so that percentage changes in costs or in productivity translate into larger percentage changes in profits.[3] Arithmetically, consider what happens to an industry with $1.00 of receipts divided between labor and capital in the proportion of 4 to 1 (labor costs of 80 cents and return-to-capital of 20 cents). An increase in labor costs of 20 percent will raise costs by 16 cents and lower profits 16 cents; but, whereas 16 cents is 20 percent of labor cost, it is 80 percent of profits. In this case, even if unions raise the productivity of capital and labor by 10 percent, so that receipts are 10 cents higher, profits will drop by 6 cents, or 30 percent. More detailed analyses of the underlying productivity, labor cost, and profit data shows that the estimates in this chapter are consistent with the estimates in earlier chapters.[4]

Another source of information on union effects on profitability is the stock market. If unionism reduces profitability, and if the stock market recognizes such an impact, the stock prices of companies becoming organized would be expected to decline relative to other stock prices. Indeed, the only analysis of this issue, by Ruback and Zimmerman (Sloan School of Management, MIT), estimates that successful organizing drives result in declines in the price of the stock of 2.7 to 3.8 percent.[5] This does not, however, imply that the rate of return on the stocks of *already* unionized firms are lower than market averages: the prices of those stocks already incorporate the impact of past unionization on profits.

Whose Profits Are Hit Hardest?

It's great that unions lower profits. Big Business has been ripping off the consumer and workers long enough. I'm glad somebody's taking them on for once.—*A radical*

184

Profits are the golden goose of capitalism. Kill profits and you kill the system. The unions are pricing themselves and American industry out of the market.
—*A conservative*

Who is right? Is it good or bad that trade unions reduce profitability in most cases?

The answer depends on the locus of the union impact on profitability. If unions reduce the profitability of industries in which firms have sufficient market power to obtain monopoly-level profits, our radical friend's commentary has some validity. In that case unions are redistributing monopoly profits from capital owners to workers. Indeed, if the industry was charging the prices of a pure monopolist, all of the union effect could come out of the pockets of owners and none out of the pockets of consumers. If, on the other hand, unions reduce profits in competitive settings to levels below the going rate of return, they will drive companies out of business, cause a reduction in the industry's output, and eventually cause a rise in the price consumers pay. In this case, our conservative friend's commentary has validity, for unions will indeed create economic problems of survival for firms and harm consumers.

To see which of the two possible cases best fits U.S. unionism, we have examined the impact of unions on profitability in industries that differ in their level of industrial "concentration," defined as the percentage of an industry's total shipments made by the four largest firms. Concentration is a widely used though imperfect measure of the market power of producers and thus an indicator of where monopoly profits are likely to be found. The impact of unionism on profitability is less likely to be harmful if it occurs in concentrated industries rather than in ones which function under more competitive conditions.

Table 12–2 presents the results of our analysis of the link between the union profit effect and market structure. It records the difference in the profitability of highly unionized and less unionized sectors of low concentration industries and of high concentration industries. A negative number implies that the highly unionized sector has lower profitability than the less unionized sector; conversely a positive number implies that the unionized sector is more profitable. The results lend considerable support to the radical commentary. Taking the low con-

TABLE 12–2

The Differential Effects of Unionism on Profitability, by
Concentration of Sector

	Approximate Percentage Difference in Profitability Between Highly Unionized and Less Unionized Sectors	
Sample, Measure of Profitability	Less Concentrated Industries	Highly Concentrated Industries
All Industries		
Quasi-Rents/Capital	5	−21
Price-Cost Margin	−7	−21
Manufacturing Industries		
Quasi-Rents/Capital	0	−26
Price-Cost Margin	−1	−17

SOURCE: Internal Revenue Service data and Survey of Manufactures data sets; see R. B. Freeman "Unionism, Price-Cost Margins, and the Return to Capital": National Bureau of Economic Research Working Paper No. 1164 (1983), 25. Approximate percentage differences were calculated as antilogs of estimated union coefficients in semi-log regression models.

centration industries first, we find no substantive difference in profitability between the highly unionized and the less unionized: for all industries the high-union sector has higher profitability than the low-union sector by one measure but lower profitability by the other; in manufacturing, the highly and less unionized industries have virtually the same profitability. These data suggest that unionism has no impact on the profitability of competitive firms. Among highly concentrated industries, by contrast, the table shows enormous differences in profitability by union density; the highly unionized industries have considerably lower profitability in all calculations. Does this mean that high-concentration high-union industries are doing especially poorly? Because concentrated industries with low unionization have exceedingly high levels of profitability, it does not. Indeed, comparisons of highly unionized concentrated industries and less concentrated industries show basically the same profitability.[6] What unions do is to reduce the exceedingly high levels of profitability in highly concentrated industries toward normal competitive levels. In these calculations, the union profit effect appears to take the form of a reduction of monopoly profits.

Using a very different approach, in which the ratio of the stock market value of a firm to the replacement value of its physical assets is taken as the measure of profitability, Salinger (Columbia Business School) has obtained comparable results for a sample of 193 manufacturing firms. In his analysis Salinger finds that unions bid away most of monopoly rents in American industry, reducing the market value of a firm with monopoly power relative to its replacement value.[7]

The relation between unionism and profits need not, however, tell the entire story about what unions do to industry profitability, particularly in the competitive sector. Low profitability in one period of time, after all, is likely to cause a sector to contract, until profitability is restored to normal levels. While higher labor costs will cause firms to substitute capital for labor, the reduction in profits will cause the total investment of resources to fall in that sector, reducing output and raising prices until normal returns are restored.[8] To the extent that unionized sectors have restored profits by contracting, our estimates have understated the true impact of unionism on the economic return from investing in the sector.

Analysis of the differential rates of growth of unionized and nonunionized sectors of the economy in the 1960s and 1970s tell a mixed story about the potential importance of this understatement. Because industry growth rates are extremely variable, unionism is only modestly related to them, and the magnitude of the relationship varies considerably across samples. In analysis of Internal Revenue Service data for the entire economy, we find unionism to be negatively related to growth in concentrated industries, but not in competitive industries (line 1 of table 12–3). In analysis of data for manufacturing, on the other hand, we find that more unionized industries in the less concentrated as well as in the more concentrated parts of the economy have grown less rapidly than less unionized industries (line 2 of table 12–3). A similar mixed picture of the relation between unionism, concentration, and growth has been found in Clark's study of 902 businesses in the 1970–80 period: his work shows unionism positively related to company growth in low market-share companies but negatively related to growth in high market-share companies.[9] In short, the evidence that our estimates of the union-profit effect should be modified in light of growth patterns is mixed.

TABLE 12–3

The Relation Between Unionism and Growth of Industries

| | Estimated Compound Annual Growth | | | |
| | High Concentration | | Low Concentration | |
Measure of Growth	Low Union %	High Union %	Low Union %	High Union %
1. Rate of Increase in Total Receipts, 1965–76, 68 manufacturing industries	6.7	2.8	2.7	3.1
2. Rate of increase in Value Added, 1958–76, 124 manufacturing industries	5.4	4.3	5.1	4.5

SOURCE: R. B. Freeman, "Unionism, Price-Cost Margins, and the Return to Capital": National Bureau of Economic Research Working Paper No. 1164 (1983).

Some Exceptions to the Rule

Every social science generalization or finding has its exceptions, and our "unionism lowers profits" result fits the pattern. There are two very different types of situations in which unionism is likely to raise rather than reduce profits: when union-induced cost increases in an industry lead the industry to charge monopoly-level prices; and when union-induced cost decreases serve to rescue firms on the brink of collapse. In the former case, the union acts, indirectly, as the cartelizing agent in the sector, forcing all firms to act in such a way as to bring the industry closer to the price and output position of a pure product-market monopolist. Since monopoly price increases are socially harmful, the resultant increase in industry profits is socially undesirable. In the latter case, the union behavior, whether reflected in wage reductions or productivity-augmenting activities on the shop floor, is socially desirable.

As an example of an industry in which union wage increases have served to raise industry prices and profits, consider over-the-road trucking during the period of intense Interstate Commerce Commission regulation. When the policy of the Commission was essentially to pass union-induced cost increases on to consumers by raising the regulated charges in the sector, profits seem to have been higher than they otherwise would have been. One study of the sector found that profitability in trucking *rose* after the Teamsters negotiated the nationwide *National Master Freight Agreement*, which brought virtually all over-the-road drivers into one agreement. Initially, the industry feared such an agreement because of the potential increase in union monopoly power, which many thought could enable the Teamsters to close down trucking in the whole country. In fact, however, the industry, as well as its workers, benefited from the union's ability to determine all over-the-road wages in one package. In the decade before the agreement, the industry profit rate was 14 percent, compared with an average manufacturing-wide profit rate of 17 percent; in the decade after the agreement, trucking had a profit rate of 19 percent compared with 16 percent for manufacturing.[10]

As an example of more socially desirable union efforts to improve profits in firms, consider the efforts to lower costs under the so-called Scanlon Plan and its close relatives. Under this plan, devised in the 1950s by a former union leader, unions and management, generally of firms facing serious economic trouble, established cost-reducing plans, with each side gaining some benefits. In numerous cases, the joint activities of the union and management has pulled companies back from the edge.[11]

That unions can raise profits by increasing or decreasing costs, with very different consequences for social well-being, demonstrates an important point about the impact of unions on profits: there is little normative content in the direction of the effect per se; rather, what matter are the market conditions and routes by which unionism alters profits.

Conclusion: The Paradox

What unions do to profits can be easily summarized: in general, they reduce profitability, especially in the more monopolized sectors of U.S. industry. This finding casts unions in a different light than our results on most other economic outcomes studied in this book. Whereas in general we have found that unionism improves diverse aspects of the economic position of workers and in many instances also improves the operation of the economy, the evidence on profitability shows that, on average, unionism is harmful to the financial well-being of organized enterprises or sectors.

Beneficial to organized workers, almost always; beneficial to the economy, in many ways; but harmful to the bottom line of company balance sheets: this is the paradox of American trade unionism, which underlies some of the ambivalence of our national policies toward the institution.

CHAPTER 13

Union Political Power: Myth or Reality?

LIKE OTHER interest groups, labor organizations operate in the political sphere as well as in the economic marketplace, seeking as best they can to obtain outcomes beneficial to their members and, in their view, to society as a whole. Many believe that unionism is a political powerhouse:

We've got the finest political organization in the country right now in the AFL-CIO.[1]

Organized labor ranks among the most powerful and active political forces in the U.S. . . . the most influential single voice in national policymaking.[2]

Yet in the 1970s, when the union movement made high priorities of passage of an amendment to enhance enforcement of the NLRA and of a bill on common situs picketing (which gave construction workers in any craft the right to strike entire construction sites), both pieces of legislation were defeated. Labor Law Reform was rejected in the Senate; Common Situs Picketing passed the Congress but was vetoed by President Ford, who had originally agreed to its provisions.

Are unions as powerful in the political arena as the quotations above suggest or as impotent as the failure of Labor Law Reform and Common Situs Picketing indicate? Have unions had greater success obtaining "special interest" legislation that strengthens their monopoly power or have they had greater success supporting "social" legislation that benefits lower-income persons and workers in general? Are unions "integral elements in a total institutional complex . . . antithetical to

191

economic freedom, to political liberty, and to world peace," as Henry Simons has argued, or do they contribute to democracy by increasing "the political position of poorer segments of society" and providing "a coordinated and coherent political voice to workers who would otherwise be largely disorganized," as Bok and Dunlop have argued?[3]

Our analysis suggests that despite all of the press given some union lobbying efforts, unions have been unable to win the legislation most important to them as institutions and to their monopoly power. As cases in point, the last major piece of legislation regulating collective bargaining and unionism, the Landrum-Griffin bill, was enacted in 1959 over the vociferous opposition of unions, while, as noted, the mild 1977 Labor-Law-Reform bill strongly favored by unions failed to clear Congress. By contrast, organized labor has been active and successful in pushing for major pieces of legislation which can be best called "social" in nature, such as the Public Accommodation Act of 1964, the Civil Rights Act of 1964, the Voting Rights Act of 1965, anti-poverty legislation, and the Occupational Safety and Health Act of 1971. This is not to deny that, like other special interest groups, unions exploit existing governmental regulations as best they can to obtain benefits for their members, often at the expense of the general public.

Unions and Economic Legislation

Unions seek to influence the political market in several ways:

1. By propagandizing their members to vote in particular ways. Because union workers tend to register and vote in particularly high proportions, and because families with one or more union members are likely to contain nonunion persons, the union influence on the electorate can be highly significant, larger than one might think on the basis of the 20-odd percent organization figure for the work force.[4]

2. By spending union funds to register voters. Since low-income persons are disproportionately represented among the unregistered and are likely to be favorably disposed to union-favored candidates, registration yields potential benefits to unions at the ballot box. A major activity of COPE (Committee on Political Education of the AFL-

CIO) has been its Register and Vote Campaign. According to one estimate, union expenditures on registration and voting averaged two-thirds as much as the sum of contributions to candidates and political action committee (PAC) expenditures.[5]

3. By contributing to pro-union candidates. Since federal law prohibits unions to donate dues to candidates for federal office, unions undertake campaigns to raise voluntary funds for such groups as COPE, the Machinists Nonpartisan League, and the like. In the past, labor was the leading contributor to political campaigns, but recently business has been the major contributor. In 1980, labor gave $13.1 million (24 percent) of the $55.3 million total PAC contributions. Corporations gave 36 percent or $19.9 million, and other interest groups gave $16.1 million (29 percent).[6] These moneys are distributed to congressional candidates, as well as to the presidential campaign.

4. By allocating union resources, including staff-time, and volunteer efforts to campaigns. While it is difficult to evaluate the amount of non-cash contributions unions have given to candidates, many regard those resources as dwarfing the value of cash contributions. It is no secret that when election time comes, union organizers often devote more time to political activity than to attempting to sign up more members.

For the union political effort to be effective, three conditions must hold. First, the union-endorsed and -aided candidates have to win a reasonable proportion of Congressional seats. Second, the union-endorsed or otherwise influenced members of Congress must vote in the direction favored by unions on at least some major issues. Third, these votes must produce at least some of the legislation favored by unions. It is important to recognize that all three conditions are necessary for unions to have true political clout. If union-favored candidates lost more often than not, or if union-favored candidates voted "wrong" on union-favored legislation as often as did other legislators, or if the union position on legislation generated a countervailing business response that defeated the union effort, one would judge union political power as being closer to myth than to the juggernaut both the AFL-CIO and its opponents claim. Let us consider these three conditions for unions to be an important political force.

1. How do union-endorsed candidates do in congressional elections? Their success varies with time, depending on national political senti-

ment. In 1974, for example, 64 percent of House members and 61 percent of Senators were favorable to the union movement. By contrast, in 1980 49 percent of the House and just 46 percent of the Senate were either COPE-supported or had voting records favorable to unions (see figure 13–1).

2. Do members of Congress from areas where unions are strong vote in accord with the labor movement? To find out the impact of unionism on the voting behavior of legislators, we have analyzed the impact of the union density in a state on the vote of senators on legislation, using the COPE *Report on Congress*, which scores the voting record

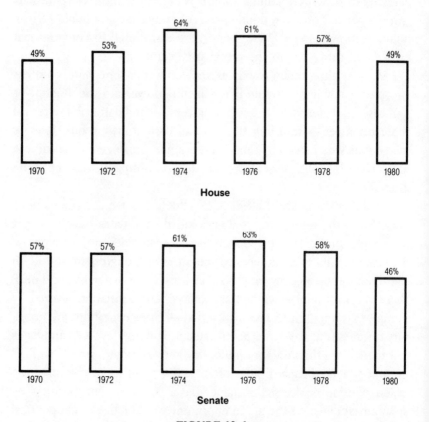

FIGURE 13–1

Members of Congress Either COPE-Supported or with Favorable Voting Record as Percentage of All Members, 1970–1980

Sources: Jeffrey L. Sheler, "Unions on the Run," *U.S. News and World Report,* 14 September 1981, pp. 61–63, and *Statistical Abstract of the United States,* various editions.

of representatives and senators on issues deemed important by the trade unions as "right" (in favor of union position) and "wrong" (opposed to union position).[7] To isolate the effect of union density, we control for diverse other factors that might influence a legislator's vote, notably: region of the country, median income in the state, percent of state residents who are black, percent of state residents who are blue-collar, and the years that the senator has been in office; in addition, because of the importance of political party in voting, in some analyses we also control for party affiliation.

The results of our analysis, summarized in table 13–1, show that senators from more heavily unionized states are, not surprisingly, much more likely to vote union than those from less heavily unionized states. The effect of the percentage of unionization is greater on Republicans than on Democrats, but because Republicans more often vote against the union position, Republicans from highly unionized states are about equally likely to vote "right" as Democrats from less highly unionized states.

The finding that union density is an important determinant of Congressional votes is consistent with other studies focused on the impact of union density on voting on minimum-wages and other pieces of legislation (see table 13–2). It is also consistent with the limited num-

TABLE 13–1

Effect of Union Density in State on Percentage of Votes "Right" on Legislation Important to Unions, 1970–1978

	Percentage Voting "Right"	Estimated Impact of One Percentage Point Increase in Union Density on Percentage Voting "Right"[a]	Percentage Voting "Right" if:	
			Unionization is 5 Percent Lower	Unionization is 5 Percent Higher
Total, Senators[b]	53	.86	49	57
Democratic Senators	69	.60	66	72
Republican Senators	31	1.00	26	36

SOURCE: Based on analysis of COPE voting records on selected issues, in R. B. Freeman, "What Unions Do to National Legislation": National Bureau of Economic Research Working Paper (Forthcoming).
[a]The estimated impact is taken from a multiple regression with controls for percent of blue-collar workers, income in state, percentage of black workers, percentage of workers employed in manufacturing, and years senator has been in office.
[b]All senator figures include dummy variable for party.

TABLE 13–2

Summary of Studies of Effect of Union Density or Campaign Contributions on Congressional Votes

	Measure of Union Strength		Votes Significantly Influenced by Union Strength?
Study and Focus	Percentage of Workforce That is Union	Contributions to Campaign	
1. Silberman and Durden (1976), Minimum Wage Legislation		X	yes
2. Kau and Rubin (1978), Minimum Wage Legislation	X		yes
3. Kau and Rubin (1979), Diverse Legislation	X		yes
4. Kau and Rubin (1981), Diverse Legislation	X	X	yes
5. Block (1980), Minimum Wage Law	X		yes
6. Uri and Nixon (1980), Amendments to Minimum Wage Law	X		yes
7. Cox and Oaxaca (1982), State Minimum Wage Laws	X		yes
8. Peltzman (1982), ADA Rating; COPE Rating	X	X	yes
9. Kau, Keenan, and Rubin (1982), Diverse Legislation	X	X	yes

SOURCES: (1) Jonathan I. Silberman and Garey C. Durden, "Determining Legislative Preferences on the Minimum Wage: An Economic Approach," *Journal of Political Economy* 84, no. 2 (April 1976): 317–29. (2) James B. Kau and Paul H. Rubin, "Voting on Minimum Wages: A Time Series Analysis," *Journal of Political Economy* 86, no. 2 (April 1978): 337–42. (3) ————. "Self-Interest, Ideology and Logrolling in Congressional Voting," *Journal of Law and Economics* 22, no. 2 (October 1979): 365–84. (4) ————. "The Impact of Labor Unions on the Passage of Economic Legislation," *Journal of Labor Research* 2, no. 1 (Spring 1981): 133–45. (5) Farrell Block, "Political Support for Minimum Wage Legislation," *Journal of Labor Research* 1, no. 2 (Fall 1980): 245–53. (6) Noel Uri and J. Wilson Nixon, "An Economic Analysis of Minimum Wage Voting Behavior," *Journal of Law and Economics* 23, no. 1 (April 1980): 1967–78. (7) James C. Cox and Ronald L. Oaxaca, "The Political Economy of Minimum Wage Legislation," *Economic Inquiry* 20, no. 4 (October 1982): 533–35. (8) Sam Peltzman, "Constituent Interest and Congressional Voting" (University of Chicago, 1982, mimeographed). (9) J. B. Kau, Donald Keenan, and Paul Rubin, "A General Equilibrium Model of Congressional Voting," *Quarterly Journal of Economics* 97, no. 2 (May 1982): 271–94.

ber of studies examining the impact of union political contributions on the voting of members of Congress (studies 1, 4, 8, and 9 of table 13–2).

Thus far, the evidence seems to support the claim that unionization is a powerful political force. But union support for a political candidate or for a piece of legislation often brings with it management opposition. The key issue in evaluating labor's success is not whether unionization influences voting but whether the influence is sufficient to pass the requisite legislation over the opposition it engenders. What matters in assessing union success in the political sphere is the impact of unionism on outcomes, not simply on the proportion of times individual congressmen vote "right." To illustrate this point, consider the situation in which union-supported members voted "right" 100 percent of the time but business-supported members voted "wrong" 100 percent of the time, and in which business-supported candidates won 51 percent of the seats. An analysis of voting would show unionization having a tremendous influence on Congress, but legislation favored by unions would be continually defeated while that favored by management would continually pass in Congress. This brings us to the key question:

3. How has union-favored legislation fared in the Congress? To answer this question we change our unit of analysis from the voting records of individual members of Congress to the legislative history of bills. Not surprisingly, union-favored legislation has done well when the Democrats are in power but poorly when Republicans are in power. Our analyses of the bills listed in the AFL-CIO's COPE Reports show that labor won 78 percent of bills from 1965 to 1968, when Lyndon Johnson was President, compared with 49 percent from 1969 to 1972, when Richard Nixon was President. Calculating the proportion of union-favored bills that have passed in Congress is, however, potentially misleading. What really matters is the contribution unions made to the outcome. Simply because a bill favored by unions is passed by Congress does not mean that union political power causes its passage; some of the bills rated by COPE are sufficiently popular (or unpopular) to pass or fail regardless of unionism. Accordingly, we have used our estimates of the impact of unionism on voting to see what might have happened if the union share of the workforce, and hence union political power, were larger or smaller. It is only by such "counterfactuals" that one can assess the contribution of a particular change to what actually happens in history. Our analysis, summarized in figure 13–2, suggests that a uniform 5 percentage point increase in unionization throughout the United States would have improved the success of union-favored bills by about 7 percentage points, while a uniform decrease of 5 percentage points would have reduced the success rate by 13 points. The greater impact of a decline in union strength than of an increase in union strength on outcomes reflects the fact that relatively more union victories than losses have been the result of close votes. Since legislators

Percentage of Union-Favored Bills Passed

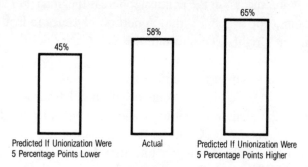

FIGURE 13–2

Assessing the Impact of Unions on Outcome of Union-Favored Legislation,
1947–1982

SOURCE: Based on regression summarized in table 13–1, which predicts the number of senators whose votes would have changed as a result of hypothesized changed union density. When the number of senators whose vote was predicted to change exceeded the vote margin, we predicted a different outcome for the bill.

often tailor bills to give them a good chance of passing, these calculations should not be interpreted as indicating that changes in unionization would actually alter the success rates of bills proposed in Congress. Rather, the more likely scenario is that the provisions of bills favored or opposed by the AFL-CIO would have been altered, with "pro-union" bills watered down when unionism is weaker and strengthened when it is stronger. The calculations in figure 13–1 are thus best viewed as "indicators" of the change in the nature of legislation, not as predictions of win-lose proportions.[8]

Where Union Political Power Matters

Granted that unions influence legislative (and executive) decisions, is that influence greater on issues relating to the monopoly face of the institution, or on issues relating to the voice face? Does union political power enhance union monopoly power in economically harmful ways, or does it provide voice for workers in ways that improve political democracy? Do unions win on important pieces of legislation, or on unimportant pieces of legislation?

We have sought to answer these questions by dividing the issues reported in the COPE ratings into several categories, ranging from national labor legislation (such as the Taft-Hartley Act) to more narrow legislation relevant to unions (such as bills to alter the Davis-Bacon Act, which obligates federal contractors to pay "prevailing" wage rates in construction and thus buttresses union rates in the industry, or bills regulating workers in the railroad and airline industries, which are covered by the Railway Labor Act), to general labor issues (i.e., unemployment insurance, minimum wage) and finally to other legislation deemed important by the AFL-CIO. Under other legislation we include bills pertaining to federal expenditures (public housing, defense, veterans' aid, and so on), taxation, and foreign policy. While there is some ambiguity among the categories (Are expenditures for job training a special interest or a general labor issue? Does union support of minimum wages, which benefit virtually no union member directly and few indirectly, reflect special interest or general labor concern?),[9] enough bills are sufficiently clearly of one type or the other to make our results impervious to changes in the categorization of ambiguous cases. Of the 280 bills reported on figure 13–2, we put 77 in one of the special union interest categories, 72 in the general labor category, and 161 in the general social legislation category. As can be seen in table 13–3, unions have had quite different success in the various areas. With

TABLE 13–3

Percentage of Bills Decided in "Right" Direction According to AFL-CIO Evaluation, 1947–1980

Bills	Percentage of Bills in Right Direction
Legislation Pertaining to Unionism	
1. National Labor Legislation	20
2. Bills to Restrict Union Political Power	100
3. Bills to Alter Davis-Bacon Act's Limits on Construction Wages	90
4. Bills Regulating Workers in Industries Covered by Railway Labor Act	55
Legislation Pertaining to General Labor Issues	58
All Non-Labor Related Legislation	55

SOURCE: Calculated by analysis of bills in AFL-CIO COPE Reports on Congress.

respect to national labor legislation, the union success rate is a sorry one: the only piece of national legislation that the union movement was able to get Congress to enact was the 1964 Amendment to Taft-Hartley, extending the law to the hospital sector, while business groups have twice managed to alter the labor law in ways opposed by unionism (the Taft-Hartley Act, 1947 and the Landrum-Griffin Act, 1959) and to deflect efforts to change the law in favor of unionism (Labor Law Reform, 1977–78). By contrast, unions have been successful in convincing Congress to turn down various bills designed to restrict unions' political expenditures. In the area of narrow industry interests, unions have been successful in halting efforts to weaken the Davis-Bacon Act, but they have had only mixed success in bills relating to the maritime, railroad, and air transport industries, which are covered by the Railway Labor Act, rather than by the Taft-Hartley Act. Various pieces of legislation affecting these industries have been prepared from time to time, some to strengthen, others to weaken union power in the sector. The success rate of unions here is around 55 percent. Finally, we find that unions have a 55 (58) percent success rate with bills that affect all of labor (the entire society), much above the success rate for national labor legislation but below that for efforts to preserve unions' existing political or economic strength.

Overall, the pattern of success in union-favored legislation shown in table 13–3 suggests that unions do much better winning general labor and social legislation and protecting their monopoly strength in some sectors than they do in winning legislation that enhances overall monopoly power. Why? What explains the fact that unions have had less success in winning major bills relating to labor law than in gaining social or general labor legislation and in defending themselves in particular sectors?

Union versus Business Lobbies

The economic analysis of legislation argues that, in general, a democratic society has an inherent weakness for special interest legislation. This is because the benefits of special interest legislation are concentrated, whereas the costs are borne by the general public. The small group that benefits from the legislation invests time and money to influence the legislature, while the potential losses to the general public are too small to motivate effective opposition.

While this analysis helps us understand why unions have succeeded in Congress on such issues as efforts to change the Davis-Bacon Act, it must be modified to explain the key phenomenon: union inability to halt legislation limiting union power and to pass legislation strengthening union power in the economy as a whole. We believe that the reason for union failure here is that major policies of union-related legislation differ substantially from particular "special interest" bills. They differ because the immediate costs, as well as the benefits, are concentrated. Legislation that strengthens unions tilts the balance of collective bargaining toward labor, while legislation that weakens unions tilts the balance toward business. Hence, when it comes to special interest legislation, unions do not face an amorphous majority but, rather, powerful business special interest groups. Supporting this thesis, a study of business lobbyists by Caves and Esty (Harvard University) found that in a large variety of industries business lobbyists regarded opposition to union proposals as a major priority, with one-quarter categorizing "defeat of labor law reform" as a major legislative priority.[10] Finally, as a test of the notion that union support generates business opposition and vice versa, we examined the impact of the proportion of "right" votes in the COPE rating of Congress on the contributions to Senators from business Political Action Committee's (PACs). This analysis showed that the higher the Senator's COPE rating, the lower was the Senator's contributions from business PACs.[11]

If, as in many European countries, unionized labor were a majority (or close to a majority) of the work force, the business opposition would be less effective. But in the United States, unions represent a distinct minority of workers, and minorities can only gain their goals through coalescing with other groups. Unions succeed in general social legislation because the more socially wide their objective, the easier it is for them to join with other groups. Moreover, unlike special interest legislation, general social legislation rarely invokes strong business opposition. On many bills, labor and business are in accord. For instance, unions have traditionally favored substantial defense expenditures and a strong anti-communist foreign policy, both of which have conservative and business support. On other social issues, such as mass transportation or public housing or civil rights legislation favored by unions, there is rarely a business concensus, as some employer groups favor while others oppose aspects of those types of legislation.

In short, while unions would like to pass laws that enhance union strength, they represent too small a proportion of the population and engender too great business opposition to succeed. Through no virtue of their own, their main political success is as the voice of workers and the lower income segments of society, not as a special interest group enhancing its own position. Our evidence supports the Bok and Dunlop statement that "the record suggests that organized labor has not been able to achieve important legislative goals unless its objectives have corresponded with the sentiments of the electorate or the *prevailing* convictions in Congress."[12]

A Case in Point: Labor Law Reform, 1977-78

In 1977 the political scene seemed opportune for unions to gain labor legislation more favorable to them than existing law. The Democratic Party had large majorities in both branches of Congress. President Carter was pledged to labor law reform. Hearings by the House Education and Labor Subcommittee on Labor Management Relations, chaired by Representative Frank Thompson (D.–N.J.), had detailed existing abuses of labor law, including the lawbreaking activities of J. P. Stevens and other notorious anti-union firms, which made a strong case for changing at least some parts of the law.

The bill introduced in the summer of 1977—the Labor Law Reform Bill of 1977–78—was a relatively mild piece of legislation, meant to facilitate union organizing activities by (1) streamlining the NLRB election procedures; (2) penalizing employers who break existing labor law more severely than they were being penalized; and (3) providing "equal time" for unions to "address employees on company time and property prior to a representation election." Unlike previous major pieces of labor legislation such as Taft-Hartley, Landrum-Griffin, or the Wagner Act, the Reform Bill of 1977–78 did not call for significant institutional changes in American industrial relations practices. It is indicative of the "mild" nature of the reforms that the Business Round Table, an organization of industrialists from the largest corporations, initially agreed not to oppose its passage. Since the reform was meant largely to ease the way for unions to organize new establishments and to penalize law-breakers, these corporations had no direct economic interest in it; they were partially unionized, and they generally obeyed existing labor laws. At first the AFL-CIO also pushed for repeal of section 14(b) of Taft-Hartley, the right-to-work section allowing states to prohibit the union shop, and for automatic certification of a union when 55 percent of workers signed union cards, but opposition forced labor leaders to drop these provisions.[13]

The bill was number one on labor's legislative agenda. Said AFL-CIO President George Meany, "We are going to fight harder for this bill than any bill since the passage of the Wagner Act."[14] The labor movement backed this up with its most vigorous lobbying effort in years. On October 6, 1977, the bill passed the House by a vote of 257 to 163, obtaining the votes of most Democrats and some Republicans as well. With a Democratic majority of 61–39 in the Senate, passage of labor law reform seemed a foregone conclusion. Here was a clearcut example of big labor using its political muscle to strengthen its own position.

But it was not to be. In the interim before the bill came to the Senate, business groups ranging from the National Association of Manufacturers to the U.S. Chamber of Commerce commenced a massive campaign to prevent passage in the Senate. Robert T. Thompson, chairman of the labor relations committee of the U.S. Chamber of Commerce, said, "Business is more unified in outright defeat of this bill than in any other labor issue I've observed over the past 25 years."[15] The most active business opposition, however, came from small businessmen. Their "grass-roots lobby" has been called "one of the most intense such campaigns in recent history," even a "holy war." Hundreds of business lobbyists worked diligently to turn back the bill, spending an estimated $5 million. The AFL-CIO, in turn, extended its initial campaign effort, which had succeeded in the House. It assessed unions one penny extra a month per 14 1/2 members over a six-month period to raise $870,000 and put eight senior staff members to work exclusively on labor law reform. Even the National Education Association put on a massive $800,000 effort to pass the bill. All told, the AFL-CIO itself spent $3 million while constituent unions together spent perhaps as much.[16]

The Senate never voted on the bill. A filibuster initiated by Senators Orrin Hatch (R.–Utah) and Richard Luger (R.–Indiana) defeated labor law reform, with the critical vote to end the filibuster, taken on June 14, 1978, failing by two votes to reach the 60 votes needed for cloture. After the cloture effort failed, 58–41, the Senate sent the bill back to Committee, where it died.

Despite a favorable political setting, the union movement was unable to gain this mild piece of special interest legislation because of the business opposition it aroused. While Senators from states that were largely unionized voted for cloture, demonstrating the union influence on voting, those from states that were less unionized voted against it in sufficient numbers to defeat the bill (see table 13–4). We could not have devised a better example of the disparity between the influence of union density on voting, which makes unions look like a powerful political force, and their inability to obtain special interest legislation over the opposition of business.

TABLE 13–4

The Defeat of Labor Law Reform, 1978

	Vote	
	Yes	No
All Senators	58	41
Democratic Senators	44	17
Republican Senators	14	24
Senators, by union density of state		
Lowest Quintile, by unionization	1	19
Second Quintile	6	14
Middle Quintile	16	3
Fourth Quintile	17	3
Top Quintile	18	2

SOURCE: Based on count of votes on Cloture Vote HR 8410, Labor Law Revision, 14 June, 1978.

Assessing the Consequences of Union
Political Success and Failure

Very well. Big Labor often fails to get what it wants on the monopoly front. Still, there are laws that strengthen union monopoly power, like Davis-Bacon, and harm the economy.—*An archetypical opponent of "Big Labor"*

It is true that unions win some special interest benefits from Congress. As table 13–3 shows, they have done a reasonable job in maintaining existing laws that strengthen union monopoly power, such as the Davis-Bacon or Walsh-Healey Acts.

In many cases, unions and management in a particular industry have united in favor of legislation to benefit their sector at the expense of the rest of the economy—sometimes successfully, sometimes not. The Teamsters and trucking industry associations have, for example, done their best to derail deregulation of trucking, which threatens their joint monopoly power. Labor and industry spokesmen often lobby together for tariffs against foreign competition. And so forth. While some of these efforts are effective, others are not. For instance, union and management efforts to obtain special advantages for American shipping have been quite unsuccessful. Moreover, since our estimates and those of others indicate that the social cost of union monopoly power, in total, is relatively modest, and since only a portion of that cost can be attributed to governmental laws strengthening union monopoly power, the harm to the economy is minuscule, indeed.

Very well. Big Labor hasn't ruined the economy through pro-union laws. It's ruined it by union-backed social legislation and income transfers to the poor. —*An archetypical opponent of "Big Labor"*

It is difficult to answer this criticism, for an evaluation of the pros and cons of the entire spectrum of laws whose passage was helped or impeded by union political power is virtually impossible. Such an evaluation depends on one's view of what the nation should be doing in various areas. Where unions have favored "liberal" legislation, liberals see social gain and conservatives see social losses. Where unions have favored conservative policies, the converse is true. In short, "union voice" can produce socially good or bad results, depending on one's perspective on the general social legislation. Our analysis can contribute nothing to that evaluation.

Conclusion

Union political power—myth or reality? Measured by resources used in the political arena, influence on congressional voting, and contributions to passage of general social legislation, unions are the political powerhouse indicated by the quotations which introduced this chapter. Measured by ability to obtain special interest legislation favorable to unions over the opposition of business groups, however, unions are far from a powerhouse. The reality is that unions have considerable political power in some areas. The myth is that they can use this power for the purpose of strengthening unionism and union economic power without general public consent.

CHAPTER 14

Blemishes on the
Two Faces

Joseph A. Yablonski, whose unsuccessful challenge last year for the presidency of the United Mine Workers of America touched off the bitterest election campaign in the union's 79-year history, was found shot to death, with his wife and daughter, in their home. . . .[1]

Nunzio Provenzano, president of one of the country's largest teamsters' union locals, was convicted yesterday of a labor racketeering conspiracy. . . .

A federal jury convicted Mr. Provenzano of conspiring to sell labor peace for $187,000 in payoffs from four interstate trucking companies.[2]

THE TWO FACES of unionism as portrayed by the media are severely scarred—the voice/response face by undemocratic practices, the monopoly face by corruption and by frequent, costly strikes. If one's perception of the labor movement came solely from media portraits, one would believe that crookedness, undemocratic behavior, and strikes flourish under unionism. Is this the correct picture of U.S. trade unions? Do union members have little access to their union's voice-making machinery? Are most unions plagued by corruption? Are strikes really very costly to the economy?

Union Democracy: The Members' Views

Union democracy depends on the extent to which members have a voice in choosing leaders and in determining union policies. On paper,

American unions offer members considerable say in both areas of decision making. Union constitutions typically specify frequent elections and often require conventions or referenda to discern the members' sentiment on important issues. Many unions require membership ratification of contracts. Since the Landrum-Griffin Act of 1959, Federal law has also mandated democratic practices within unions. Landrum-Griffin contains provisions that require unions to hold elections at fixed, reasonably short intervals; that guarantee members a reasonable opportunity to nominate candidates, run for office, and criticize union leaders and their policies freely; that prohibit incumbents from using union funds to support the election of a given candidate for office in the union and from disseminating propaganda for one candidate without doing as much for his or her opponent; and that require officials to file information on the financial affairs of the union and its leaders and on its constitutional provisions. In addition, judicial decisions obligate unions to represent all members fairly and to give due process to members in internal union affairs.[3] Do these *de jure* guarantees of union democracy indeed make unions bastions of democratic procedures, or are unions boss-ridden, nondemocratic institutions, as their critics often claim?

According to the results of several surveys of union members by the University of Michigan Survey Research Center, unions are closer to the "bastions of democracy" model than to the "union boss" model. First, a large proportion of union members participate in union activities (table 14–1). While attendance at any particular meeting may be small, within a two-year period about three-quarters of the members went to meetings at one time or another, roughly three-quarters voted in union elections, while 16 percent were elected to, nominated for, or chosen for a union office. In the same two-year period, 28 percent expressed their voice through the filing of a grievance. Looking at participation by groups, nonwhites participated roughly as much as whites, while women participated only slightly less than men. The biggest difference in participation is by seniority, with employees with more than twenty years of service significantly more likely to attend union meetings and to vote in union elections than those with less seniority. This is consistent with the argument that union voice grows as the exit option declines, because senior workers generally have fewer opportunities in the outside market than junior workers.

TABLE 14–1
Percentage of Members Participating in Union Activities: Blue-Collar Private Sector Unions

Union Activity	Total	Men	Women	White	Nonwhite	20 or More Years
In the last two years have you ever . . .						
Gone to a union meeting	76	77	72	76	73	82
Voted in a union election	73	75	67	74	68	97
Been elected to, nominated for, or chosen for an office in a union	16	17	11	15	18	15
Filed a grievance through a union	28	26	36	28	27	24

Source: Based on tabulations of microdata from the 1977 Quality of Employment Survey. We have restricted the sample to members with more than three years of company service, because the question asked about behavior in the last two years.
Note: The heading "20 or More Years" refers to company service.

Surveys that ask members about the management of their unions also indicate considerable democracy in the internal operation of unions (see table 14–2). While some blue-collar private sector union members felt that there were some problems with the management of their union (21 percent in 1969–70 and 30 percent in 1972–77), only a bare 3 percent in each year specifically mentioned a lack of democracy as the difficulty. Moreover, of those who mentioned problems, roughly one-third (30 percent in 1960–70 and 42 percent in 1972–73) regarded the problem as slight or "really no problem at all."

Members' responses to the question "How satisfied are you with your union?" analyzed in chapter 9 also support the claim that unions are responsive to their members' needs. Roughly three-fourths of union members report themselves as somewhat or very satisfied with their union (see table 9–4 in chapter 9).

Other Evidence of Union Democracy

The opinion of union members is not our only source of information on union democracy. Evidence can be found in the turnover of union

TABLE 14-2

*Evaluation of Democracy and Corruption in Own Union By
Blue-Collar Private Sector Union Members (Percentages)*

	1969–70	1972–73
Members Who Mention One or More Problems with Union Management	21	30
Members Who View Problem(s) as:		
Really No Problem at All	5	10
Slight	25	32
Sizable	30	34
Great	39	24
Specific Problem Mentioned— Democracy Related:		
Not Democratic Enough	3	3
Election Procedures	0.4	0.0
Minority Group Representation	0.4	0.4
Flow of Information	0.7	0.8
Handing of Grievances	3	3
Specific Problem Mentioned— Corruption Related:		
Graft or Corruption	3	3
Officials Paid Too Much	0.4	0.8
Officials Too Close to Company	3	5
Coercive Behavior Toward Present or Potential Members	0.0	0.0

SOURCE: Based on tabulations of microdata from the 1969–70 and the 1972–73 Quality of Employment Surveys. The "blue-collar" category includes service and farm workers. The percentages reflect the responses of 282 and 241 wage and salary workers in 1969–70 and 1972–73, respectively.

leaders, in the number of charges of improper conduct of unions under the Landrum-Griffin Act, and in case studies of specific unions, all of which provide important information on the internal operation of unions.

Turnover of leadership

Turnover of leadership is an imperfect but useful indicator of union democracy. While there may be exceptions, a union run by a single "boss" or clique is likely to experience fewer changes in leadership than a democratic union.[4] Is there considerable leadership turnover in unions, or do unions tend to have the same leadership, year in and year out?

There have been several studies of the length of tenure of union leaders. One study, which examined 94 locals in the Milwaukee, Wisconsin area between 1960 and 1962, found that approximately 20 percent of the officials in office at the beginning of a year were not in office at the end of the year; another study based on a random sample of 2,018 local unions in Ohio and Wisconsin revealed an average annual turnover rate of roughly 7 percent during the 1962–67 period; a comparable study for 1971–73 yielded a similar annual rate.[5]

Given that local unions must hold elections every three years to be in accordance with the Landrum-Griffin Act of 1959, these turnover rates imply that from 20 percent to 60 percent of union officials are replaced each time they come up for election. This is consistent with 1973 evidence for local unions in the United States Steelworkers, which showed that 42 percent of the local presidents, 55 percent of the vice presidents, 37 percent of the recording secretaries, 35 percent of the financial secretaries, and 40 percent of the treasurers were new to their offices.[6]

At the national level, there is less union-leadership turnover. Some national leaders have held their offices for decades, while others leave office only upon serious illness or death. Still, an average of the annual turnover rate of national presidents is about 9 to 12 percent a year. Between 1975 and September 1980, the turnover rate on the thirty-five-member executive council of the AFL-CIO, whose members are almost all national union presidents, was 12 percent. Rates of turnover of this magnitude suggest that, on average, national union leaders hold their jobs for about eight years, the same length of time permitted an individual in the Presidency of the United States.[7]

Measures of Election Conduct

As part of its monitoring of trade union democracy, the U.S. Department of Labor issues reports on charges of improper conduct (as defined by the Landrum-Griffin Act of 1959) in union elections. In a well-functioning democracy, we would expect improper conduct in election proceedings to be very small. Is this what the government data tell us?

The evidence on election conduct suggests that the vast majority of local and international unions in the United States suffer very few breaches of internal democracy. From fiscal years 1965 to 1974, only 239 charges of improper conduct affecting the outcome of a union election were judged to have merit, according to information issued by the Department of Labor.[8] Since approximately 200,000 elections were held by locals, intermediate bodies, and internationals during this period, the percentage of elections in which there were proven violations is approximately 0.1 percent. These figures are consistent with the assessments of union members in table 14–2, which revealed that less than one half of one percent of union members had a problem with their union's election procedure.

Case Studies

Case studies of the internal affairs of unions provide an additional source of information on union democracy. Perhaps the most famous such work was conducted by Sayles (Columbia University) and Strauss (University of California, Berkeley) in the 1950s. Their large-scale study was based on participant observation and informal interviewing in twenty local industrial unions, primarily from the manufacturing sector. Sayles and Strauss summarized their findings as follows:

In general . . . locals are more democratic than their parent internationals. In fact, a majority of those we examined maintained an energetic political life, with lively (although often poorly directed) debate in their meetings and a substantial turnover of officers. Although only a small proportion of the members were active in union affairs, there was nothing to prevent others becoming more active if they wished. There were many opportunities for dissatisfied members to protest decisions—even more than those specified in the contract grievance procedure. A determined member could take his case to many levels of the local hierarchy.[9]

Sayles and Strauss's belief that union democracy flourishes to a much greater extent at the local than at the national level was expanded upon by Barbash (University of Wisconsin), who analyzed numerous case studies in 1967.

Popular control and politics in collective bargaining are real in the national union. There is extensive local participation in the various processes, including bargaining conferences, strike votes, and contract ratification votes; and there is considerable local supplementation and enforcement of national bargaining, all of which acts to make this popular control effective. However, the national union's internal administration—unlike its collective bargaining processes—suffers from several deficiencies in democracy, specifically: the large area of unreviewable power exercised by the president; the failure of the executive board, and in turn of the convention, to serve as checks on the executive authority; the use of the union periodical as an instrument of the administration in power, and the failure of the constitution to reflect the full range of union functions.[10]

While one can find explicit cases of unions that have not operated democratically either at the local or at the national level, the case evidence suggests that these are the exceptions rather than the rule.

Taken together, the reports of union members, turnover data, measures of improper conduct, and case studies imply that democracy is alive and well in the U.S. labor movement. They also indicate, however, that the extent of democracy may be greater at the local level than at the national level. In light of this fact, the following statement by Sayles and Strauss seems appropriate:

When the proverbial man of the street thinks of the word "union" he thinks of the International and the men like Hoffa and Reuther, who make the headlines. But for the average member in the factory, his union is his *local* —and when he talks about the union he talks about his *local* officers and his *local's* problems.[11]

This observation helps to explain why "unions" appear more democratic to a union member than to someone whose perception of the institution is based solely on media portrayals.

Corruption: The Exception or the Rule?

Honesty is dull; corruption is exciting. This could explain why much more is written about corrupt unionism than about honest unionism; why the presidents of the Teamsters are household names while those of the International Ladies Garment Workers Union or United Food and Commercial Workers are not.

The illegal union activities receiving the greatest publicity involve embezzling resources from a union treasury or a union-management health, welfare, or pension fund; selling out a membership's well-being with a "sweetheart contract"; and selling protection against union-sponsored violence or disruption. Clearly, these crimes differ along a number of dimensions. Perhaps the most important is that embezzlement of union funds and negotiation of "sweetheart" contracts are generally nonviolent activities, while the shaking down of an employer will involve either the act or the threat of violence.

Just how rampant is corruption among union leadership? In the eyes of the membership, not very. The statistics in table 14–2 show that just 3 percent of blue-collar employees reported a corruption-related problem with the management of their union. Despite the publicity given corruption in unions, most experts on unionism agree with the members' view. In a statement made at hearings before the Permanent Subcommittee on Investigations of the Senate Committee on Governmental Affairs, which was studying racketeering, former Attorney General Benjamin Civiletti estimated that 300 local unions in our country "are severely influenced by racketeers."[12] Given that there are about 65,000 local unions in the United States, the Civiletti estimate implies that less than 1 percent of local unions are severely plagued by corruption. Consistent with this finding, Bok and Dunlop have written:

Although the record in this country compares unfavorably with that of many other nations, legal safeguards now go far to curb dishonest and encourage democratic behavior. Probably only a tiny fraction of all union officials in America would stoop to serious abuse. The overwhelming majority of labor leaders are honest men who take seriously their obligation to represent the interest of the members who have elected them to office.[13]

Still, some unions are corrupt, and some union leaders belong behind bars. But the same can be said of some businesses and business leaders. Is labor more corrupt than business, or less?

In 1980 *Fortune* magazine conducted a study of corrupt acts in 1,043 large U.S. corporations. It defined "corporate corruption" to include five crimes "about whose impropriety few will argue: bribery (including kickbacks and illegal rebates); criminal fraud; illegal political contributions; tax evasion; and criminal anti-trust violations."[14] The last category is made up entirely of price-fixing and bid-rigging conspiracies and excludes the vaguer area of monopolistic practices that are the subject of civil anti-trust suits. Also excluded are Federal Trade

Commission complaints that have to do with the ways companies 'signal' price changes to the competitors.

The *Fortune* survey revealed that 117, or 11 percent, of the large corporations studied had been involved in at least one major delinquency in the period under analysis; some of the companies had been cited more than once. In total there were 188 citations covering 163 separate offenses: 98 antitrust violations, 28 cases of kickbacks, bribery, or illegal rebates, 21 instances of illegal political contributions, 11 cases of fraud, and 5 of tax evasion. This count is limited to domestic citations; it would have been higher if it had included foreign bribes and kickbacks. Each of the charges resulted either in conviction on federal charges or in consent decrees (or similar administrative settlements).

The *Fortune* study deals only with large U.S. corporations. What would one find in companies of more modest size? According to *Fortune,* probably more crime would be found in smaller businesses, since "the bribing of purchasing agents by small manufacturers and the skimming of receipts by cash-laden small retail business are a commonplace of commercial life." Moreover, in trucking, in construction and on the docks, where time is of the essence, on-time bribes seem to flourish. And, *Fortune* contends, "Where bribes are not freely offered, they are often extorted."[15]

Another study of business crime was done by American Management Associations. Their dollar estimates for 1975 of the key forms of corruption are as follows: commercial bribery and kickbacks, $3.5 to 10 billion; securities theft and fraud, $5 billion; embezzlement (including computer crime), $4 billion; arson for profit, $3.5 billion; and insurance fraud $2 billion. The total for these categories was $18 to 24.5 billion, between 1 and 2 percent of the entire 1975 gross national product.[16]

The point is not that American business is riddled with crime, but that against the backdrop of business crime, crime and corruption in unions does not look anywhere near as significant as it does judged in isolation. Indeed, logic suggests—and the *Fortune* and American Management Associations data support—the notion that business crime far exceeds union crime. After all, businesses deal with much larger sums of money than unions and thus offer greater potential for crime.

The Nature and Locus of Union Corruption

Union corruption may be small, but it still exists. What type of crime is it? Where is it found?

Table 14–3 provides some answers to these questions. The information is based on Department of Labor reports on convictions for criminal activity (which obviously understate the total number of union illegalities, but which still have valid implications about union corruption, as long as the understatement of crimes does not vary greatly by type or convicted union). The table shows that union crimes likely to be associated with violence—extortion and, to a lesser degree, kickbacks—represent a very small fraction of total union corruption; the overwhelming majority of criminal actions take the form of nonviolent

TABLE 14–3

Total Convictions for Criminal Activity in Labor Unions, July 1969–September 1978

Union	Criminal Action Involved			
	Embezzlement	Benefit Plans	Kickbacks	Extortion
All Unions	292	29	52	12
Four Major Sources of Problems	83	15	29	9
Teamsters	10	5	12	1
Longshoremen	2	0	1	0
Hotel and Restaurant Workers	7	2	1	0
Building Trades	64	8	15	8
Percentage of All Convictions Due to the Four Major Sources	28	52	56	75

Source: Based on authors' tabulations of information in U.S. Department of Labor, Labor-Management Services Administration, *Compliance, Enforcement, and Reporting Under the Labor-Management Reporting and Disclosure Act*, each report year from 1967 to 1978.
Notes: Convictions are pleas of findings of guilt and pleas of *nolo contendere*. Embezzlements include non-fund-related embezzlement and theft of over $50. Benefit plans include embezzlement from a union benefit plan or kickbacks from the plan. Kickbacks include non-fund-related kickbacks and other payoffs from employers. Extortion includes extortion as defined under the Hobbs Act, arson, and extortionate picketing. The Building Trades figures are weighted averages that reflect the unions operating in the contract construction industry and the fraction of their members in this industry. Each time a contract construction union is cited, a number equal to the fraction of its members in contract construction is added to the relevant total. See U.S. Department of Labor, Bureau of Labor Statistics, *Directory of National Unions and Employee Associations, 1975*, Appendix I, table 1, p. 115 for the information on unionism in contract construction, which was used in these calculations. The four "major sources" listed represented approximately 24 percent of all private-sector union members in 1974.

crimes concerning the administration of cash. The table also reveals that crimes in which violence or the threat of it is likely to be present are highly concentrated among representatives of the Teamsters, the Longshoremen, the Hotel and Restaurant Workers, and some unions in contract construction. However, an above-average amount of criminal activity in these unions does not imply that they are crime-ridden. In fact, the existing data suggest that the vast majority of the unions' national and local officers carry out their duties in a law-abiding responsible manner.

Why do we find violent union crimes where we do? What is it about the trucking, longshoring, hotel and restaurant, and construction industries that increases the probability that a union leader will commit a violent criminal act? One reason is that in these industries, local unions generally help to determine who gets jobs, either through a hiring hall or through a system under which potential employees are recommended to unionized employers. Any such arrangement creates possibilities for union leadership to try to extract part of the compensation differential between union and nonunion workers for themselves. In industries where wages are negotiated nationally and where employers control hiring, there is much less possibility for such union corruption.

Strikes: How Common Are They?

But I am not worried about crime. I am worried about all those strikes unions call.—*The man in the street*

No one—neither workers, management nor the public—likes strikes. How common are strikes? How costly are they, and to whom? Why can't labor and managment reach agreement without recourse to the strike?

From headline news stories, one might expect the amount of time lost due to strikes to be sizable. U.S. Department of Labor data show it is not. In the decade from 1971 to 1980, just 2.6 percent of workers in the United States were on strike in a typical year, and just 0.18 percent of total working time was lost because of strikes—less time lost than that lost from worker absences for the common cold. Since most strikes occur in unionized sectors, however, the work loss under unionism is larger: in the 1980s about 11 percent of unionized workers went on strike in a typical year, reducing work time by an average of 0.9 percent.[17] About two-thirds of the recorded strikes involved contract negotiations, while one-third took place during the term of a contract. In terms of numbers of workers and time lost due to strikes, however, strikes over contract negotiations made up the vast bulk of strike activity: some 80 percent of workers and 95 percent of time lost occurred as part of disputes over contracts.[18] On average, a typical union worker is employed in an enterprise which is likely to be struck during contract negotiations once every eleven years. For a firm that has a three-year contract, this implies one strike every three to four negotiations. The average, however, conceals considerable diversity in both the nature and locus of strikes. Much of strike time lost occurs as a result of long strikes with many workers. In 1980 the average strike lasted 35 working days and involved 352 workers. Much strike time lost is concentrated in a small number of industries, notably construction and mining. Many companies bargain with unions for decades without a strike. Infrequent but long strikes are characteristic of the United States; in many other countries, by contrast, strikes are frequent but of short duration.

In the 1960s, some observers claimed that the strike was diminishing as a tool of conflict between management and labor. Union and management negotiators were said to have learned about each other's bargaining positions and built a more mature relationship that did not require strikes. While there is some downward trend in strike-time lost, the notion that strikes are diminishing is now recognized to be inaccurate. Strikes remain part of labor-management relations.[19]

The Cost of Strikes

Consider two possible strike scenarios. In the former, when management and labor are unable to reach agreement and workers strike, the lost output causes a major hardship to the public, with demonstrably adverse effects upon the health or safety of the nation. In the latter, when workers strike, the cost of the strike falls largely on management and labor in the form of lower profits and lost wages, respectively. Which of these cases best fits U.S. strike experience? Are strikes relatively more costly for the public or for workers and management?

Researchers have examined these questions by studying specific strikes and by statistical analysis of large numbers of strikes. Both types of studies focus on output lost as the key social loss. The case studies, many of which have dealt with disputes considered so critical to the nation as to induce the President to invoke the "emergency dispute" provision of the Taft-Hartley law, have almost invariably found that the costs of the strike to the nation are small. The most recent such analysis, evaluating the 1977–78 coal strike, concluded that "employer predictions of strike effects proved to be consistently exaggerated; these effects probably never constituted an actual emergency."[20] Statistical calculations designed to evaluate the impact of strikes on output in manufacturing industries yield comparable results.[21]

There are two basic reasons why strikes have only a modest impact on the economy. First, firms and consumers often alter their production or purchase plans in advance of a strike, building up inventories so as not to run short during the dispute. Second, sufficient substitutes exist for most goods to allow people to "make do" in the face of lost output. If truckers are on strike, one can ship goods by rail or sea or air; if miners strike, one can stockpile coal in advance and use it during the strike period. In short, strikes are by no means the major problem that they are sometimes alleged to be, except to the parties to the dispute. While some strikers may significantly harm third-party consumers or producers, just as some marital squabbles upset close relatives or neighbors, the major cost of a strike is on the direct participants.

Indeed, it is precisely because both management and labor lose from strikes that economists have trouble understanding the pattern of strikes in the economy. Why should both sides engage in an activity that costs each something? Wouldn't they do better to reach the agreement that settles the strike before actually striking? The conceptually plausible answer to those questions, advanced by Nobel Prize-winning economist Sir John Hicks in 1932, was that strikes are "accidents," errors in negotiating strategies by labor and management. If both sides fully understood the situation, they would come to agreement without a strike. Unfortunately, this "rational man" answer is inconsistent with the timing of strikes. For one thing, most researchers find strikes to be more frequent during economic booms than during recessions. When unemployment is low, strikes tend to be more frequent than when it is high. Strikes also tend to be more frequent when inflation is high than when it is low. If strikes were simply "errors of calculation," there should be no such pattern. True, labor might view the strike as a more fruitful weapon during booms than during recessions, but by the same token, management should be aware of this possibility and be willing to offer higher settlements in boom than in recession periods.[22]

Conclusions

This chapter has reached four conclusions about democracy and corruption in unions and about strikes:

1. There is a great deal of democracy, defined as access to a union's voice-making machinery, throughout the labor movement, particularly at the local union level.

2. While there is some hand-in-the-till corruption in unions, the amount of union corruption is no more than, and probably less than, business corruption.

3. Crime involving violence is relatively rare, and it seems to be concentrated in four industries—local trucking, longshoring, hotel and restaurant, and contract construction.

4. While costly to those directly involved, strikes cost the economy relatively little in terms of lost output.

In sum, the potential ugly scars on "The Two Faces of Unionism" appear to be blemishes upon closer examination. Moreover, these blemishes do not cover both of the two faces; rather, they are quite isolated.

CHAPTER 15

The Slow Strangulation of Private-Sector Unions

Labor Nemesis—When the Boss Calls in This Expert, the Union May Be in Real Trouble (*Wall Street Journal,* 19 November, 1979)

Preventive-Maintenance Techniques for Staying Union-Free (*Personnel Journal,* June 1980)

Unions on the Run (*U.S. News and World Report,* 14 September, 1981)

THE HEADLINES tell the story. Since the mid-1950s, private sector unionism in the United States has been on the decline (see figure 15–1). While the absolute number of union members has increased, the labor force has grown so much more rapidly that the union share of employees has dropped precipitously. In 1956, 34 percent of private nonagricultural workers were organized, and in 1980, just 24 percent —a 10-point decline in union density that is unprecedented in American history. Even in traditional union strongholds such as construction, transportation, and mining, the union proportion of workforces has fallen, often dramatically, as "open shop" or "union-free" environments have grown.[1]

Union success in National Labor Relations Board (NLRB) representation elections has shown a commensurate deterioration (see table 15–1). In the 1950s unions were victorious in 65 to 75 percent of the elections, organizing approximately 1.0 percent of the workforce annu-

**Percentage of Private
Nonagricultural Workers
Organized**

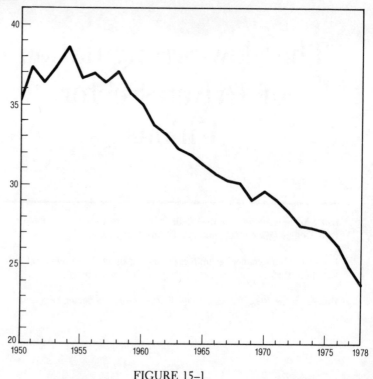

FIGURE 15–1

The Decline in Private Sector Unionization in the United States.

SOURCE: U.S. Bureau of Labor Statistics, *Handbook of Labor Statistics* Bulletin 2070 (1980), tables 72, 162, and 165; and Bulletin 2000 (1978), table 42. The percentage of private nonagricultural workers organized is calculated as (all union members, excluding Canada, multiplied by the percentage of union members in nongovernment industries) divided by (all nonagricultural employees minus government nonagricultural employees).

ally through the election procedure. In the early 1980s, unions were engaged in so few elections and were winning so few (4.5 percent) that just 0.14 percent of the unorganized work force became organized via NLRB elections—a percentage below that needed for unions to maintain their share of the work force, much less to grow proportionately.[2]

What has caused this dramatic fall in unionization in the United States—a fall that contrasts sharply with increases in unionism in most other Western countries, including Canada? Is the decline due to changes in the structure of the economy, such as the rise of white-collar employment, the growth of the Sunbelt, and the increased proportion of women in the workforce? Is it due to failings by the unions? Have

TABLE 15-1

From NLRB Elections to New Union Representation

	Number of Elections	Workers Eligible to Vote as Percentage of Private Wage and Salary Workers	Workers in Union Victories as Percentage of Those Eligible to Vote	Workers in Union Victories as Percentage of Private Wage and Salary Workers
1950	5,731	2.4	84	2.0
1955	4,372	1.4	73	1.0
1960	6,617	1.2	59	0.7
1965	7,776	1.1	61	0.7
1970	8,074	1.2	52	0.6
1975	8,061	1.1	38	0.4
1980	7,296	0.5	37	0.2

SOURCE: *Annual Reports of the National Labor Relations Board* (NLRB), 1951, 1961, 1971, 1981. Figures for private wage and salary workers from U.S. Department of Labor, *Employment and Training Report of the President, 1981*, with private household workers excluded from the total.

they fallen down on the job of organizing the unorganized? Is it due to a decline in workers' desires for unions? Or to the increased strength and effectiveness of managerial opposition?

To answer these questions, it is necessary to understand the process of unionization in the United States. Consider first how a group of workers becomes organized through an NLRB election. In most cases, the first step occurs when some workers decide that they want a union and ask an existing union to organize their work group. The union organizer will try to get two-thirds of the individuals to sign cards requesting an election. While only a third need sign such cards for the NLRB to hold an election, experience has shown that unless two-thirds sign the union will have no chance to win. When management learns of the union activity, it will mount a counteroffensive to convince workers to vote "no" on election day, often calling in labor-management consultants to run the campaign against the union. The management may object to the "election district"—the makeup of the eligible-to-vote workforce—sought by the union, arguing that some workers (favorable to the union) should not be included while others (unfavorable to the union) should. By challenging the election district and through other legalistic means, management can delay an election for months. Finally, even if management loses the election, it need not enter into a collective bargaining agreement; employers are required to bargain "in good faith," not to reach agreement with the union.

While in principle the Taft-Hartley law makes workers the sole determinants of whether or not to organize through the elections, in fact, unionization depends on management as well as on labor. Accordingly, any explanation of the decline of U.S. unionism must treat the activities of both parties.

So, why has the proportion unionized in the private sector been falling?

The First Suspect: Changing Economic Structure

The first and simplest explanation of the decline in unionism is that it resulted from broad economic changes, which reduced the proportion of the workforce in groups traditionally highly unionized and increased the proportion in groups traditionally nonunion. The explanation is simple because it ties the decline to the changing structure of the economy with no need to bring in changes in union or management behavior or the desires of workers for unions. It is a "technocratic" explanation, and technocratic explanations are invariably the easiest and least controversial.

To estimate the potential impact of structural changes on unionization, we performed a two-part analysis. First, we estimated the impact of personal, job, and geographic factors on the probability an individual is unionized, using data on over 100,000 workers from the May 1973–75 Current Population Survey tapes. Second, we multiplied the estimated impacts of the factors by the changed proportion of workers in that category since 1954. The logic of the procedure is simple: if, as turns out to be the case, female workers are (all else the same) 8 percentage points less likely to be union members than male workers and if the proportion of the workforce that is female increases from .30 to .40, our calculations attribute 0.8 [= 8 × (.40 − .30)] percentage points of the decline in unionization to the rising female share of the workforce.[3]

At first blush, the changing structure of the workforce appears to be the principal cause of the decline in unionization, with the growth of white-collar employment the major culprit (see table 15–2). Over the period 1954–79 we estimate that if the probability that workers with differing personal, job, and geographic characteristics were union was constant, the changing composition of the workforce would have reduced the union density by 8.2 percentage points, or 72 percent of the observed decline. While, as figure 15–2 makes clear, there were substantial declines in unionization among production workers within traditional union strongholds, which require a different explanation, a simple reading of table 15–2 places most of the blame, or gives most of the credit, for the falling percentage of workers unionized on structural changes.

TABLE 15–2

Estimates of the Impact of Structural Changes in the Workforce on the Decline in Unionism, 1954–1979

Characteristic	Relation to Unionism	Estimated Impact on Percentage Organized
Personal		
Age	Younger workers less likely to be union	−0.4
Education	Better educated less likely to be union	−0.7
Sex	Women less likely to be union	−0.8
Race	Nonwhites more likely to be union	0.0
Total Personal		−1.9
Job		
Occupation	White-collar less likely to be union	−3.0
Industry	Manufacturing, construction, mining, transport more likely to be union than services, trade, finance	−1.9
Total Job		−4.9
Geography	South less likely to be union; SMSAs more likely to be union	−1.4
Total Related to Structural Changes		−8.2
Total Change		−11.3

Sources: Calculated by estimating the impact of each factor on the probability of being unionized, with all information coming from the 1973–75 May Current Population Surveys and then applying the estimates to changes in the composition of the workforce. For the period 1954–74 we used composition figures from U.S. Department of Labor, *Employment and Training Report of the President* and unionism figures from U.S. Department of Labor, *Handbook of Labor Statistics* (1980). For the period 1974–79 we used composition figures from the May CPS surveys.
Notes: The 11.3 point drop in this table differs from the 10.0 point drop shown in figure 15–1 because the table and figure use different data sets. In the table we measured the change in unionization from 1954–74 using Department of Labor figures but measured the change from 1974–79 using CPS figures. In the figure we used Department of Labor figures throughout.
SMSA stands for Standard Metropolitan Statistical Area.

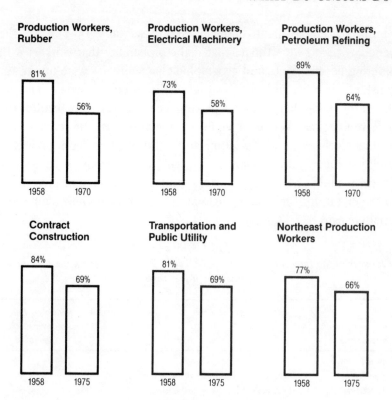

FIGURE 15–2

Decline in Unionization in Traditional Areas of Union Strength

SOURCES: Figures for Rubber, Electrical Machinery, and Petroleum Refining refer to percentage of production workers covered by collective bargaining, as reported in R.B. Freeman and J. L. Medoff, "New Estimates of Unionization in the U.S.," *Industrial and Labor Relations Review* 32 (January 1979): table 4. Figures for Northeast production workers also refer to percentage of production workers covered, from U.S. Department of Labor, *Handbook of Labor Statistics*, 1977. Construction and transportation-and-public-utility figures are ratios of union workers to nonagricultural employment, as reported in R. B. Freeman "The Evolution of the American Labor Market, 1948–1980," in M. Feldstein, ed., *The American Economy in Transition* (Chicago: University of Chicago Press, 1980), 349–96. The "1970" figures actually refer to 1968–72; the "1975" figures actually refer to 1974–76.

Objections to the Structural-Change Explanation

Simple technocratic explanations rarely explain important social phenomena, and upon closer examination the "structural-change" hypothesis turns out to be no exception.

Problem number one: The major structural changes in the U.S. labor market—growth of white-collar jobs, decline of manufacturing, increased number of women in the labor force—have occurred in virtually all major western economies. If structural changes were the chief factor behind the decline in unionism, the proportion organized would fall everywhere. Instead, outside the United States unionization has increased, often in large numbers. Perhaps most telling is the fact that in the country most like the United States, Canada, where many of the same unions and firms operate, the percentage unionized went from below the U.S. percentage unionized to above it.[4]

Problem number two: The structural argument postulates that the proportion of workers of a given type who are unionized does not change over time. But union growth has historically taken the form of sudden organization of traditionally nonunion groups, rather than of growth of already-unionized sectors. In the 1960s and 1970s one group of workers with a traditionally low unionization rate—public sector employees—organized in unprecedented numbers.[5] Why didn't the proportion of traditionally unorganized groups of private sector employees rise as did the proportion of public sector workers?

Problem number three: Some of the changes in the structure of the workforce that tend to reduce the proportion of workers unionized have opposite effects on the proportion who would vote for a union in a NLRB representation election. In particular, in surveys asking if workers would vote for a union in a NLRB election, young and female workers, who are less likely to be organized than older and male workers, express as much pro-union sentiment as older or male workers, if not more, while nonwhites, whose unionization rate is comparable to that of whites, express exceptional desire for unions. Evidence from actual representation elections also shows that nonwhite and young workers are more likely to vote "yes" than others, while women are as likely to vote "yes" as men.[6] As can be seen in table 15–3, the result is that the structural changes that "accounted for" 72 percent of the decline in the percentage organized can explain none of the decline in the union share of votes in NLRB elections. Since lack of success in NLRB elections is one of the chief causes of the decline in union density, something is evidently wrong with a pure structuralist explanation of the decline in union success in the United States.

The problem is that the structuralist explanation assumes, erroneously, that structural changes are the sole determinants of unionization and does not allow other factors, such as union organizational activity or management opposition, to affect unionization. A more realistic

TABLE 15-3

Estimates of the Impact of Personal, Job, and Geographic Factors on Percentage Voting Union in NLRB Elections

Characteristic	Relation to Vote for Unionism	Estimated Impact on Proportion Voting Union in Elections
Personal		
Age	Young more likely to vote union	0.3
Education	Little relation to vote	0.2
Sex	Women more likely to vote union	0.8
Race	Nonwhites much more likely to vote union	0.3
Total personal		1.6
Job		
Occupation	Blue-collar more likely to vote union	−2.1
Industry	Mining, transportation, and communications *below* average desire to vote union	−0.4
Total job		−1.7
Geography	In South most likely to vote union; in Central least likely; SMSA residents more likely to vote union	0.7
Total Change in Percentage Who Would Vote Union as a Result of Structural Changes		−0.6
Total Changes in Percentage of Voters Who Voted Union in NLRB Elections, 1954–80		−22.1

SOURCE: Calculated by estimating the impact of each factor on the probability of stating would vote for a union in the 1977 Quality of Employment Survey and then applying the estimates to changes in the composition of the work force for the period 1954–80, as in table 15-2.

reading of the evidence is that structural factors increase or decrease the difficulty of organization but do not determine unionization.

The Decline of Union Organizing Efforts

NLRB elections generally involve active campaigns by both unions and management. To what extent does the result of an election depend on union organizing efforts? How have these efforts changed over time? How much, if any, of the decline in private sector unionism can be attributed to a decline in union organizing activity?

Voos (University of Wisconsin) has analyzed these questions in some detail. Her investigation of the yearly expenditures on organizing by twenty different international unions during the 1953–77 period suggests that resources spent to organize the unorganized in a union's jurisdictions is, indeed, a major determinant of unionization. Roughly, a 10 percent increase in dollars spent per potential union member raises the proportion for whom the union wins representation rights by 7 percent. Moreover, Voos finds that in the 1950s and 1960s organizing expenditures per nonunion worker, deflated by wages to reflect the labor intensity of organizing activity, fell sharply. In 1953 unions spent $1.03 (in constant wage-deflated dollars) per nonunion member for organizing; in 1963, they spent $0.91; in 1974, spent $0.71, for an overall decline of 30 percent. Using these figures we estimate that the decline in union organizing effort contributed substantially to the drop over the past quarter century in the percentage of nonagricultural workers newly organized through NLRB elections. In the early 1950s, unions organized roughly 1.0 percent of the workforce annually through elections; in the early 1970s, they organized roughly 0.3 percent of the workforce annually through elections. Voos's figures suggest that the decline in organizing effort reduced the proportion of newly organized by between 0.1 and 0.2 points of the 0.7 point drop.[7] While crude, these figures indicate that possibly as much as a third of the decline in union success through NLRB elections is linked to reduced organizing activity.

Another related statistic can be brought to bear on the issue of union organizing effort and electoral success. In some NLRB elections, more than one union contests the right to represent workers. In this situation organizing effort is undoubtedly much higher than in elections which pit unions against management only. In 1980 the victory rate in elections with two or more unions on the ballot was 74.2 percent, compared with a rate of 47.4 percent where only one union was seeking representation rights. Prior to unification of the AFL and CIO, employers would often express a desire to work with unions associated with one rather than the other federation ("The CIO is too leftist," "The AFL is too corrupt" or "too craft-oriented.") After unification, the number of elections with two or more unions on the ballot fell, from 23.7 percent of NLRB elections in 1953 to 6.2 percent of elections in 1980, implying less choice for workers (and employers) among unions and less organizing activity per election.[8] All else the same, the drop of 17.5 percentage points in the proportion of elections with two or more unions on the ballot would, at 1980 rates of victory, reduce the proportion of elections won by unions by 5 percentage points, or a quarter of the actual drop in the percentage of elections won by unions—an estimate surprisingly close to that obtained from Voos's analyses.[9]

All told, reduced organizing activity appears to have contributed to the decline in union representation.

The Growth of Managerial Opposition

I've been called the biggest no-good union busting S.O.B. that ever lived.—
A labor management consultant charging $150/hour

While trade union organizing effort per nonunion worker has fallen, managerial opposition to unionism has increased by leaps and bounds. In the 1950s many managements did relatively little to discourage their workers from unionizing—after all, did the law not specify that the decision was for the workers to make? In ensuing decades, however, as courts and the NLRB gave management increasing power to oppose organization under the "free speech" provision of the Taft-Hartley Act (which allows employers to voice opposition to unionism, but not to threaten workers who want a union), management has come to contest hotly nearly every significant NLRB election. Labor-management consultants who specialize in defeating unions in certification elections are routinely brought in to run anti-union election campaigns. Because these consultants rarely comply with the Landrum-Griffin Act by reporting their activities to the Department of Labor, solid estimates of the number and receipts of such firms are unavailable.[10] That they have grown to become an important part of the labor-relations scene is, however, incontestable.

What is the nature of the modern "union-prevention" business? Management opposition to union organizing drives takes three basic forms. The first, sometimes called "positive labor relations," attempts to beat unions at their own game by offering unorganized workers most of the benefits of unionism—high wages, good fringes, seniority protection, and the like—with none of the associated costs. As noted in chapter 10, positive labor relations has resulted in sizable spillovers of union-won gains to nonunion labor in some segments of the economy. While union leaders occasionally rant and rave against employers who practice positive labor relations, in private they do not condemn "good" nonunion employers. They believe, however, that at the first sign of economic trouble, even the most well-meaning employer will drop "positive" labor relations and break promises of no layoffs, seniority protection, and the like.

A second employer strategy is to conduct tough legal campaigns to convince workers that their interests might be better served by voting against unions. A typical campaign might involve:

- frequent written and verbal communication with workers, particularly by their immediate supervisors;
- predictions about the possible dire effects of unionism on worker well-being;
- presentation of information about strikes designed to make workers fear that unionism will bring active conflict to the firm;
- efforts to obtain voting districts most favorable to management;
- delay of the representation election, on the (correct) assumption that the greater the time between initial petitions for an election and the holding of the election, the more likely it is that union fervor will fall.

Many major U.S. companies, including such giants as Dupont, General Electric, and B.F. Goodrich, to name just three, campaign hard using these and related legal tactics to influence NLRB elections in favor of management.

Assume that a management has done all it can within the law to defeat a union organizing drive but still foresees a likely union victory. Is there anything else it can do to ward off unionization? There is.

The third way to try to defeat unionism is to break the law, in particular to identify and fire leading pro-union workers, in direct contradiction of section 8(a)(3) of the National Labor Relations Act, which states in part:

It shall be an unfair labor practice for an employer, by discrimination in regard to hire or tenure or employment or any term or condition of employment to encourage or discourage membership in any labor organization. . . .[11]

Beginning in the 1960s the relative number of illegal activities committed by management, after declining for years, rose at phenomenal rates (figure 15–3). From 1960 to 1980 the number of charges of all employer unfair labor practices rose fourfold; the number of charges involving a firing for union activity rose threefold; and the number of workers awarded back pay or ordered reinstated to their jobs rose fivefold. By contrast, the number of NLRB elections scarcely changed in the same period. Despite increasingly sophisticated methods for disguising the cause of such firings, more employers were judged guilty of firing workers for union activity in 1980 than ever before. To obtain an indication of the risk faced by workers desiring a union, one may divide the number of persons fired for union activity in 1980 by the number of persons who voted for a union in elections. The result is remarkable: one in twenty workers who favored the union got fired. Assuming that the vast bulk of union supporters are relatively inactive,

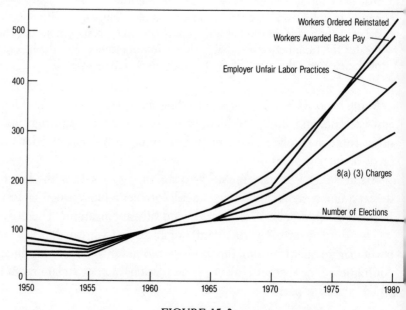

FIGURE 15-3

Employer Unfair Labor Practices and Number of NLRB Representation Elections,
1950–1980

SOURCE: *Annual Reports of the National Labor Relations Board, 1950–80.*

the likelihood that an outspoken worker, exercising his or her legal rights under the Taft-Hartley Act, gets fired for union activity is, by these data, extraordinarily high. Put differently, there is roughly one case of illegal discharge deemed meritorious by the NLRB for every NLRB representation election.[12]

One reason why firing workers for union activity has become increasingly popular is that the penalties for such activities are slight. Employers who are found guilty of firing union workers are forced to reinstate the workers and to pay them limited back pay (the wages they would have received minus whatever income they received on other jobs), often several years later. In addition the employers must post a notice that they will not engage in such illegal activity again. Such notices are jocularly referred to as "hunting licenses"; rather than convincing workers that management will forego such tactics in the future, they warn workers of how far management is willing to go to defeat unionism. Another reason for the growth of illegal management opposition is that it is an exceedingly effective way to chill an organizing campaign, as we shall see next.

The Effect of Management Opposition on Union Decline

To determine what impact, if any, legal and illegal managerial opposition has on NLRB elections, we and other researchers have examined diverse data linking management activities to election outcomes. Some studies compare success rates across elections where management employed different tactics; others analyze the determinants of the vote of individual workers (reported after the secret ballot election); others relate management activity in a geographic area to union organizing success in the area; while yet others study changes over time. Despite considerable differences among studies, however, virtually all tell the same story: managerial opposition to unionism, and illegal campaign tactics in particular, are a major, if not the major, determinant of NLRB election results.

Table 15–4 presents a capsule summary of these studies, divided

TABLE 15-4
Legal and Illegal Company Opposition and Union Success in NLRB Elections:
Twelve Studies

Study	Finding	
1. Conference Board, Study of 140 Drives Attempting to Organize White-Collar Units, 1966–67.	Percentage of wins for union depends on amount of company communication.	
	Written or no communication	85
	Meetings with workers	51
	Meetings and written communication	39
2. AFL-CIO, Study of 495 NLRB Elections, 1966–67.	Percentage of wins for union depends on extent of company opposition.	
	No opposition	97
	Some opposition	50
	Wages increased	37
	Surveillance of union, firing workers	43
3. Prosten, Analysis of Probability of Union Win in 130,701 Elections, 1962–77.	Percentage of wins for union falls with time delay between election and petition; is lower in election in which management argues about district before Regional Board (stipulated elections).	
4. Lawler, Study of 155 NLRB Elections, 1974–78.	Percentage of wins for union falls if company hires consultant.	
	If no consultant	71
	If consultant	23
5. Drotning, Study of 41 Elections Ordered Void and Rerun by NLRB, 1956–62.	Nature of employer's campaign influences voting.	
	Average number of employer communications per election	
	Union losses	12.5
	Union wins	8.6
6. Roomkin and Block, Study of 45,115 Union Representation Cases, 1971–77.	Percentage of wins for union decreases with delay between petition and actual election.	
	0–1 months	50
	2 months	45
	3 months	41
	4–7 months	30
	8–12 months	30
7. Seeber and Cooke, Analysis of Proportion of Workers in States Voting for Union Representation, 1970–78.	One percentage point increase in proportion of elections to which employers "consent" to the election district (rather than objecting to NLRB) increases union success by one-half percentage point.	
8. U.S. General Accounting Office, Analysis of 400 8(a)(3) Illegal Firings or Other Cases of Discrimination for Union Involvement, 368 Representation Elections, 1981.	Unions were more successful in campaigns in which no employer discrimination occurred than in those which involved an unfair labor practice charge.	
	Success rate:	
	no violation	45
	violation	38

TABLE 15-4

Legal and Illegal Company Opposition and Union Success in NLRB Elections: Twelve Studies (continued)

Study	Finding	
9. Aspin, Study of 71 NLRB Elections in Which Reinstatements Were Ordered, 1962–64.	Percentage of wins for union depends on firing, with unions doing worse unless reinstatees return to job before election.	
	All elections in region	62
	With 8(a)(3) firings	48
	Election held before 8(a)(3) case is settled or discriminatee refuses to return to job	41
	Election held after discriminatee returns to job	67
10. Getman, Goldberg, and Herman, Analysis of 1,293 Workers in 31 Elections in 1972–73.	Percentage of workers voting union reduced by sizable, but statistically insignificant, amount by management campaign tactics.	
11. Dickens, Analysis of 966 Workers in 31 Elections, 1972–73.	Percentage of workers voting union reduced by employer activities.	
	Legal campaign	−10%
	Illegal campaign	−4%
	Employer threatening acts against pro-union workers	−15%
	Percentage of elections unions would win in simulation model.	
	No campaign or light campaign against	53–67%
	Intense campaign	22–34%
	Campaign with violations	4–10%
12. Catler, Study of 817 NLRB Elections Reported on AFL-CIO Organizing Reports, 1966–77.	Company campaigning activities, unfair labor practices and delay reduce union success, with the percentage of union wins lowered by 10 points by unfair labor practice.	

SOURCES: (1) Edward R. Curtin, *White-Collar Unionization,* (New York: National Industrial Conference Board, 1970). (2) Statement of William Kirchner, Director of Organization, AFL-CIO, on *A Bill to Amend the National Labor Relations Act in Order to Increase Effectiveness of the Remedies: Hearings on H.R. 11725 Before the Special Subcommittee on Labor of the House Committee on Education and Labor,* 90th Cong., 1st Sess., 1967 12, 15. (3) Richard Prosten, "The Longest Season: Union Organizing in the Last Decade," *Proceedings of the Thirty-first Meeting of the Industrial Relations Research Association* (Madison, Wisconsin, 1978): 240–49. (4) John Lawler, "Labor-Management Consultants in Union Organizing Campaigns" (Paper presented at the Thirty-fourth Annual Meeting of the Industrial Relations Research Association, Washington, D.C., 1981). (5) John Drotning, "NLRB Remedies for Election Misconduct: An Analysis of Election Outcomes and their Determinants," *Journal of Business* 40, no. 2 (April 1967): 137–48. (6) Myron Roomkin and Richard Block, "Case Processing Time and the Outcome of Elections: Some Empirical Evidence," *University of Illinois Law Review* 5, no. 1 (1981): 75–97. Calculated from tables 2 and 4. (7) R. Seeber and W. Cooke, "The Decline of Union Success in NLRB Representation Elections," *Industrial Relations* 22, no. 1 (Winter 1983): 33–44. (8) United States General Accounting Office, *Concerns Regarding Impact of Employee Charges Against Employers for Unfair Labor Practices* (Washington, D.C.: GAO-HRD 82–80, June 21, 1982). (9) Leslie Aspin, *A Study of Reinstatement Under the National Labor Relations Act* (Ph.D. diss. MIT, 1966). (10) Jules Getman, Steven Goldberg, and Jeanne Herman, *Union Representation Elections: Law and Reality* (New York: Russell Sage Foundation, 1976). (11) William F. Dickens, *Union Representation Elections: Campaign and Vote* (Ph.D. diss. MIT, 1980). (12) Susan Catler, "Labor Union Representation Elections: What Determines Who Wins?" (Senior thesis, Harvard University, 1978).

between those focused on legal management opposition and those focused on illegal opposition. The studies of legal opposition show the following:

1. The amount of company communication influences the election results, with unions winning most elections in which management opposition is light but less than half in which opposition is severe (studies 1, 2, 4, 6; also 11 and 12).

2. Union success is lower the longer the delay between the initial petition and the actual holding of the election (studies 3 and 6).

3. Elections to which companies accede readily to the election district proposed by the union (consent elections) produce greater chances of union wins than elections in which the company battles the election district until the NLRB in Washington stipulates who can or cannot vote (studies 3 and 7).

4. Companies that bring in labor-management consultants to fight unionization are more likely to defeat an organizing drive than companies that do not use such consultants (study 4).

The studies of illegal company opposition show that employer discrimination against union activists, particularly firing, also has a great impact on the success rate of unions, though the magnitude of the impact varies. Two studies estimate a drop in union success in the area of 7–10 points (studies 8 and 12), while two others estimate declines in union success by 14–24 points (studies 9 and 11). Only in the rare case where a fired worker is ordered reinstated by the NLRB and actually returns to his job *before* the election does breaking the law backfire (study 9). Because of long delays before workers are ordered reinstated and because of workers' fears that management will be out to get them if they go back to the job, however, relatively few return to their job before the election.

The evidence that company campaign activities affect election results is substantial and, on the face of it, compelling. Both labor and management practitioners agree that what the company does is important, and companies back this belief by spending time and money on NLRB election campaigns. Given all this, one might expect the point to go unchallenged.

It has not. In 1976 Getman (Yale Law School), Goldberg (Northwestern Law), and Herman (Northwestern) published a book that argued the opposite: that even deceptive and illegal campaign tactics do not matter (see study 10). They based this conclusion on analysis of the votes of over 1000 workers in 33 elections that indicated that, while company opposition reduced the probability workers would vote union, it did not do so by what they viewed as statistically significant amounts. On the basis of their findings they recommended sweeping changes in NLRB regulation of election campaigning. In an intellectual climate favorable to deregulation, this study won considerable attention, and for a period of time it may have influenced NLRB policies.[13] More recent analyses of their findings indicate, however, that they reached faulty conclusions from the data. First, they erred by placing too great a stress on statistical significance as opposed to estimated effects: statistics that show company opposition *reduces* voting for a union by "statistically insignificant" amounts do not mean that opposition does not matter, but rather that its true effect cannot be estimated with great precision. Second, re-analysis of their data by Dickens (Berkeley) found that some forms of company opposition do indeed have statistically significant effects and that, because many NLRB elections are decided by relatively small margins, even modest *statistical* effects on individual voters can cumulate to have powerful effects on the proportion of elections won by unions (see study 12). Viewed from this perspective, the Getman-Goldberg-Herman data are consistent with, rather than inconsistent with, the other work listed in the table.

Granted that company opposition matters, how much of the decline in union electoral success can be attributed to rising management opposition? The answer is from a quarter to a half, according to our analysis of the impact of one major indicator of illegal opposition—unfair labor practices committed by employers—on the proportion of nonagricultural workers choosing representation in NLRB elections (table 15–5). Our estimates are based on three distinct studies of the relation between unfair practices and union success in elections: an analysis of success rates across states; an analysis of success rates over time; and an analysis of success rates within states over time. All of our calculations control for diverse other potential determinants of union electoral success, such as region of the country, proportion of workers who are blue-collar, and so on.

We have focused on unfair management practices not because we believe they are management's only effective anti-union weapon—the

TABLE 15-5

Estimates of the Effect of Management Unfair Labor Practices on Percentage of the Nonagricultural Work Force Newly Organized in NLRB Elections

Analysis and Period	*Estimated Impact of 10% Increase in Unfair Practices per Election on Proportion of Workers Newly Organized in NLRB Elections* %	*Estimated Percentage Decline in Nonagricultural Work-force Organized in NLRB Elections Due to Increased Management Unfair Labor Practices* %
1. Comparison of Union Success Across States, 1950–78[a]	−2.5	28
2. Comparison of Union Success Within States Over Time, 1950–78	−3.4	38
3. Comparison of Union Success over Time, 1950–80[b]	−6	49

SOURCE: R. B. Freeman, "The Simple Economics of Declining Union Density" National Bureau of Economic Research Working Paper (Forthcoming)). For corroborating estimates of the effect of unfair labor practices on new unionization using a different model, see David Ellwood and Glenn Fine, "Impact of Right-to-Work Laws on Union Organizing": NBER Working Paper No. 1116 (1983). We thank Ellwood and Fine for providing us with their data set for the analysis in lines 1 and 2.
[a]The measure of management unfair practices is all CA cases, as reported in *Annual Reports of the National Labor Relations Board*, where CA cases relate to charges that employers violated section 8(a)(3) of the Act, divided by nonagricultural work force. 8(a)(3) cases involve alleged employer penalization of one or more workers for union activity.
[b] The measure of management unfair practices is 8(a)(3) cases divided by workers in elections.

studies in table 15–4 show that legal opposition also has a substantial impact on union success—but, rather, because information on those practices, but not on legal opposition, exists over time and across states. As legal and illegal opposition have presumably grown together, we interpret the analysis as showing the effect of "total" management opposition on union success, not of illegal opposition only.

So interpreted, the analyses show that employer opposition has a substantial and highly statistically significant depressant effect on union success rates (the first column) and accounts for a large part of the decline in union organization of new workers in NLRB elections. For every 10 percent change in unfair labor practices per election, our estimates suggest that unionization of new workers falls from about 3 percent to 6 percent. From 1950 to 1980, when unfair labor practices per election increased by sixfold, we further estimate that the rise in management opposition explains from over a quarter to nearly a half of the decline in union success organizing through NLRB elections.

The point is not that unfair practices per se have hurt unions in NLRB elections, though they obviously have, but that opposition, broadly defined, is a major cause of the slow strangulation of private sector unionism. Analysis with other indicators of opposition (workers ordered reinstated because they had been fired for union activity; workers awarded back pay for the same reason; the proportion of elections not consented to by management) also show that company opposition affects NLRB election results significantly.[14]

Finally, our analysis suggests that part of the increased management opposition to unions is attributable to the increased union wage differential documented in chapter 3: multivariate statistical analysis shows that about 40 percent of the rise in management unfair labor practices is due to the rise in the union premium. When unions are more costly to employers, employers are more hostile to unions.[15]

From Elections to Contracts to Decertification

Damn it. We lost the NLRB election to the [expletive deleted] union. I can't let those [expletive deleted] run my company. Do I have to deal with them?
—*An archetypical anti-union employer*

Not really. Under the law, employers have a "duty to bargain" with the union elected to represent its workers, but they are not obligated to reach agreement or sign a collective bargaining contract. An employer who is vehemently anti-union can bargain over wages and terms of work but refuse to give in to worker demands and continue to operate nonunion. If he does this, the workers can strike, but the employer has the right to hire replacements and try to continue operating. If the union lacks the muscle to close down the plant, the secret ballot election results may be annulled de facto. Moreover, one year after the NLRB election, another election can be held to decertify the union, with strike replacements voting (and strikers possibly voting, possibly not). Union victory in an NLRB election is *not* the final word in establishing collective bargaining. Because a sizable number of employers refuse to accept unions even after an NLRB election and have the economic strength to resist union efforts, there is a leakage from elections to contracts.

How great is the leakage? According to two AFL-CIO "tracer" studies of elections won by unions, the leakage is surprisingly large. Five years after workers have voted for a union, workers are covered by signed collective contracts in only two-thirds of the election districts won.[16] In one of three elections, the employer has continued to operate nonunion. Thus unionization from NLRB elections is considerably lower than indicated in the voting statistics. Whereas the 1980 election data show 400,000 workers becoming organized in NLRB elections, in fact only 280,000 are likely to end up working under a union contract.

Finally, an increasingly large number of workers have decertified their unions through NLRB decertification elections. Until the 1970s and 1980s, decertification was a rare event. In 1955 there were just 5,324 workers in districts that voted to decertify unions. During the 1970s, however, the number of decertification elections increased greatly, so that by 1980, 21,249 workers were in such districts. In 1980 unions gained 0.17 percent of the private nonagricultural work force through NLRB elections but lost 0.02 percent through decertification. The same management consultants who direct management campaigns against unions in representation elections provide assistance in decertification elections as well.[17]

Taking account of the leakage from election to contracts and of decertifications, net union gain in membership from NLRB elections was minuscule for the early 1980s, leading one union organizer to refer to the election process as "the graveyard of worker hopes" and unions to call for various forms of "labor law reform" designed to restore their chances of winning.

From Elections to Unionization

Organization of workers through NLRB elections is not the only determinant of unionization in the United States. From 1960 to 1961 unions won over 218,000 members through NLRB elections, but union membership fell by 746,000. From 1967 to 1968 unions won 271,695 members through NLRB elections, but union membership rose by 549,000. Despite increased membership from 1967 to 1968, however, the proportion of workers organized remained virtually constant.[18] Membership also changes because of cyclical and sectoral changes in employment in already organized plants; in the 1960–61 period, indeed, it was the recession in manufacturing and construction that reduced union membership despite considerable success on the organizing front. Organization of workers outside of NLRB elections (as in construction, where unions organize employers by convincing them that the union represents local craftsmen and can provide the employer with skilled workers for jobs) can also be an important factor in changes in union membership. The potential importance of organizing employees implies that unions can gain by reducing management's misperceptions of how bad life must be under unionism, in addition to telling workers how good it will be. Finally, the union share of the labor force changes not only when union membership changes but also when nonunion employment changes. Because some union (as well as nonunion) plants close down every year, and new plants are "born" nonunion, there is a normal attrition in membership each year, which requires a certain amount of new organization by unions simply to maintain their share of the work force.

Taking all these factors into consideration we estimate that, in the absence of new organization of workers through NLRB elections, the union share of the workforce in the United States tends to decline by roughly 3 percent a year.[19] That is, if in one year 35 percent of the workforce were organized, this proportion would decline to 34 percent [= 35 percent × (1 − .03)] in the following year. The pattern of change in the union share of the workforce depends on the relationship between the rate of attrition of the union share of the workforce and the rate of new organization. When the rate of attrition multiplied by the existing union share exceeds the proportion of the workforce newly organized, the union share will fall over time. When the rate of attrition times the share is smaller than the proportion newly organized the union share will rise over time. When organization just balances out the attrition, the union share will be constant.[20]

With a 3 percent attrition, what do late 1970s–early 1980s levels of organization portend for unionism? The answer is a disastrous decline. In the late 1970s and early 1980s, unions organized just 0.3 percent of the workforce through NLRB elections. With an attrition rate of 3 percent, our analysis shows that, if the patterns of structural change, organization, and normal loss of membership relative to a growing workforce continue, the union share would fall to a bare 10 percent of the nonagricultural workforce. If the unions organized 0.6 percent of the workforce through NLRB elections, as they did in the 1950s, the union share would stabilize at 20 percent.[21]

We are not predicting such a decline in membership. To the contrary, we would not be surprised to see a sudden burst in union organization. But such a decline is the logical consequence of 1980s patterns of change. If these patterns continue, the American labor movement will experience a precipitous decline in the next decade, of a magnitude comparable to the decline from the mid-1950s to the 1980s.

The Role of Public Policy

No different today

In 1978 the AFL-CIO and its affiliated unions and the major nonaffiliated unions made a major push for "Labor Law Reform," designed to strengthen penalties against firms that break the labor law and to extend protection to workers in smaller firms. As we saw in chapter 13, the bill was defeated. Underlying the AFL-CIO effort was a belief that public policy as reflected in U.S. labor law and its interpretation by the courts is an important factor in the increased ability of management to defeat drives.

What evidence, if any, is there that legal changes can determine union organization?

First, there is evidence from Canada, once again. The principal difference between unionization in the United States and in Canada is that U.S. laws allow management to conduct lengthy, well-funded election campaigns against unions. Canadian labor laws do not permit such activity. Indeed, in most provinces a union is certified without any secret ballot campaign at all: it requires only that 60 or so percent of the workers sign authorization cards. The result is growing private-sector unionization in Canada.

Second, there is the experience of "right-to-work" laws. Under the Taft-Hartley law, states are allowed to pass so-called "right-to-work" laws, which outlaw union shops (workplaces where workers must join a union or pay the equivalent of dues within 30 days to maintain their jobs). In these states unions face serious "free-rider" problems that weaken them financially and make organizing more difficult. A free-rider is a worker who enjoys all the benefits of unionism but does not pay dues for those benefits. In Right-to-Work states, upwards of 20 percent of workers covered by collective bargaining are not union members, compared with 10 percent elsewhere in the country. A careful analysis of unionization across states and over time by Ellwood and Fine (Harvard University) finds that new organizing in a state falls by about one-third with the passage of a right-to-work law.[22]

Third, we have the evidence of the great growth of public sector unionization in the United States. It was preceded by new public sector labor laws, which often required municipalities to bargain with workers who had chosen to unionize. Before these laws, municipalities could simply refuse to bargain with public sector unions; since strikes were generally illegal, workers had no easy way of "forcing" management to recognize them. Analyses of the relationship between the presence of law favorable to bargaining and unionization across states and of the relationship between the timing of union growth and passage of laws within states shows that public sector unionization is greatly enhanced by changes in the law.[23] Similarly, the dramatic growth in unionization among Canadian public sector employees since 1967 can be closely linked to a new governmental posture toward the organizing of civil servants.

From these diverse alternative legal environments—Canada, right-to-work versus non-right-to-work states, U.S. public sector—we conclude that labor law does indeed influence the success of unions in representing workers. Under a different legal environment, U.S. employers would behave differently and unions might fare better in organizing the workforce.

An Historic Perspective on Union Decline

American trade unionism is slowly being limited in influence by changes which destroy the basis on which it is erected. It is probable that changes in the law have adversely affected unionism . . . I see no reason to believe that American trade unionism will . . . become in the next decade a more potent social influence (1932, Presidential Address, American Economic Association).[24]

The recent decline of one-third in union representation of the workforce is a serious setback to American unionism, but it is not without historic precedent. In the 1920s American unions also suffered serious setbacks: both the union share of the workforce and the absolute number of union members fell sharply, and major unions like the United Mine Workers and International Ladies Garment Workers virtually disappeared. Then, as in the 1970s and 1980s, unions faced a two-pronged attack by management; on the one hand were efforts to fight unionism with good employee relations, company unions, representation plans; on the other was the virulent anti-union activity of so-called "American shop" employers, many of whom hired goons, labor spies, strike breakers, and the like in their effort to fight organization.[25] By 1932 unions were so weak that at the annual meeting of the American Economic Association economists saw only doom and gloom in their future. Yet shortly thereafter the CIO was formed, and unions successfully organized the major industries in the country.

Historically, unions have rarely grown at a moderate steady pace. Instead, they have advanced in fits and starts—in sudden spurts, generally during improving conditions following significant recessions,[26] and during the two world wars. These spurts have been spurred by organizational innovations, new unions led by new unionists along somewhat different lines than the traditional unions. In the 1930s and 1940s the new form of organization was the industrial union, with most AFL unions responding to the CIO challenge by becoming themselves industrial unions. In the recent spurt in the U.S. public sector, professional associations such as the Professional Nurses Association, the National Education Association, and the American Association of University Professors, together with various police and fire associations and unions like the American Federation of State, County, and Municipal Employees, have played the role of "new unions." The spurts have also gone hand in hand with governmental policies favorable to unionization. If unionism is to grow in the future, history suggests that the growth will occur suddenly, among groups new to unionism in a legal setting supportive of the collective organization of workers.

What group of workers might possibly form the basis of such a spurt in the future? While we are loathe to make any explicit prediction, one possible group is the white-collar workers of the "baby boom" generation, particularly those with some college education whose wages and career advancement have been far below their expectations.[27] As the baby boom generation is a group that has turned to collective action in the past, it is conceivable that they will do so again, relying on unions to remedy the gap between their economic aspirations and the reality of the labor market.

[handwritten margin note: focus on this group]

[handwritten note: 1. Retiring Now 2. Information Age]

CHAPTER 16

Conclusion and Implications

Question 2

IN THE BEGINNING of this book, we argued that trade unionism has two faces: a monopoly face and a voice/response face. If one looks only at the monopoly face, most of what unions do is socially harmful. If one looks only at the voice/response face, most of what unions do is socially beneficial. The debate over the merits of unionism has been inconclusive because critics of unionism have focused exclusively on the monopoly costs while "friends of labor" have focused exclusively on the voice/response benefits. In our view, there is some truth to both sides of the debate. The central question is not, "Who in principle is right?" but rather, "Which face is quantitatively more important in particular economic outcomes?" and, given the diversity of experiences with collective bargaining, "What factors lead to the predominance of one face over the other in different settings?" Because the debate about the two faces of unionism is ultimately empirical, we have attacked it by applying modern statistical techniques to computerized data files on thousands of workers and establishments, obtaining the specific findings outlined in chapter 1 and detailed in the succeeding chapters.

We believe that the results of our book raise a host of important issues for public policy regarding the key worker institution in the American capitalist system. While some of our specific results will surely be altered by additional research and some (few, we hope) may even be proven wrong, we do believe that our findings present a reasonably valid picture of what unions do in the United States. It stands in sharp contrast to the unidimensional monopoly view of trade unions and to many popular opinions about them. According to our analysis, in most settings the positive elements of the voice/response face of unions offset or dominate the negative elements of the monopoly face. As a result we come out with the following assessment—generally positive though not uniformly so—of what unions do to the three major outcomes about which debate has raged: efficiency, distribution of income, and social organization.

- Efficiency. Our analysis has shown that unionism does three things to efficiency: on the monopoly side, it reduces employment in the organized sector; on the voice/response side, it permits labor to create, at no extra cost to management, workplace practices and compensation packages more valuable to workers; and in many settings it is associated with increased productivity. Although it is difficult to sum up these three effects, our evidence suggests that unionism on net probably raises social efficiency, and if it lowers it, it does so by minuscule amounts except in rare circumstances. This conclusion contradicts the traditional monopoly interpretation of what unions do to efficiency.
- Distribution of Income. On the question of distribution, we have found a definite dominance for the voice/response face of unions, with unions reducing wage inequality and lowering profits, which generally go to higher-income persons. For readers to whom greater economic equality is a plus, what unions do here is definitely good. For readers to whom greater equalization of incomes is undesirable, what unions do is definitely bad.
- Social Organization. Our analysis of the internal affairs of unions has dispelled some of the negative myths about undemocratic practices and discriminatory and corrupt behavior. It has shown that unions, for the most part, provide political voice to all labor and that they are more effective in pushing general social legislation than in bringing about special interest legislation in the Congress.

All our conclusions are based, we stress, on comparisons of what happens under trade unions with what happens in comparable nonunion settings, not on comparisons with some theoretical construct the real world has yet to witness. In an economy where governments, business, and unions work imperfectly—sometimes for, sometimes against the general welfare—there is a place for unions to improve the well-being not only of their members but of the entire society, to increase the total amount of goods and services, including the dignity and rights of workers.

While our research suggests that unionism generally serves as a force for social and economic good, it has also found that unions benefit labor

247

negative mind

at the expense of capital. Unions reduce the profitability of organized firms, particularly those in concentrated sectors where profits are abnormally high. In addition, while some nonunion workers lose from unionism, our investigations indicate that many nonunion workers, especially those in large firms, benefit from the threat of organizing and from the information about workers' desires that comes from unionism.

Should someone who favors, as we do, a thriving market economy, also favor a strong union movement and be concerned with the ongoing decline in private sector unionism? According to our research findings, yes.

Should someone who wants a thriving, profitable company, as managers and stockholders rightly do, oppose the unionization of his or her firm? According to our research findings, the answer is generally yes.

The paradox of American unionism is that it is at one and the same time a plus on the overall social balance sheet (in most though not all circumstances) and a minus on the corporate balance sheet (again, in most though not all circumstances). We believe that this paradox underlies the national ambivalence toward unions. What is good for society at large is not necessarily good for GM (or any other specific company).

future implication

What policies might better enable society to benefit from the pluses of unionism and to reduce the minuses of the institution? How should society deal with the paradox of an institution that is socially valuable but that conflicts with the private interests of firms?

Our answer is twofold. First, we should develop policies that strengthen the voice/response face of unionism and weaken the monopoly face. Second, we should change the mode of organizing in ways that permit workers to choose union status, without undue management pressure on them.

Strengthening the voice/response face of unionism requires creative action by union leaders and managers of unionized firms. After many years in which union leaders and management paid lip-service to efforts to improve the voice of workers on shop floors and to encourage positive management response to worker involvement, U.S. collective bargaining has witnessed a sudden burst of voice/response related activity. Whether such activities are sold as "Quality of Working Life," "Employee Involvement," or "New Industrial Relations," they represent a needed effort to shake up traditional labor-management relations. Perhaps more than ever before in our past, both management and labor appear willing to entertain innovations in their modes of dealing with one another. How many of these new efforts will succeed is hard to say. We believe that some will be successful and, if accepted widely, will offer hope for improving industrial relations in the future. As improvements in the voice/response face of unions are for the general good, we recommend continued experimentation and monitoring of relevant experiments, not only in times of recession but in good times as well. It is important that innovations in labor-management relations not be discarded when times get better, as has often happened in the past.

As all sides potentially stand to benefit from strengthening the voice/response face of unionism, few will disagree with this prescription.

Our recommendations for weakening the monopoly effect of unionism and for enhancing workers' say in deciding "to be or not to be union" are, by contrast, more controversial and will be opposed by those to whom such changes will be costly. While our analysis, and that of other researchers, has found the monopoly costs of unionism to be relatively small to the society as a whole, even small social costs should, where possible, be cut. As the principal weapon against monopoly power is competition, we favor continued governmental efforts to reduce industry (and therefore union) monopoly power through deregulation; we oppose efforts to reduce foreign competition for the purpose of bailing out particular sectors. At the same time, however, we recognize the inequity of placing the burden of increased competitiveness on small groups of workers and firms, particularly in a period of slow economic growth and high unemployment, and we believe greater effort should be made to provide a "cushion" for displaced labor. Protection of workers dislocated by competition, not protectionism, is the appropriate policy in a dynamic economy.

Government policies aside, we believe that the burden of reducing the costs of the monopoly face of unionism, particularly the loss of jobs, lies with unionized labor and management. Unions pushed the union wage premium to extremely high levels from the mid–1970s to the early 1980s, gaining more and more for an increasingly small share of the workforce. We believe that union leaders gave insufficient weight to the job side of the job/wages tradeoff facing them, with dire long-term consequences for the well-being of their membership and the union movement in general. As we stated in chapter 3, we believe the union wage advantage will decline in the 1980s, in large part because of competitive pressures. It is our hope that union workers and leaders will have learned from the experience that always extracting "more" is harmful in the long run, not only to society as a whole, but to labor itself, and that they will use their economic power more judiciously in the future.

Turning to the ongoing decline in union density in the U.S. private sector, we believe that current labor law should be substantially revised. As we saw in chapter 15, the key factor in many representation elections is the extent of management opposition, as reflected in both legal and illegal actions. We believe that steps should be taken to limit the power of management to oppose unionization, returning to workers a greater say in choosing to unionize or not. Since existing penalties against managements that break U.S. labor law have failed to deter a rising tide of illegal firings and other unfair practices, we favor substantial increases in these penalties. To reduce the ability of management to conduct lengthy campaigns against unions, we also recommend that NLRB elections be conducted quickly—within, say, fifteen days of the petition date. There are, of course, other possible remedies for the current imbalance in the unionization decision, and we believe that Congress should be open to a wide variety of changes that would give back to workers the right to decide their union status without undue interference from management.

We favor legal changes that will make it easier to unionize because we believe continued decline in unionization is bad not only for unions and their members but for the entire society. Because our research shows that unions do much social good, we believe the "union-free" economy desired by some business groups would be a disaster for the country. We also think that 100 percent (or virtually 100 percent) unionization would also be economically undesirable for the United States. While we are not sure what the optimal degree of unionization is in this country, we are convinced that current trends have brought the union density below the optimal level. In a well-functioning labor market, there should be a sufficient number of union and of nonunion firms to offer alternative work environments to workers, innovation in workplace rules and conditions, and competition in the market. Such competition will, on the one hand, limit union monopoly power and on the other, limit management's power over workers.

Unionization involves the policies and practices of labor and management. On the labor side, we believe unions must take steps to improve the efficiency of their organizing efforts, particularly in meeting and countering management opposition. On the management side, many nonunion managements respond viscerally to a union drive, focusing solely on the costs of a union victory. We believe their virulence would be defused if they understood the possible ways management can respond positively to unions. Resources spent fighting unions may, in many instances, be better spent devising fruitful ways to deal with these worker organizations.

All told, if our research findings are correct, the ongoing decline in private sector unionism—a development unique to the United States among developed countries—deserves serious public attention as being socially undesirable. We believe the time has come for the nation to reassess its implicit and explicit policies toward unionism, such as it has done several times in the past. And we hope that such a reassessment would lead to a new public posture toward the key worker institution under capitalism—a posture based on what unions actually do in the society and on what, under the best circumstances, they can do to improve the well-being of the free enterprise system, and of us all.

APPENDIX

Key Sources of
Data Analyzed

THIS APPENDIX provides the following information about the key sources of data used in this book: who conducted the survey, when the survey was conducted, to whom the survey was addressed (for example, individuals, establishments, or companies), how many units were surveyed, and what characteristics of the survey make it unique.

Annual Survey of Manufactures

Conducted by: U.S. Department of Commerce, Bureau of the Census

Survey years: Annually since 1949; selected years 1849–1947

Unit surveyed: Companies, with separate reports required for each establishment within the company

Number of units in survey: 50,000 to 70,000 establishments per year since 1958

Unique characteristics of survey: Provides data on such subjects as value of shipments, value added, number of employees, number of production workers, production worker hours, total and production worker wages, and expenditures for plant and equipment. Data are available on an industry, area, industry-by-area, and national basis.

Census of Manufactures (COM)

Conducted by: U.S. Department of Commerce, Bureau of the Census

Survey years: Every five years since 1967; selected years, 1809–1963

Unit surveyed: Companies, with separate reports required for each establishment within the company

Number of units in survey: Approximately 4,000,000 establishments per survey since 1958

Unique characteristics of survey: Provides data on same subjects as Annual Survey of Manufactures and also gives information on industry concentration ratios. Data are available for the same industry/area aggregations as in the Annual Survey.

Census of Population

Conducted by: U.S. Department of Commerce, Bureau of the Census

Survey years: Every ten years since 1790

Unit surveyed: Individuals, by household

Number of units in survey: Between 5 and 100 percent of the population, depending on the question

Unique characteristics of survey: Provides data on individuals' labor force status (employed, unemployed, or out of the labor force), demographic characteristics, industry of employment, occupation, and area of residence. Data are available on an industry, industry-by-area, area and national basis.

Committee on Political Education (Cope) "Report on Congress"

Conducted by: COPE, a division of AFL-CIO

Survey years: Annually since 1947

Unit surveyed: Congress members

Number of units in survey: 100 percent of Congress

Unique characteristics of survey: Provides information on Congress members' votes on various pieces of legislation.

Current Population Survey (CPS)

Conducted by: U.S. Department of Commerce, Bureau of the Census, for the U.S. Department of Labor, Bureau of Labor Statistics (BLS)

Survey years: Monthly since 1943

Unit surveyed: Individuals 16 years or older, by household

Number of units in survey: From 1969 to 1976, approximately 100,-000 individuals (47,000 households); since January 1977, approximately 120,000 individuals (60,000 households)

Unique characteristics of survey: Each CPS file provides data on some or all of the following: union membership, coverage by collective bargaining, wages, labor force status, demographic characteristics, establishment and company size, industry, region, state, and occupation.

Expenditures for Employee Compensation (EEC)

Conducted by: U.S. Department of Labor, Bureau of Labor Statistics (BLS)

Survey years: Biannually, 1959–1977

Units surveyed: Establishments

Number of units in survey: Approximately 4000 in each sampling

Unique characteristics of survey: Provides information on all significant aspects of employee compensation, separately for production and nonproduction workers. These include: wages, legally required fringe benefits (such as Social Security), life and accident insurance, vacation pay, holiday pay, overtime pay, sick leave pay, shift premiums, and other fringe benefit programs. Also provides information on whether each employee group is covered by collective bargaining and on the industry and region of the establishment.

Freeman-Medoff Unionization Estimates

Conducted by: Richard B. Freeman (Harvard) and James L. Medoff (Harvard)

Survey years: Published as "New Estimates of Private Sector Unionism in the United States," *Industrial and Labor Relations Review* 32 (January 1979): 143–74

Units surveyed: Establishments, using the 1968–1972 EECs, and individuals, using the May 1973–1975 CPSs

Number of units in survey: Approximately 13,000 establishments in the EEC pool; 119,706 individuals in the CPS pool

Unique characteristics of survey: Provides unionization and collective bargaining coverage rates for detailed industries, occupations, states, and SMSAs. Data are available for all workers and production workers alone.

Industry Wage Survey

Conducted by: U.S. Department of Labor, Bureau of Labor Statistics (BLS)

Survey years: Every five years for selected industries; every three years for certain low-wage industries.

Unit surveyed: Establishments in forty manufacturing and twenty-five nonmanufacturing industries, mostly defined at the 4–digit SIC level

Number of units in survey: Varies

Unique characteristics of survey: Provides information on wages, work schedules, shifts, paid holidays and vacations, and health, insurance, and pension plans. Data are available for the nation, regions, and major areas of industrial concentration. Separate estimates are provided by size of establishment, union status, and type of product.

Labor Turnover Survey

Conducted by: U.S. Department of Labor, Bureau of Labor Statistics (BLS)

Survey years: Monthly since 1958 (for manufacturing, since 1930; for telephone and telegraph, since 1943); discontinued in 1981

Unit surveyed: Establishments

Number of units in survey: Approximately 38,000 establishments in 1975

Unique characteristics of survey: Provides data on separations rates (total, layoffs, quits, discharges) and accessions rates (total, new hires) for manufacturing, major manufacturing industry groups, manufacturing industries, and industry groups in mining and communications. Data are available on state and national basis.

Medoff-Abraham Layoff/Promotion Survey

Conducted by: James L. Medoff (Harvard) and Katharine G. Abraham (MIT)

Survey years: 1980, 1982

Unit surveyed: Managers in private, nonagricultural, nonconstruction companies

Number of units surveyed: 377 in 1980, 553 in 1982

Unique characteristics of survey: Collects data on how layoff and promotion practices affect workers with different amounts of seniority. Also gathers information on the occupation category and collective bargaining coverage of the workers and the industry and size of their company.

National Labor Relations Board (NLRB) Annual Reports

Conducted by: U.S. NLRB
Survey years: Annually since 1946
Unit surveyed: Election, voter, or worker covered by election
Number of units in survey: Varies by year and unit surveyed
Unique characteristics of survey: Provides information on number of elections, eligible voters, and votes cast in different NLRB elections; on claims of unfair labor practices; and various other activities under NLRB supervision. Most data available by industry and state.

National Longitudinal Survey (NLS)

Conducted by: Center for Human Resource Research, Ohio State University, for the U.S. Department of Labor. Field work by the Bureau of the Census.
Survey years: Occasionally since 1965
Unit surveyed: Individual men aged 14 to 24 in 1966 (young men), individual men aged 45 to 59 in 1966 (older men), individual women aged 14 to 24 in 1966 (younger women), individual women aged 30 to 44 in 1966 (mature women)
Number of units in survey: Approximately 5000 in each of the four groups of units, for each survey
Unique characteristics of survey: Provides information on union status, wages, fringe benefits, job separations, job satisfaction, and demographic characteristics. The NLS surveys the same individuals each time it is repeated, rather than creating new random samples. Hence, a "longitudinal" record of each individual is created.

Panel Study of Income Dynamics (PSID)

Conducted by: Survey Research Center, Institute for Social Research, University of Michigan (Ann Arbor)

Survey years: Annually since 1968

Unit surveyed: Heads of households

Number of units in survey: 4802 families in 1968 and 6373 in 1979. The sample grows as family members leave home and set up new families, which are then included in the new survey.

Unique characteristics of survey: Provides information on employment and unemployment, job satisfaction, earnings, fringe benefits, and job separations, among other topics. Families interviewed in 1968 are followed thereafter, so that a "panel" of data is available on each family (including newly formed families which are offshoots of original families).

Quality of Employment Survey (QES) (original 1969 title: Survey of Working Conditions)

Conducted by: Survey Research Center, Institute for Social Research, University of Michigan (Ann Arbor)

Survey years: 1969–70, 1972–73, 1976–77

Unit surveyed: Individual workers

Number of units in survey: 1,533 in 1969; 1,496 in 1972; 1,515 in 1976

Unique characteristics of survey: Provides information on work life, including job satisfaction, attitudes toward employers and unions, personal habits, wages, health and safety, discrimination, and employment status. Data are available separated by workers' sex, age, race, education, occupation, and industry. The data from 1973 to 1977 may be used as a "panel"—a continuous record of specific individuals.

NOTES

Chapter 1

1. For examples of economists with generally negative views of labor unions, see Henry C. Simons, *Economic Policy for a Free Society* (Chicago: University of Chicago Press, 1948); Gottfried Haberler, "Wage Policy and Inflation," in P. D. Bradley, ed., *The Public Stake in Union Power* (Charlottesville, Va.: University of Virginia Press, 1959), 63–85; Milton Friedman and Rose Friedman, *Capitalism and Freedom* (Chicago: University of Chicago Press, 1962), 123–25, and *Free to Choose* (New York: Harcourt Brace Jovanovich, 1980), 228–47; W. H. Hutt, *The Theory of Collective Bargaining* (London: P. S. King,1930); Fritz Machlup, *The Political Economy of Monopoly* (Baltimore: Johns Hopkins University Press, 1952).

2. For examples of economists with generally positive outlooks on labor unions, see Lloyd G. Reynolds and Cynthia H. Taft, *The Evolution of Wage Structure* (New Haven: Yale University Press, 1956); Sumner H. Slichter, James J. Healy, and E. Robert Livernash, *The Impact of Collective Bargaining on Management* (Washington, D.C.: The Brookings Institution, 1960); and Derek C. Bok and John T. Dunlop, *Labor and the American Community* (New York: Simon and Schuster, 1970).

3. Mr. Murphy's statement was made at the GM-UAW Contract Anniversary Dinner, in Detroit, Michigan, on February 11, 1977. The text of his comments was provided by the General Motors Corporation Public Relations Library.

4. The results of a recent Gallup poll illustrate the growing ambivalence about unions. In August, 1978, only 59 percent of people polled approved of unions. By contrast, in January, 1957, 76 percent of people polled approved of unions. See *The Gallup Index*, August 1978, Report Number 157.

5. This work has been reviewed in several places. See H. Gregg Lewis, *Unionism and Relative Wages in the United States*, (Chicago: University of Chicago Press, 1963) for a discussion of pre-1960s studies. See George E. Johnson, "Economic Analysis of Trade Unionism," *American Economic Review*, 65 (May 1975): 23–38, for a brief description of many post-1960s studies. H. Gregg Lewis, *Union Relative Wage Effects: A Survey* (Forthcoming) and R. B. Freeman and J. L. Medoff, "The Impact of Collective Bargaining: Illusion or Reality?" in J. Steiber, R. B. McKersie and D. Q. Mills, *U.S. Industrial Relations 1950–1980: A Critical Assessment* (Madison, Wis.: Industrial Relations Research Association, 1981), 47–97, also provide summaries of recent work.

6. The empirical investigations referred to are summarized in R. B. Freeman and J. L. Medoff, "The Impact of Collective Bargaining: Can the New Facts be Explained by Monopoly Unionism?" in Joseph D. Reid, Jr., ed., *Research in Labor Economics: New Approaches to Labor Unions*, supp. 2 (Greenwich, Conn.: JAI Press, 1983).

7. For a discussion of possible union maximands see John T. Dunlop, *Wage Determination Under Trade Unionism* (New York: Augustus M. Kelley, 1950), 28–44; and Wallace N. Atherton, *The Theory of Union Bargaining Goals* (Princeton, N.J.: Princeton University Press, 1973).

8. The concept of economic rent refers to the returns to a relatively fixed factor. A union can raise wages and therefore lower returns of a firm with economic rent without putting the enterprise out of business.

9. See Albert O. Hirschman, *Exit, Voice, and Loyalty* (Cambridge, Mass.: Harvard University Press, 1971).

10. Protection for collective action without union status is found in section 7 as well, which guarantees "the right to engage in other concerted activities for the purpose of collective bargaining or other mutual aid or protection. . . ." Individuals acting alone are not protected by law. For

a more detailed discussion, see Archibald Cox and Derek Bok, *Labor Law Cases and Materials* (Mineola, N.Y.: The Foundation Press, 1969), 858–904. A text of the NLRA is contained in A. Cox and D.C. Bok, *1966 Statutory Supplement, Labor Law Cases and Materials* (Brooklyn, N.Y.: The Foundation Press, 1966), 38–59.

11. Among the studies that make this point are Peter Kuhn, "Malfeasance in Long Term Employment Contracts: A New General Model With An Application to Unionism" (National Bureau of Economic Research Working Paper No. 1045, December 1982); Edward P. Lazear, "Why Is There Mandatory Retirement," *Journal of Political Economy* 87 (December 1979): 1261–84; Benjamin Eden, "Competitive Price Setting, Labor Contracts and Trade Unions" (University of Iowa, mimeographed 1983); James M. Malcomson, "Trade Unions and Economic Efficiency," *Economic Journal*, supp. (March 1983): 51–65. Melvin W. Reder, "Unionism, Wages and Contract Enforcement," in Joseph D. Reid, Jr., ed., *Research in Labor Economics: New Approaches to Labor Unions*, supp. 2 (Greenwich, Conn.: JAI Press, 1983).

12. The idea that human resources management involves the mediation between various groups within the firm is central in the literature of organizational behavior. See, for example, Michael Beer, Paul R. Lawrence, D. Quinn Mills, and Richard Walton, *Human Resources Management* (Free Press, forthcoming). This point is also important in the work of a number of economists who focus on the internal operations of firms. See, for example, Harvey Leibenstein, *Beyond Economic Man* (Cambridge, Mass.: Harvard University Press, 1976); Oliver E. Williamson, "Efficient Labor Organization," University of Pennsylvania Discussion Paper No. 123 (Revised) (Philadelphia: Center for the Study of Organizational Innovation, April 1982), 21–22; and Herbert Simon, "Rational Decision Making in Business Organizations," *American Economic Review* 69 (September 1979): 493–513.

13. The response of management is a decisive determinant of whether unions have positive or negative effects on the operation of enterprises, a point most strongly stressed by Harvard's Slichter, Healy, and Livernash in their classic study, *The Impact of Collective Bargaining on Management.* On the potential role of any form of external pressure on management, see H. Leibenstein, "Allocative vs. X-Efficiency," *American Economic Review* 56 (June 1966): 392–415.

14. F. A. Hayek, *A Tiger by the Tail* (London: Institute of Economic Affairs, 1972), 72.

15. Alfred T. Marshall, *Elements of Economics*, 3rd ed. (London: Macmillan, 1899), 1: 381–82.

16. Slichter, Healy, and Livernash, *Impact of Collective Bargaining*, 951.

17. Lloyd G. Reynolds, *Labor Economics and Labor Relations*, 8th ed., (Englewood Cliffs, N.J.: Prentice-Hall, 1982), 474.

18. Friedman and Friedman, *Capitalism and Freedom*, 124.

19. Reynolds and Taft, *Evolution of Wage Structure*, 194.

20. Henry C. Simons, "Some Reflections on Syndicalism," *Journal of Political Economy* 52 (March 1944): 23.

21. Bok and Dunlop, *Labor and the American Community*, 425–26.

22. The view of unions as coercive forces was expressed at an early date. See Henry George, *The Condition of Labor: An Open Letter to Pope Leo XIII* (New York: United States Book Co., 1891), 86. For a later version of this opinion, see Mancur Olson, *The Logic of Collective Action* (Cambridge, Mass.: Harvard University Press, 1971), 71.

23. For a description of the data sets, see appendix.

Chapter 2

1. For other analyses of the extent to which nonunion workers want unions, see Thomas A. Kochan, "How American Workers View Labor Unions," *Monthly Labor Review* 102 (April 1979): 22–31; Henry S. Farber, "The Determination of the Union Status of Workers," National Bureau of Economic Research Working Paper No. 1006 (October 1982). For analyses of actual voting, see Henry S. Farber and Daniel H. Saks, "Why Workers Want Unions: The Role of Relative Wages and Job Characteristics," *Journal of Political Economy* 88 (April 1980): 349–69;

Notes

Julius G. Getman, Steven B. Goldberg, and Jeanne B. Herman, *Union Representation Elections: Law and Reality* (New York: Russell Sage Foundation, 1976); and Edward R. Curtin, *White-Collar Unionization* (New York: National Industrial Conference Board, Personnel Policy Study No. 220, 1970).

2. Based on Current Population Survey data similar to those in table 2–1, but for May 1979. We used 1979 data because the May 1979 CPS contains data on company size, tenure, and benefits not available on other CPS tapes. Linear regression of a 0–1 union status variable on sex, age, race, and years of schooling yielded a 16-point difference in unionization between men and women. The addition of nine industry and eight occupation dummy variables reduced the differential to 7 points; addition of variables for number of workers at the firm and job site reduced the differential to 6 points; addition of years with a firm reduced it to 5 points; addition of the presence of pension and health plans reduced it to 3 points. Thus, 82 percent of the initial 16-point difference can be attributed to the factors examined. The sample size for this analysis was 15,471. For a study yielding comparable results see W. Mellow, J. Antos, and R. Chandler, "Sex Differences in Union Membership," *Industrial and Labor Relations Review* 33, no. 2 (January 1980); Farber, "Determination of the Union Status," finds no significant male/female differences in desire for unionization.

3. Calculated from figures on the distribution of employment for white and nonwhite workers from *Employment and Training Report of the President,* 1981, (Washington, D.C.: Government Printing Office, 1982), 151.

4. This is found in Farber and Saks, "Why Workers Want Unions," Farber, "Determination of Union Status," and Kochan, "How American Workers View Labor Unions."

5. The Hill quotation is from "New Insights on Black Unionists," *Labor World* 20, (October 1979): 7. Frederick O'Neal and Bayard Rustin of the Philip Randolph Institute support both unions and seniority rules. O'Neal goes so far as to state, "There is no hope for the black workers outside of the American trade union movement . . . a Negro labor alliance must be made a firm and enduring reality. It must be made a reality simply because the black man has been dispossessed in this country and the labor movement is the primary vehicle through which the dispossessed can advance themselves economically." Frederick O'Neal, "The Role of the Black Trade Unionist," *American Federationist,* 77 (July 1970), 10.

6. The unionization rates are from R. B. Freeman and J. L. Medoff, "New Estimates of Private Sector Unionism in the United States," *Industrial and Labor Relations Review* 32 (January 1979): table 9. The growth rates of employment are from *Employment and Training Report of the President, 1981,* table C–1. The average ages are from Bureau of the Census, *Census of Population: 1970,* vol. 1 *Characteristics of the Population,* part 1 (Washington, D.C.: Government Printing Office, 1973), 239.

7. For studies of actual NLRB voting showing young workers more likely to vote union than older workers in the same plant, see Farber and Saks, "Why Workers Want Unions," and Getman, Goldberg, and Herman, *Union Representation Elections.*

8. *Labor in the South* (Cambridge, Mass.: Harvard University Press, 1967), viii. Marshall goes on to state, "The South's environment had important effects on the growth of unions. The unity of white managers and workers, the race problem, the surplus of labor in low-income agriculture, the nature and composition of southern industry, the undemocratic tradition, the idea that employers were benefactors, all created relatively unfavorable conditions for the growth of unions."

9. Right-to-work laws presently exist in Alabama, Arizona, Arkansas, Florida, Georgia, Iowa, Kansas, Louisiana, Mississippi, Nebraska, Nevada, North Carolina, North Dakota, South Carolina, South Dakota, Tennessee, Texas, Utah, Virginia, and Wyoming. *Handbook of Labor Statistics* (Washington, D.C.: Department of Labor, Bureau of Labor Statistics, 1980), 414. Statistics on coverage of nonunion workers by union contracts are from Freeman and Medoff, "New Estimates of Private Sector Unionism," 171.

10. For evidence on the extent of unionism in the U.S. economy, see Amy K. Taylor and Walter R. Lawson, Jr., "Employer and Employee Expenditures for Private Health Insurance," *National Medical Care Expenditure Study* Data Preview no. 7 (Washington, D.C.: Government Printing Office, 1981). See also Audrey Freedman, *Managing Labor Relations: Research Report from the Conference Board* (New York: The Conference Board, 1979), vi, 2. In Freedman's non-random sample of 778 companies in 1978, 5.8 million of the 9.26 million employees (63 percent) worked in companies with some workers unionized.

11. Figures on the size of union locals in 1966 may be found in Derek C. Bok and John T. Dunlop, *Labor and the American Community* (New York: Simon and Schuster, 1970), 153. Figures for 1982 appear in D. Quinn Mills, *Labor-Management Relations* (New York: McGraw-Hill, 1982), 228. The quotation is from Martin Estey, *The Unions: Structure, Development, and Management*, 3rd ed., (New York: Harcourt Brace Jovanovich, 1981), 50.

12. The 1980 figures for U.S. union membership were obtained by courtesy of George Rubin of the Bureau of Labor Statistics (phone interview, April 20, 1982). They will appear in the *Directory of National Unions and Employee Associations, 1981* (Washington, D.C.: Department of Labor, Bureau of Labor Statistics, forthcoming).

13. These are 3-digit Standard Industrial Classification (SIC) industries, a categorization system published by the Office of Management and Budget of the Executive Office of the President. A 2-digit industry is relatively broad in nature (for example, "Transportation Equipment"), a 3-digit industry is narrower (for example, "Automobiles and Parts"), while a 4-digit industry is a very specific division (for example, "Truck and bus bodies"). In manufacturing, there are 20 2-digit SIC groups, 143 3-digit SIC groups, and several hundred 4-digit ones. The percentage of United Steelworkers members employed in non-steel industries was obtained by courtesy of the Steelworkers Public Relations Department. The information on the dispersion of various unions into different 3-digit SIC groups, and the figures on increased 5-union concentration, are from Marie-Paule Joseph Donsimoni, *An Analysis of Trade Union Power: Structure and Conduct of the American Labor Movement*, (Ph.D. diss., Harvard University, 1978), p. 37 (dispersion) and p. 15 (concentration).

14. The evidence on variation in contracts and on the influences of the union involved and the firm's market position comes from Donsimoni, *Analysis of Trade Union Power*, p. 59. Martin S. Estey, in "Trends in Union Concentration of Union Membership," *Quarterly Journal of Economics* 80 (August 1966): 347–49 and in *The Unions*, pp. 45–46, argues that the increase in the concentration of union membership is relatively significant from data on the six and ten largest unions. Jack Barbash, in "A Commentary," in Gerald G. Somers, ed., *Collective Bargaining: Contemporary American Experience* (Madison, Wis.: Industrial Relations Research Association, 1980), 583, sees a decentralization in union power of late.

15. The 1980 AFL-CIO and Teamsters membership data were obtained from George Rubin of the Bureau of Labor Statistics (phone interview, April 20, 1982) and will appear in the *Directory of National Unions and Employee Associations, 1981*. The UMW figure is from the *Directory of National Unions and Employee Associations, Bulletin 2079, 1979* (Washington, D.C.: Department of Labor, Bureau of Labor Statistics, 1980).

16. For a discussion of pattern bargaining, see Mills, *Labor-Management Relations*, 246–57, 466, 473–75. See also Harold M. Levinson, "Pattern Bargaining: A Case Study of Automobile Workers," *Quarterly Journal of Economics* 74, no. 2 (May 1960): 296–317.

17. For a summary of groups opposing labor unions, see Charles McDonald and Dick Wilson, "Peddling the 'Union-Free' Guarantee," *American Federationist*, 86 (April 1979): 12–19.

18. For a discussion of the government's involvement in labor-management relations, see Edwin F. Beal and James P. Begin, *The Practice of Collective Bargaining* (Homewood, Ill.: Richard D. Irwin, 1982), 127–73, and Lloyd G. Reynolds, *Labor Economics and Labor Relations*, 8th ed., (Englewood Cliffs, N.J.: Prentice-Hall, 1982), 501–98.

19. For a discussion of NLRB policy making, see Merton C. Bernstein, "The NLRB's Adjudication–Rule Making Dilemma Under the Administrative Procedure Act," *The Yale Law Journal* 80 (March 1970): 572–622; also William N. Cooke and Frederick H. Gautsch Ill, "Political Bias in NLRB Unfair Labor Practice Decisions," *Industrial and Labor Relations Review* 35, no. 4 (July 1982): 539–49.

Chapter 3

1. Among the early studies are Paul Douglas, *Real Wages in the United States, 1890–1926* (New York: Houghton Mifflin, 1930), 562–63, and Henry L. Moore, *Laws of Wages* (New York:

Notes

Macmillan, 1911), which discusses the effect of union strikes on wages. In the 1940s and 1950s the important studies included J. T. Dunlop, *Wage Determination Under Trade Unionism* (New York: Macmillan, 1944), and a number of doctoral theses at the University of Chicago, Harvard and elsewhere, which examined different groups or industries. These are discussed in H. Gregg Lewis, *Unionism and Relative Wages in the United States* (Chicago: University of Chicago Press, 1963). In the 1960s there were numerous other studies, some based on data for individuals. They are discussed in George E. Johnson, "Economic Analysis of Trade Unionism," *American Economic Review* 65 (May 1975): 23–38. For the more recent studies, see R. B. Freeman and J. L. Medoff, "The Impact of Collective Bargaining: Illusion or Reality?" in J. Steiber, R. B. McKersie, and D. Q. Mills, *U.S. Industrial Relations 1950–1980: A Critical Assessment* (Madison, Wis.: Industrial Relations Research Association, 1981, 47–97. Of particular note are the following studies: Leonard Weiss, "Concentration and Labor Earnings," *American Economic Review* 56 (March 1966): 96–117; George E. Johnson and Kenneth Youmans, "Union Relative Wage Effects by Age and Education," *Industrial and Labor Relations Review* 25 (January 1971): 141–79; Orley Ashenfelter, "Union Relative Wage Effects: New Evidence and a Survey of Their Implications for Wage Inflation," in *Economic Contributions to Public Policy*, R. Stone and W. Peterson, eds. (New York: Macmillan, 1978); and Wesley Mellow, "Employer Size and Wages," *The Review of Economics and Statistics* 64 (August 1982): 495–501.

2. Charles E. Lindblom, *Unions and Capitalism* (New Haven: Yale University Press, 1949), 4; Henry C. Simons, "Some Reflections on Syndicalism," *Journal of Political Economy* 52 (March 1944): 2; and Gottfried Haberler, "Wage Policy and Inflation," in *The Public Stake in Union Power*, P. D. Bradley, ed. (Charlottesville, Va.: University of Virginia Press, 1959), 63.

3. The information on the union/nonunion wage differential in various occupations comes from Lewis, *Unionism and Relative Wages*, 7–8 and 293.

4. Some analysts have tried to deal with the problems of cross-sectional data by formulating complicated econometric models, which involve a system of equations instead of a single equation. These efforts have not succeeded in providing useful information, as is documented in Freeman and Medoff, "The Impact of Collective Bargaining," 47–97.

5. For an analysis of the problems with longitudinal data, see R. B. Freeman, "Longitudinal Analyses of Trade Union Effects," *Journal of Labor Economics* (January 1984).

6. The choice among these alternative comparisons depends on one's assumption about the actual operation of the market and the nature of the "ability bias" problem. Many analysts prefer comparisons of "changers"—that is, comparisons of persons moving from union to nonunion jobs with persons moving from nonunion to union jobs—on the hypothesis that changers have similar characteristics. For other studies finding similar results, see, for example, Gary H. Chamberlain, "Multivariate Regression Models for Panel Data," *Journal of Econometrics* 18 (1982): 5–46; Gregory M. Duncan and Frank P. Stafford, "Do Union Members Receive Compensating Wage Differentials?" *American Economic Review* 70 (June 1980): 355–71; Duane E. Leigh, "Do Union Members Receive Compensating Wage Differentials? Note," *American Economic Review* 71 (December 1981): 1049–55.

7. For a survey of dozens of studies of union wage effects by group with results generally consistent with ours, see H. Gregg Lewis, "Union Relative Wage Effects: A Survey" (Forthcoming).

8. One of the first studies to examine the relationship between the union wage effect and an employee's age was George E. Johnson and Kenneth Youmans, "Union Relative Wage Effects by Age and Education."

9. The effect of unionization on black/white earnings differentials was first discussed in Orley Ashenfelter, "Racial Discrimination and Trade Unionism," *Journal of Political Economy* 80 (May–June 1972): 435–64. Ashenfelter concluded that "using several bodies of data it has been found that the average wage of black workers relative to the average wage of white workers is consistently higher in unionized than in nonunionized markets" (p. 461). The union wage effects by sex are discussed in Martin S. Estey, *The Unions: Structure, Development, and Management*, 3rd ed. (New York: Harcourt Brace Jovanovich, 1981), 134.

10. Based on regression analysis using May 1979 Current Population Survey data for white-collar workers, conducted with the same basic model as for blue-collar workers (except that it included white-collar occupation categorical variables). The size of the sample was 6,544.

11. We limited the analysis discussed in the text to industries with at least five union and five nonunion sample members. Only four industries were dropped because of this requirement. The

approximate percentage effects were calculated by taking the antilog of estimated union coefficients in semi-log hourly wage regressions, which had controls for sex, race, labor market experience, education, region of residence, occupation, and survey year.

12. R. B. Freeman and J. L. Medoff, "The Impact of the Percentage Organized on Union and Nonunion Wages," *Review of Economics and Statistics* 63 (November 1981): table 1.

13. Calculated from Marie-Paule Joseph Donsimoni, *An Analysis of Trade Union Power: Structure and Conduct of the American Labor Movement* (Ph.D. diss., Harvard University, 1978), 127. For a more detailed explanation of the impact of industry-wide bargaining on wages, see Donsimoni, *An Analysis of Trade Union Power*, 86–87; and Estey, *The Unions*, 139.

14. Estimated by authors with May 1979 CPS data with the same controls as used for the figure 3–1 results, including those indicating company or site size.

15. Studies discussing the influence of the employer's market power on union wage gains include Joseph W. Garbarino, "A Theory of Intermediary Wage Structure Variation," *Quarterly Journal of Economics* 64 (May 1950): 282–305; William G. Bowen, *Wage Behavior in the Postwar Period: An Empirical Analysis* (Princeton, N.J.: Industrial Relations Section, Princeton University, 1960); Harold M. Levinson, "Postwar Movements of Prices and Wages in Manufacturing Industries": *Study Paper No. 21 of the Joint Economic Committee*, 86th Cong., 1st sess., 1960; Martin E. Segal, "The Relation Between Union Wage Impact and Market Structure," *Quarterly Journal of Economics* 78 (February 1964): 96–114; Leonard W. Weiss, "Concentration and Labor Earnings," *American Economic Review* 56 (March 1966): 96–117; and Albert Rees, *The Economics of Trade Unions* (Chicago: University of Chicago Press, 1977) 78–82. The most recent empirical analysis, which includes a summary of earlier results, is John E. Kwoka, Jr., "Monopoly, Plant and Union Effects on Worker Wages," *Industrial and Labor Relations Review* 36, no. 2 (January 1983): 251–57.

16. The wage data are from *Monthly Labor Review* 105 (May 1982): table 1, p. 4, and table 2, p. 6. For data on COLA clauses see Ronald Ehrenberg, Leif Danziger, and Gee San, "Cost-of-Living Adjustment Clauses in Union Contracts": National Bureau of Economic Research Working Paper No. 998 (October 1982).

17. An early analysis of the relationship between the union/nonunion wage differential and the rate of unemployment and the rate of inflation is found in Lewis, *Unionism and Relative Wages*, chapter 5. The impact of these two variables on the wage effect through the 1970s has been analyzed by George E. Johnson in "Changes Over Time in the Union/Nonunion Wage Differential in the United States" (University of Michigan, February 1981, mimeographed). More discussion of union wage policy through the business cycle is provided by Estey, *The Unions*, 137.

18. This analysis is based on correspondence with George E. Johnson (University of Michigan).

19. "Teamsters Clear Pact that Yields on Wages, Rates," *Wall Street Journal*, 2 March, 1982.

20. "GM, Union Reach Tentative Pact Giving Concessions Generally Paralleling Ford's," *Wall Street Journal*, 22 March, 1982.

21. *Layoffs, Plant Closings and Concession Bargaining* (Washington, D.C.: Bureau of National Affairs, 1983), 16.

22. Daniel J. B. Mitchell in *Union Wages and Inflation* (Washington, D.C.: Brookings Institution, 1980) comments on the impact of bargaining in 1973 and 1976. Mitchell discusses the 1982 givebacks in this perspective in "Recent Union Contract Concessions," *Brookings Papers on Economic Activity* 1 (1982): 165–201. See also Rees, *Economics of Trade Unions*, 55–57; and John T. Dunlop, "Remarks by Former Secretary of Labor Dunlop on 1982 Wage Developments Before Conference of Business Economists," *Daily Labor Reports No. 56* (Washington D.C.: Bureau of National Affairs, February 23, 1982) and "Wage Moderation in 1982— Temporary or Lasting?" (Harvard University, 1982, mimeographed).

23. Calculated from data on employment from the Bureau of Labor Statistics, *Employment and Earnings*, relevant years.

24. Our figures for the percentage decrease in labor costs due to concessions in the automobile and airline sectors are taken from a number of periodicals. For example, the *Wall Street Journal* ("Pan Am Asking Help of Unions to Stem Losses," 16 February, 1982, and "Trans World Air Pilots Agree to Wage Freeze and Labor Concessions," 25 February, 1982) discusses givebacks on the order of 12 to 20 percent in labor negotiations with Pan American Airlines and Trans World Airlines. Concessions in the auto industry of between 7 and 12 percent are discussed in

Notes

articles on negotiations with General Motors ("GM Workers' Narrow Vote for Concession Might Hinder Further Cost Cuts at Plants," 12 April, 1982), Ford ("Tentative Ford-UAW Pact Seen Showing Rise in Firm's Costs, May Cut Many Jobs," 16 February, 1982) and American Motors, ("UAW Concessions Will Provide AMC Up to $11 Million," 19 April, 1982). For a more complete discussion of the recent giveback phenomenon, see Mitchell, "Recent Union Contract Concessions."

25. The fact that most new contracts still call for wage increases comes from "First-Year Wage Gains Averaged 10.1% in 1981 for Major Contracts": *Daily Labor Report*, (Washington, D.C.: Bureau of National Affairs, January 29, 1982), B1–B7. The construction sector data are from *Employment and Earnings, March 1982* (Washington, D.C.: Department of Labor, Bureau of Labor Statistics, 1982), 79.

26. While the construction industry average hourly earnings data include nonunion workers, its movement has been quite similar to that of the *Index of Union Hourly Wages, All Building Trades*, published by the Bureau of Labor Statistics, (Washington, D.C., various years).

27. The general procedure for estimating welfare loss or gain is described in detail in Arnold C. Harberger, "Three Basic Postulates for Applied Welfare Economics: An Interpretive Essay," *Journal of Economic Literature* 9 (September 1971): 785–97. Under the assumptions of this approach, the economic cost of the resource misallocation associated with the union monopoly wage effect is:

$$1/2 \ \times \ \frac{\text{union wage}}{\text{effect} \ / \ 100} \ \times \ \begin{array}{c}\text{decline in employment}\\ \text{in union sector due to}\\ \text{wage effect} \ / \ 100\end{array} \ \times \ \begin{array}{c}\text{fraction of}\\ \text{labor force}\\ \text{in unions}\end{array} \ \times \ \begin{array}{c}\text{fraction of}\\ \text{total costs}\\ \text{associated}\\ \text{with labor.}\end{array}$$

This formula estimates the size of the triangle under the demand curve for union labor, which provides an estimate of what the social loss would be if all output were produced under collective bargaining, and then multiplies this amount by an estimate of the fraction of all output produced in unionized settings. Our calculations assume a union wage effect of 20 to 25 percent; a decline in employment of workers of 13 to 17 percent, a union share of the work force of 25 percent, and a labor share of GNP of three-fourths. Using the formula above we obtain for the social cost:

$$1/2 \ (.20) \ (.13) \ (.25) \ (.75) = .0024 \tag{1}$$

$$1/2 \ (.25) \ (.17) \ (.25) \ (.75) = .0040 \tag{2}$$

Rees's calculations are in "The Effects of Unions on Resource Allocation," *The Journal of Law and Economics* 6 (October 1963): 69–78. The 1957 estimate is very close to the one for 1981, largely because the increase in the union wage effect was offset by the declining importance of unionism.

28. The GNP deflator figure is from the *Economic Report of the President, February 1982* (Washington, D.C.: Government Printing Office, 1982), table B–3.

29. *Union Wages and Inflation*, 174.

Chapter 4

1. *Employee Benefits, 1981* (Washington, D.C.: U.S. Chamber of Commerce, Economics Policy Division), tables 8 and 20, and *Employee Benefits, 1982*, chart 2. We have recalculated their figures to reflect benefit share of compensation, as opposed to payroll.

2. Two sides have been voiced on the union pension fund issue. One side is epitomized by Jeremy Rifkin and Randy Barber, *The North Will Rise Again: Pensions, Politics and Power in the 1980s* (Boston: Beacon Press, 1980). This work encourages private and public unions to use their control of pensions to prevent corporate flight to the West and thus to revitalize the East. A contrasting view of union pensions is offered by George T. Borjas, *Union Control of Pension Funds: Will the North Rise Again?* (San Francisco: The Institute for Contemporary Studies, 1979).

3. Work by Steven G. Allen of North Carolina State University has shown that the rate of unpaid absenteeism is higher for unionized than for nonunion employees. This is not necessarily inconsistent with the text's claim that unionism discourages sick leave, because sick leaves are usually paid absences and can be expected to be more closely monitored in unionized settings. See Steven G. Allen, "Trade Unions, Absenteeism, and Exit-Voice": North Carolina State University Department of Economics and Business Faculty Working Paper No. 7 (February 1982).

4. See Edward R. Curtin, *White Collar Unionization* (New York: National Industrial Conference Board, 1970), 63.

5. These data are based on analyses of 886 workers in the Quality of Employment Survey Matched 1973–77 sample. The number of workers covered and of fringes for various groups are as follows:

	Sample Size	Number of Fringes	
		1973	1977
Union in Both Years	193	3.64	3.28
Nonunion in Both Years	561	3.01	2.56
Union to Nonunion	83	3.16	2.55
Nonunion to Union	49	2.59	3.02

The decline in number of fringes in both union and nonunion settings reflects changes in definitions in the surveys. The detailed analysis of these longitudinal data is given in R. B. Freeman, "Longitudinal Analyses of Trade Union Economic Effects," *Journal of Labor Economics* (January 1984).

6. For other studies showing that unions increase fringe benefits, see Greg J. Duncan, "Earnings Functions and Nonpecuniary Benefits," *Journal of Human Resources* (Fall 1976): pp. 462–83; R. B. Freeman, "The Effect of Trade Unionism on Fringe Benefits," *Industrial Labor Relations Review* 34, no. 4 (July 1981); Gerald Goldstein and Mark Pauly, "Group Health Insurance as a Local Public Good," in R. Rosett, ed., *The Role of Health Insurance in the Health Services Sector* (New York: National Bureau of Economic Research, 1976), 73–110; Duane E. Leigh, "Labor Unions and the Value of Pension Benefits" (Washington State University, April 1980 mimeographed); Loren M. Solnick, "Unionism and Employer Fringe Benefit Expenditures," *Industrial Relations Review* 32 (February 1978): 102–17; W. Kip Viscusi, "Unions, Labor Market Structure and the Welfare Implications of the Quality of Work," *Journal of Labor Research* 1 (Spring 1980): 175–92; and Marie-Paule Joseph Donsimoni, *An Analysis of Trade Union Power: Structure and Conduct of the American Labor Movement* (Ph.D. diss., Harvard University, 1978).

7. See R. B. Freeman, "Unionism, Pensions, and Union Pension Funds": National Bureau of Economic Research Working Paper No. 1226 (1983).

8. See Freeman, "Unionism, Pensions, and Union Pension Funds."

9. The data on health insurance are from Amy K. Taylor and Walter R. Lawson, Jr., "Employer and Employee Expenditures for Private Health Insurance," *National Medical Care Expenditure Survey* Data Preview No. 7, (Washington, D.C.; GPO, 1981). The data on disability plans are from Daniel Smith and Lawrence Kotlikoff, *Pensions in the American Economy*, (Chicago: University of Chicago Press, tables 3.9.1 and 4.11.22.

10. Based on analysis of Expenditures for Employee Compensation data for 1972–1973 with same controls in regressions as for figure 4–1.

11. With wages held fixed, unionism raises fringe spending in construction by 47 percent and in trucking by 53 percent, compared with an effect of 32 percent in the entire economy. These estimates are based on regressions for 164 trucking service companies and 386 construction firms in the EEC sample.

12. Information was provided by the Public Disclosure Department of the Office of Pension and Welfare Benefit Programs, Department of Labor.

13. For a discussion of the link between measures of union market power and fringe expenditures, see Donsimoni, "Analysis of Trade Union Power," p. 170. We have calculated the differential at 20 percent and 80 percent organized using her regression coefficient estimate.

Notes

14. The effect of the demographic characteristics of organized workers on the size of the union fringe effect is discussed in William T. Alpert, "Unions and Private Wage Supplements": Working Paper No. 9 (Department of Economics, Washington University in St. Louis, 1980), 18.

15. See Richard Lester, "Benefits in a Preferred Form of Compensation," *Southern Economics Journal* 33 (April 1967): 494; Edward Lawler and Edward Levin, "Union Officers' Perceptions of Members' Pay Preferences," *Industrial Labor Relations Review* 22 (July 1968): 517; and Duane E. Leigh, "The Effect of Unionism on Workers' Valuation of Future Pension Benefits," *Industrial Labor Relations Review* 35 (1981): 510–21.

16. Based on tabulations for the same sample as in table 4–4.

17. Asked how good a job their union does in getting better wages, 83 percent of older members compared with 66 percent of younger members rated the union "good." This 17 percentage point differential is less than the 22 point differential in the ratings for fringes.

18. See Olivia S. Mitchell and Emily S. Andrews, "Scale Economics in Private Multi-Employer Pensions," *Industrial and Labor Relations Review* 34, no. 4 (July 1981): 522–30; and Oliver D. Dickerson, *Health Insurance*, 3rd ed. (Homewood, Ill.: Richard D. Irwin, 1968), 591–92; David A. Weeks, "Rethinking Employee Benefits Assumptions" (New York: Conference Board, 1978) 35; Augustine K. Fosu, "Choice of Fringe Benefits as a Form of Labor Earnings," (Northwestern University, 1979 mimeographed).

19. For discussions of the rising power of union pension funds, see Peter Drucker, *The Unseen Revolution: How Pension Fund Socialism Came to America* (New York: Harper and Row, 1976), and Rifkin and Barber, *The North Will Rise Again.*

20. "Targeting Pension Investments," *Business Week*, 7 September 1981, 87–88.

21. See Daniel Smith and Laurence Kotlikoff, *Pensions in the American Economy*, table 7.5.5.

22. For a detailed analysis of the pension plans, see Freeman, "Unionism, Pensions, and Union Pension Funds."

23. For the union pension fund investments to generate more jobs, they must offer contractors a better deal than can be gotten elsewhere, such as a lower interest rate. It can be shown that under some conditions the optimal monopoly union strategy is to offer such low-interest loans, recouping the funds through high wages. See Freeman, "Unionism, Pensions, and Union Pension Funds."

Chapter 5

1. See Friedman, *Capitalism and Freedom* (Chicago: University of Chicago Press, 1962), 124.

2. To see how the median voter model predicts a policy of greater increases for the lower paid, consider a situation with five workers, two who are paid $10.00 an hour; two who are paid $5.00 an hour and one who is paid $6.50 an hour. The "median" voter in this situation is the man paid $6.50. Since his wage is below the average (mean) wage ($7.30), he will favor wage policies that bring the median closer to the mean.

3. See R. B. Freeman, "Union Wage Practices and Wage Dispersion Within Establishments," *Industrial and Labor Relations Review* 36, no.7, (October 1982).

4. See *Wage and Salary Administration*, Personnel Policy Forum Survey No. 97 (Washington, D.C.: Bureau of National Affairs, 1972), 14, and *Characteristics of Major Collective Bargaining Agreements, July 1, 1974* (Washington, D.C.: Department of Labor, Bureau of Labor Statistics, 1975), 33.

5. The lognormal distribution states that the very common "bell-shaped" or "normal" curve describes the distribution of wages better if we express wages in logarithmic (log) units (or points) as opposed to dollars. In log units, small differences between people or groups, when multiplied by 100, tell us percentage (as opposed to dollar) differentials.

6. Unions have a large effect on overall inequality because within-plant inequality constitutes about 40 percent of overall inequality and thus they affect a large proportion of overall inequality among blue-collar workers.

7. Sumner H. Slichter, James J. Healy, and E. Robert Livernash, *The Impact of Collective Bargaining on Management* (Washington, D.C.: Brookings Institution, 1960), 606.

8. For a discussion of the Cooperative Wage Study, see Jack Steiber's various works, including "Steel," in Gerald G. Somers, ed., *Collective Bargaining: Contemporary American Experience* (Madison, Wis.: Industrial Relations Research Association, 1980), 177; *The Steel Industry Wage Structure* (Cambridge: Harvard University Press, 1959); and *The Development, Impact and Administration of the Steel Industry Wage Inequity Program* (Ph.D. diss., Harvard University, 1955); see also Slichter, Healy, and Livernash, *The Impact of Collective Bargaining*, 566–67.

9. See table 2–5 for a breakdown by type of bargaining unit, and also *Characteristics of Major Collective Bargaining Agreements, January 1, 1980.* (Washington, D.C.: Department of Labor, Bureau of Labor Statistics, 1981). The Teamsters information is from Harold M. Levinson, "Trucking," in Somers, ed., *Collective Bargaining.* The clothing industry information is from Slichter, Healy, and Livernash, *The Impact of Collective Bargining*, 523–24.

10. Exceptions to wage standards are discussed in David H. Greenberg, "Deviations from Wage-Fringe Standards," *Industrial and Labor Relations Review* 22 (January 1968): 197–209; Morris A. Horowitz, *The New York Hotel Industry: A Labor Relations Study* (Cambridge, Mass.: Harvard University Press, 1960), 165–66; and Kenneth Alexander, "Market Practices and Collective Bargaining in Automotive Parts," *Journal of Political Economy* 69 (February 1961): 15–29. Wage contours are discussed by John T. Dunlop in "The Task of Contemporary Wage Theory," in John T. Dunlop, ed., *The Theory of Wage Determination* (London: Macmillan, 1957), 3–27.

11. We included industries in this analysis only if at least five union and five nonunion plants reported compensation. The industry discussion was at the 2-digit SIC code level.

12. For the multivariate analysis, see R. B. Freeman, "Unionism and the Dispersion of Wages," *Industrial and Labor Relations Review* 34 (October 1980): 3–23.

13. See Freeman, "Unionism and the Dispersion of Wages." The first study that showed unionism reducing the effects of standard wage-determining factors was George E. Johnson and Kenneth Youmas, "Union Relative Wage Effects by Age and Education," *Industrial and Labor Relations Review* 25 (January 1971): 171–79.

14. See, for example, E. Wight Bakke, "Why Workers Join Unions," *Personnel Journal* 22 (1944): 2–11; and William F. Whyte, "Who Goes Union and Why?," *Personnel Journal* 23 (1945): 215–30.

15. See Henry S. Farber and Daniel H. Saks, "Why Workers Want Unions: The Role of Relative Wages and Job Characteristics," *Journal of Political Economy* 88 (April 1980): 349–69. The quotation is from page 363. Our analysis is based on 731 workers from the Quality of Employment survey data file.

16. Because variances are readily additive whereas standard deviations are not, we have changed our measure of inequality from standard deviation to variances for mathematical ease. The formula is:

Change in variance due to unionism	=	Proportion of workers who are union	×	Reduction in variance among workers who are union due to unionism
	+	Proportion of workers who are union	× Proportion of workers who are nonunion blue-collar ×	Increase in the squared differential of log of wages between union and nonunion blue-collar workers due to union wage effect
	+	Proportion of workers who are union	× Proportion of workers who are white-collar ×	Decrease in the squared differential of log of wages between union blue-collar workers and nonunion white-collar workers due to union wage effect.

Notes

Chapter 6

1. This recognition underlies much of modern economic theorizing about the labor market, implicit labor contracts, and unemployment. On these subjects see *Quarterly Journal of Economics* 98, supp. (1983).

2. In terms of probability theory, if P is the chance of quitting in a year, then the chance a worker has T years of *completed* tenure is $(1-P)^{T-1}$. P, while the chance a worker has T years of *uncompleted* tenure (i.e., has not yet left the firm) is $(1-P)^T$. For further analysis see R. B. Freeman, "The Exit-Voice Tradeoff in the Labor Market: Unionism, Job Tenure, Quits, and Separations," *Quarterly Journal of Economics* 94 (June 1980): 643–73.

3. Our analyses make use of a linear probability model that can be criticized because it does not bound the dependent variable between 0 and 1. Analyses with other functional forms, such as the probit or logistic, which can take on only values between 0 and 1, yield comparable results.

4. The equations that compare the effect of unionism and of wages on tenure assume that high wages cause high tenure, rather than the reverse. But of course tenure is a major determinant of wages, and that fact can lead to a biased (on average, wrong) estimate of the impact of both wages and unionism on tenure. In Freeman, "The Exit-Voice Trade Off," it is shown that this problem raises the estimated impact of wages and reduces the estimated impact of unionism by modest amounts.

5. Duane E. Leigh, in "Unions and Nonwage Racial Discrimination," *Industrial and Labor Relations Review* 33 (July 1979): 439–50, obtains a similar result.

6. In fact, a study by Burton and Parker obtained an insignificant union effect. Pencavel correctly criticized their aberrant finding and reported different results. Our re-estimation of their model produced the findings presented in the text. See John Pencavel, "Comment," *Industrial and Labor Relations Review* 23, no. 1 (October 1969): 78–83 as well as the citations in the table notes.

7. Specifically, our analysis has focused on the Michigan Panel Study of Income Dynamics, the National Longitudinal Survey of Older Men, 1971–73, and the Quality of Employment Survey Panel, 1973–77. We used linear probability models like those given in table 6–1. The union coefficient fell in the Michigan PSID analysis but not in the other two analyses. In Freeman "The Exit-Voice Tradeoff," an alternative analysis yields the same conclusion.

8. We have estimated the extent of these better opportunities by comparing the wages of union and nonunion workers who change jobs, controlling for their personal and job characteristics and for their initial wage. We find a 13 percent union advantage in the Michigan PSID (sample = 525). See R. B. Freeman, "The Exit-Voice Tradeoff," 643–73.

9. Our analysis suggests that we double the estimated impact of wages on quits to correct for this problem. Since the estimates in table 6–1 show a union impact that is generally more than twice the impact of a 20 percent wage increase, even doubling the estimated wage effect still leaves a larger union effect.

10. These analyses use two functional forms, the linear probability model and the logistic model. In the linear probability model, we have added intercept terms for each individual. In the logistic model, we eliminate workers who do not change jobs because their behavior is attributed entirely to an individual propensity to stay on-job in this functional form. See R. B. Freeman, "The Exit-Voice Tradeoff."

11. Measured by absolute changes, unionism has a greater impact on the quits of dissatisfied than of other workers. Measured by differences in log odds ratios the differential impact is less clear.

12. See Thomas A. Kochan and David E. Helfman, "The Effects of Collective Bargaining on Economic and Behavioral Job Outcomes," (Paper prepared for the New York State School of Industrial and Labor Relations, Cornell University, October 1979).

13. For the grievance system data, see the Bureau of Labor Statistics, *Major Collective Bargaining Agreements—Grievance Procedures:* Bulletin No. 1425–1 (Washington, D.C.: Department of Labor, Bureau of Labor Statistics, November 1964), 6. For analysis showing union workers accruing greater tenure in sectors with wide grievance procedures, see R. B. Freeman,

"The Effect of Unionism on Worker Attachment to Firms," *Journal of Labor Research* 1 (Spring 1980).

14. Richard N. Block, "Job Changing and Negotiated Nonwage Provisions," *Industrial Relations* 17 (October 1978): 296–307, and "The Impact of Seniority Provisions on the Manufacturing Quit Rate," *Industrial and Labor Relations Review* 32 (July 1978): 474–88.

15. See Edward R. Curtin, *White-Collar Unionization:* Personnel Policy Study No. 220 (New York: National Industrial Conference Board, 1970).

16. For a discussion of 1920s efforts at employee representation, see *Collective Bargaining Through Employee Representation* (New York: National Industrial Conference Board, 1933). For a discussion of how company unions became "real" unions, see Walter Galenson, *The AFL Response to the CIO Challenge* (Cambridge, MA: Harvard University Press, 1963).

17. See "Policies for Unorganized Employees": *Personnel Policies Forum Survey No. 125* (Washington, D.C.: Bureau of National Affairs, April 1979), 1, 12.

18. This is based on two estimates: (1) the impact of quits on productivity, in the Brown-Medoff productivity regressions; see Charles Brown and James Medoff, "Trade Unions in the Production Process," *Journal of Political Economy* 86, no. 3 (June 1978): 335–78; (2) the impact of unions on quits and the potential savings in recruitment and training costs, using data on costs from P. Doeringer and M. Piore, *Internal Labor Markets* (Lexington, Mass.: D.C. Heath, 1972).

Chapter 7

1. *Wall Street Journal,* 26 February, 1970, p. 2.

2. *Wall Street Journal,* 23 September, 1980, p. 1.

3. See R. B. Freeman and Kim B. Clark, "How Elastic is the Demand for Labor?" *Review of Economics and Statistics* 62, (November 1980): 509–20.

4. The significant drops in shipments (and employment) in typical manufacturing firms occurred in 1953–54, 1957–58, 1960–61, 1969–70, 1973–75, 1980, and 1981–82. The unemployment rates in manufacturing and the change in the number of workers in construction are from U.S. Department of Labor, *Employment and Training Report of the President,* 1981, pp. 9–10.

5. We have obtained estimates of the cyclical variability of product demand in 68 industries with regressions of log (real [deflated] shipments) on a time trend and season dummy variables using quarterly data from 1958 to 1975. Regressions using these figures reveal that the cyclical variation in the log of shipments is five to six times larger under unionism than in nonunion settings. We have obtained the hours and wages response estimates by regressions of log (annual hours) or log (hourly wages divided by the CPI) on current and lagged values of the log (real shipments), a time trend and season dummy variables. Regressions using these estimates indicate a response of hours to shipments in union plants of .59 compared with .64 in nonunion plants; this difference was not statistically significant. For our hourly wage variable, we find responses of .02 in unionized establishments and .12 in those that are nonunion; this difference was significant.

6. By a layoff we refer to a suspension without pay for an extended period of time (at least seven consecutive calendar days in the Bureau of Labor Statistics definition) initiated by the employer without prejudice to the worker. In manufacturing, where layoffs are important, about 70 percent lead to a recall or rehire; on this issue see David Lilien, "The Cyclical Pattern of Temporary Layoffs in United States Manufacturing," *Review of Economics and Statistics* 62 (February 1980): 24–31.

7. The calculation is discussed in J. L. Medoff, "Layoffs and Alternatives Under Trade Unions in U.S. Manufacturing," *American Economic Review* 69 (June 1979): 390–93.

8. Sumner H. Slichter, James J. Healy, and E. Robert Livernash, *The Impact of Collective Bargaining on Management* (Washington, D.C.: Brookings Institution, 1960), 152.

9. The data on the major 1954–55 contracts are from BLS, "Analysis of Layoff, Recall, and Work-Sharing Procedures in Union Contracts": *Bulletin 1209* (Washington, D.C.: Government Printing Office, March 1957), 2, 8, and 9. The 1970–71 agreements data are from BLS, "Layoff,

Notes

Recall, and Work-Sharing Procedures": Bulletin *1425–13* (Washington, D.C.: Government Printing Office, 1972), 22 and 24.

10. See J. L. Medoff, "Layoffs and Alternatives," table 4, p. 391.

11. See R. B. Freeman and J. L. Medoff, National Bureau of Economic Research "Unionism, Employment and Unemployment Across Geographic Area": Working Paper (Forthcoming).

Chapter 8

1. Agreement between the Amalgamated Food and Allied Workers Union Local 56 and the Maxwell House Division of General Foods Corporation, for 1973–76, Section 4.4, p. 19.

2. Agreement between the International Brotherhood of Electrical Workers Locals 2222 and 2320–2327 and the New England Telephone and Telegraph Company, effective August 7, 1977, Article 25, p. 60.

3. Agreement between the United Rubber, Cork, Linoleum, and Plastic Workers of America Local 2 and the Goodyear Tire and Rubber Company, as of July, 1978, Article IX, Section 1(a).

4. Figures on promotion clauses in collective bargaining agreements were derived with data from "Seniority in Promotion and Transfer Provisions": *Bulletin 1425–11* (Washington, D.C.: U.S. Department of Labor, Bureau of Labor Statistics, 1970), 4–7 and 36–38. The BLS figures were based on a sample of 1,763 collective bargaining contracts each covering 1,000 workers or more; these contracts cover a total of 7,105,100 workers. Contracts with references to promotions but subject to local negotiations, as well as contracts for which there were no details or unclear details given about the promotion provisions, were omitted. The all-company figures were derived with data from "Employee Promotion and Transfer Policies": *Personnel Policies Forum No. 120* (Washington, D.C.: Bureau of National Affairs, January 1978), 16–17. The BNA figures were based on responses from 166 personnel executives who were members of the 1977–78 panel of BNA's Personnel Policies Forum.

5. These figures are from Katharine G. Abraham and J. L. Medoff, "Length of Service and the Operation of Internal Labor Markets," IRRA Series, Thirty-fifth Annual Proceedings (December 1982): 308–18.

6. See Craig A. Olson and Chris J. Berger, "The Relationship Between Seniority, Ability, and the Promotion of Union and Nonunion Workers," in *Advances in Industrial and Labor Relations*, vol. 1, ed. David B. Lipsky and Joe M. Douglas (Greenwich, Conn.: JAI Press, 1982).

7. J. L. Medoff and K. G. Abraham, "Are Those Paid More Really More Productive? The Case of Experience," *Journal of Human Resources* 16 (Spring 1981): 186–216; "Experience, Performance, and Earnings," *Quarterly Journal of Economics* 94 (December 1980): 703–36.

8. These figures are based on counts from the 1977 Quality of Employment Survey, which reflect the survey's sampling weights.

9. That these figures are plausible can be seen by comparing their magnitude with the actual percentage of total compensation that goes for vacation pay. In table 4–1, we saw that 3 percent of the total compensation of union workers and 2 percent of the total compensation of nonunion workers is spent on vacation pay.

10. For example, for life insurance, see the rate schedules of Aetna Life Insurance Company, published in *Best's Flitcraft Compendium* (Oldwick, N. J.: A.M. Best Co., 1983): 37.

11. There is some difficulty in making these comparisons, due in part to problems of valuing contingency clauses and in part to problems of translating purchases of deferred benefits into "simple" wages. Our procedure, discussed in R. B. Freeman and J. L. Medoff, "The Returns to Seniority Under Unionism": National Bureau of Economic Research Working Paper (Forthcoming), is to value benefits at different ages at the increase in the present value of their worth or change in cost, under the Henry Simons approach in which income is the *change* in capital value.

12. See Freeman and Medoff, "The Returns to Seniority."

13. See Peter J. Kuhn, "A New Integrated Theory of Unions and Life Cycle Employment Contracts: Voice, Malfeasance and Welfare" (Ph.D. diss., Harvard University, 1983).

14. Quoted in *Labor Relations Yearbook, 1975* (Washington, D.C.: Bureau of National Affairs, 1976), 197.

15. In some data sets, such as the older male National Longitudinal Survey, black men actually have as much or more seniority than white men, while in others, such as the young male NLS, they have notably less.

Chapter 9

1. For a general discussion of job satisfaction as an economic variable, see R. B. Freeman "Job Satisfaction as an Economic Variable," *American Economic Review* 68 (May 1978): 135–41.

2. Among the studies are George Borjas, "Job Satisfaction, Wages, and Unions," *The Journal of Human Resources* 14, no. 1 (Winter 1979): 21–39; David G. Mandelbaum, "Responses to Job Satisfaction Questions as Insights into Why Men Change Employers" (Honors thesis, Harvard College, 1980); Freeman, "Job Satisfaction"; Thomas Kochan and David Helfman, "The Effects of Collective Bargaining on Economic and Behavioral Job Outcomes" (Paper prepared at the New York State School of Industrial and Labor Relations, Cornell University, October 1979), 36; James Hughes, "An Exit-Voice Model of the Labor Union: Some Implications for the Individual Member" (Honors thesis, Harvard College, 1976).

3. "Job Satisfaction," 25.

4. "Effects of Collective Bargaining," p. 36.

5. See Chris J. Berger, Craig A. Olson, and John W. Boudreau, "Effects of Unions on Job Satisfaction: The Role of Work-Related Values and Perceived Rewards": (Paper prepared principally at the Krannert Graduate School of Management, Purdue University, 1982).

6. Based on the responses of 244 union workers in the Quality of Employment Survey 1973–77 matched file.

7. The .06 estimate is based on the following formula:

$$\text{Proportion of workers dissatisfied in } 1977 = \alpha + P_{dd} + (1-\alpha)(P_d)$$

where P_{dd} = proportion of workers who were dissatisfied in 1973 and stayed with their firm and were dissatisfied in 1977

P_d = proportion of all other workers who were dissatisfied in 1977

α = ratio of workers who were dissatisfied in 1973 and stayed with the firm to all workers in the firm.

The exit-voice tradeoff will raise the proportion who are dissatisfied in 1977 by

$$\Delta\alpha (P_{dd} - P_d)$$

where $\Delta\alpha$ = differences in proportion of union members who are dissatisfied and quit and nonunion members who are dissatisfied and quit.

In the 1973–77 Quality of Employment Panel Survey, 40 percent of dissatisfied union workers compared to 75 percent of dissatisfied nonunion workers quit their jobs, making $\Delta\alpha = .35$. In the same data we estimate $P_{dd} = .30$ and $P_d = .12$. Hence our final estimate is .18 (.35) $\approx$ .06.

8. Consistent with this finding, a study by Olson found that job satisfaction is significantly positively correlated with union satisfaction and with the extent to which the unions achieve certain worker demands. See Craig A. Olson, "The Relationship Between Union Member Preference for Bargaining Outcomes, Union and Job Satisfaction," (Paper presented at the Thirty-fourth Annual Winter Meeting of the Industrial Relations Research Association, Washington, D.C., December 28–30, 1981).

9. Based on tabulations for the same workers covered in table 9–4. Specifically, with respect to satisfaction with one's union we find:

Satisfaction With Union

	Workers Under 40 %	Workers Over 40 %	Black Workers %	Workers in Bottom 25 percent of Earnings Distribution %
Very Satisfied	18	33	14	24
Somewhat Satisfied	50	47	62	40
Not Too or Not At All Satisfied	32	20	24	36

10. Tabulations for the table 9–5 group of workers show:

Satisfaction with Say in Union

	Workers Under 40 %	Workers Over 40 %	Tenure Less than 5 Years %	Tenure More than 5 Years %
Very Good	18	21	16	21
Somewhat Good	35	43	32	43
Not Too or Not At All Good	47	36	52	36

11. See Thomas I. Chacko and Charles R. Green, "Perceptions of Union Power, Service and Confidence in Labor Leaders: A Study of Member and Nonmember Difference," *Journal of Labor Research* 3, no. 2 (Spring 1982): 211–22.

12. Jeanne M. Brett, "Behavioral Research on Unions and Union Management Systems," in Barry M. Straw, ed., *Research in Organizational Behavior,* vol. 2 (Greenwich, Conn.: JAI Press, 1980), 181.

Chapter 10

1. Fred K. Foulkes, *Personnel Policies in Large Nonunion Companies.*

2. D. Q. Mills, "Management in Performance," in Steiber et al, eds., *U.S. Industrial Relations 1950–1980: A Critical Assessment.*

3. Edward R. Curtin, *White-Collar Unionization* (New York: National Industrial Conference Board, 1970), 68.

4. The studies would still correctly measure the gain to an *individual* of switching from nonunion to union status. However, they give incorrect measures of the gain to a *group* of workers who changed status, since their change would also alter the wages of nonunion workers. The correct measure in the latter case is the economic well-being of the workers before unionization and after unionization.

5. The Burlington example is based on discussion with John T. Dunlop, who points out that

management in companies like Burlington often deals with the unions in their industry on industry problems relating to trade and technology.

6. "Wage and Salary Administration": *Personnel Policy Forum No. 131* (Washington, D.C.: Bureau of National Affairs, July 1981), 3.

7. F. K. Foulkes, *Personnel Policies in Large Nonunion Companies* (Englewood Cliffs, N.J.: Prentice Hall, 1980), 47, 151, 154, 165.

8. Charles L. Hughes, quoted in National Organizing Committee, *The AFL-CIO Report on Union Busters* (Washington, D.C., March 1979). For comments in a similar vein, see Hughes' *Making Unions Unnecessary* (New York: Executive Enterprises Publishing Co., 1976): 102–3.

9. Curtin, *White-Collar Unionization*, 60.

10. The wage comparisons are based on May 1979 Current Population Survey data. For a discussion of the pension data, see R. B. Freeman, "Unionism, Pensions, and Union Pension Funds"; National Bureau of Economic Research Working Paper No. 1226 (1983). The estimates of fringe spending are based on the Expenditures for Employee Compensation tapes for 1974–78.

11. It is, however, important to remember that the statistical comparison of union effects by size of firm or establishment neither proves the existence of a positive spillover to large firms nor estimates that spillover. They are consistent with the positive spillover and can be interpreted as reflecting its impact, but they may be interpreted in other ways as well.

12. *Personnel Policies*, 341.

13. Benjamin Calkins, Economics 1650 Term Project, Harvard University, 1977.

14. *Personnel Policies*, 61–62.

15. The eligible-to-vote figures are from *Annual Report of the National Labor Relations Board*, 1980. Note that the text estimates are based on all workers covered in the NLRB elections. A more sophisticated analysis would adjust for the fact that the number of workers affected also depends on the extent to which the 150,000 to 250,000 workers who are eligible to vote had been eligible to vote in recent years. Our estimates are that perhaps 15 percent of the workers in an NLRB election in a given year have participated in an election in their plant within the past several years. Thus, any adjustment for this fraction is modest.

16. Sumner H. Slichter, James J. Healy, and E. Robert Livernash, *The Impact of Collective Bargaining on Management* (Washington, D.C.: Brookings Institution, 1960), 445.

17. Loren M. Solnick, "The Effect of Blue-Collar Unions on White-Collar Wages and Fringes," (Paper prepared at the Center for Forensic Economic Studies, for the Assistant Secretary for Policy, Evaluation, and Research at the U.S. Department of Labor, May 1979), 13–14.

18. Daniel J. B. Mitchell, *Union Wages and Inflation* (Washington, D.C.: Brookings Institution, 1980), 278.

19. See *Wall Street Journal:* "UAW Attacks Plan by GM to Continue Executive Bonuses," 21 April, 1982; "GM Agrees to Forgo Richer Bonus Pay After UAW Objects," 23 April, 1982; and "GM's Bonus Flap: 'The Timing Was Wrong,' " 30 April, 1982.

20. Harry J. Holzer, "Unions and the Labor Market Status of White and Minority Youth," *Industrial and Labor Relations Review* 36 (April 1982): 392–405; and Lawrence M. Kahn, "The Effect of Unions on the Earnings of Nonunion Workers," *Industrial and Labor Relations Review* 32 (January 1978): 205–16.

21. Harry G. Johnson and Peter Mieskowski develop the model without trade in "The Effects of Unionization on the Distribution of Income: A General Equilibrium Approach," *Quarterly Journal of Economics* 84 (November 1970): 539–47. Alan A. Carruth and Andrew J. Oswald develop a model with trade in "The Determination of Union and Nonunion Wage Rates," *European Economic Review* 16 (June–July 1981): 285–302.

Chapter 11

1. Derek C. Bok and John T. Dunlop, *Labor and the American Community* (New York: Simon and Schuster, 1970), 260.

Notes

2. We recognize that decreases in turnover that benefit a firm could reduce mobility in the economy to a point where they reduce national output.

3. See Sumner H. Slichter, James J. Healy, and E. Robert Livernash, *The Impact of Collective Bargaining on Management* (Washington, D.C.: The Brookings Institution, 1960), 841–78.

4. See Allan B. Mandelstamm, "The Effects of Unions on Efficiency in the Residential Construction Industry: A Case Study," *Industrial and Labor Relations Review* 19 (July 1965): 503–21; and Robert Cochran, "Productivity Among Union/Nonunion Construction Workers" (Paper, Harvard University, 1979).

5. Bok and Dunlop, *Labor and the American Community*, 261.

6. Ibid.

7. Investment to modernize plants was especially important in the recent giveback negotiations of the Steelworkers.

8. Nestor E. Terlecky, in "Sources of Productivity Advance: A Pilot Study of Manufacturing Industries, 1899–1953" (Ph.D. diss., Columbia University, 1960), found a negative correlation. John W. Kendrick and Elliot S. Grossman, in *Productivity in the United States: Trends and Cycles* (Baltimore, Md.: Johns Hopkins University Press, 1980), report finding a positive relationship between growth of productivity and growth of unionism. From their data, however, it is apparent that there is a positive correlation between the level of unionism and productivity *growth* as well as between changes.

9. Lest the reader think our critic is a straw man, note the statements by Leo Troy, C. Timothy Koeller, and Neil Sheflin in "The Three Faces of Unionism," *Policy Review* 14 (Fall 1980): 95–109.

10. R. B. Freeman and J. L. Medoff, "Substitution Between Production Labor and Other Factors in Unionized and Nonunionized Manufacturing," *Review of Economics and Statistics* 64 no. 2 (May 1982), table 4, 231, 220–33.

11. In technical parlance, if we have a *general* production function, the first-order Taylor series expansion terms do not include the elasticity of substitution. It enters with the second-order terms.

12. Mandelstamm, "The Effects of Unions on Efficiency," 512.

13. Clinton C. Bourdon and Raymond E. Levitt, *Union and Open-Shop Construction* (Lexington, Mass.: D.C. Heath, 1980), 63.

14. See C. Brown and J. Medoff, "Trade Unions in the Production Process," *Journal of Political Economy* 86, no. 3 (June 1978): 355–78; and S. Allen, "Unionization and Productivity in Office Building and School Construction," (North Carolina State University, January 1983, mimeographed), 27–30.

15. Slichter, Healy, and Livernash, *Impact of Collective Bargaining*, 951.

16. "Labor-Management Response to Productivity Change," a lecture delivered at Utah State University, April 1, 1982, and published in "George S. Eccles Distinguished Lecture Series, 1981–82" (Logan, Ut.: Utah State University, 1982), 34.

17. Harry Katz, Thomas Kochan, and Kenneth Gobeille, "Industrial Relations Performance, Economic Performance and the Effects of Quality of Working Life Efforts: An Inter-Plant Analysis": Sloan School Working Paper 1329–82 (Massachusetts Institute of Technology, July 1982); Bernard Ichniowski, "How Do Labor Relations Matter? A Study of Productivity in Eleven Paper Mills": National Bureau of Economic Research (Summer Workshop, August 1983); Michael Schuster "The Impact of Union-Management Compensation on Productivity and Employment," *Industrial and Labor Relations Review* 36, no. 3, (April 1983): 415–30.

18. For a history of coal see William H. Miernyck, "Coal," in Gerald G. Somers, ed., *Collective Bargaining: Contemporary American Experience* (Madison, Wis.: Industrial Relations Research Association, 1980), especially pp. 17–23. An explanation of Lewis' views may be found in "More Machines, Fewer Men—A Union That's Happy About It," *U.S. News and World Report*, 9 November, 1959, 60–64. The data on work stoppages are from "Collective Bargaining in the Bituminous Coal Industry": Bureau of Labor Statistics Report No. 514 (Washington, D.C.: GPO, 1977).

19. See Peter A. Navarro, "Union Bargaining Power in the Coal Industry, 1945–1981," *Industrial and Labor Relations Review* 36, no. 2 (January 1983): 214–29.

Chapter 12

1. For a discussion of the problems in measuring profits, see Leonard Weiss, "The Concentration-Profits Relationship and Antitrust," in Harry S. Goldschmidt, H. Michael Mann, and J. Fred Weston, eds., *Industrial Concentration: The New Learning* (Boston: Little, Brown, 1974), 184. For discussion of some of the problems in capital evaluation, see Henry G. Grabowski and Dennis C. Mueller, "Industrial Research and Development, Intangible Capital Stocks, and Firm Profit Rates," *Bell Journal of Economics* 9 (Autumn 1978): 328–43; and L. W. Weiss, "Advertising, Profits, and Corporate Taxes," *Review of Economics and Statistics* 51 (November 1969): 421–30.

2. For a critical view of the price-cost margin, see J. J. Leibowitz, "What Do Census Price-Cost Margins Measure?" *Journal of Law and Economics* 25, no. 2 (October 1982): 231–46. For a more positive view, see Weiss, "The Concentration-Profits Relationship and Antitrust."

3. Formally we can relate the union effect on compensation and on productivity to its effect on profitability with the following equation:

$$
\begin{pmatrix} \text{Percentage Change in} \\ \text{Return to Capital} \\ \text{Due to Unionism} \end{pmatrix} = \left(\frac{1}{\text{Capital's Share of Cost}} \right) \begin{pmatrix} \text{Percentage Change in} \\ \text{Output per Worker} \\ \text{Due to Unionism} \end{pmatrix}
$$

$$
- \begin{pmatrix} \text{Labor's} \\ \text{Share of} \\ \text{Cost} \end{pmatrix} \begin{pmatrix} \text{Percentage Change in} \\ \text{Compensation per Worker} \\ \text{Due to Unionism} \end{pmatrix}
$$

$$
- \begin{array}{l} \text{Percentage Change in} \\ \text{Capital per Worker} \\ \text{Due to Unionism} \end{array}
$$

or

$$
\begin{pmatrix} \text{Percentage Change in} \\ \text{Return to Capital} \\ \text{Due to Unionism} \end{pmatrix} = \left(\frac{1}{\text{Capital's Share of Cost}} \right) \begin{pmatrix} \text{Percentage Change in} \\ \text{Total Factor Productivity} \\ \text{Due to Unionism} \end{pmatrix}
$$

$$
- \begin{pmatrix} \text{Labor's} \\ \text{Share of} \\ \text{Cost} \end{pmatrix} \begin{pmatrix} \text{Percentage Change in} \\ \text{Compensation per Worker} \\ \text{Due to Unionism} \end{pmatrix}
$$

This equation shows that the union effect on profitability is positive or negative depending on whether changes in worker productivity are sufficiently greater than changes in compensation to counterbalance a likely increase in the capital/labor ratio, or alternatively whether total factor productivity changes are larger or smaller than cost changes.

4. Indeed, in the same data set, we obtain the following union effects: increases in wages, increases in value added per worker, and decreases in profits.

5. The 3.8 percent figure represents the change in equity of a successful drive compared to what might have happened in the absence of any organizing drive. The 2.7 percent figure represents the difference between changes in equity value of companies which become organized and companies which defeat a drive. If one believes that organizing drives indicate poor labor-management relations, with likely negative effects on profits, the latter comparison is better. The study is Richard Ruback and Martin Zimmerman, "Unionization and Profitability: Evidence from the Capital Market," (Sloan School of Management, MIT, October 1982, mimeographed).

6. See Richard B. Freeman, "Unionism, Price-Cost Margins, and the Return to Capital": National Bureau of Economic Research Working Paper No. 1164 (1983).

7. Michael Salinger, "Tobin's q, Unionization and the Concentration-Profits Relationship," Columbia Graduate School of Business Research Working Paper No. 514A, February 1983. A contrary result is obtained by Kim B. Clark, "Unionization and Firm Performance: The Impact of Profits, Growth, and Productivity," Harvard Business School HBS 83–16, (1983), table 7, whose data are, however, limited to a special group of businesses rather than to the entire economy.

Notes

8. Whether total capital rises or falls depends on whether the reduction in the scale of the sector is larger or smaller than the induced substitution of capital for labor.

9. "Unionization and Firm Performance," table 7.

10. See James F. Hayden, *Collective Bargaining and Cartelization: An Analysis of Teamster Power in the Regulated Trucking Industry* (Undergraduate thesis, Harvard University, 1977), appendix B.

11. For further discussion of the Scanlon Plan and its derivatives, see Thomas A. Kochan, *Collective Bargaining and Industrial Relations* (Homewood, Ill.: Richard D. Irwin, 1980), 428–30; and D. Quinn Mills, *Labor Management Relations* (New York: McGraw-Hill, 1982), 453–55.

Chapter 13

1. George Meany, Washington Daily News, 29 April, 1971.

2. Douglas Caddy, *The Hundred Million Dollar Payoff: How Big Labor Buys Its Democrats* (New Rochelle, NY: Arlington House, 1979).

3. These quotations are from Henry C. Simons, "Some Reflections on Syndicalism," *Journal of Political Economy* 52 (March 1944): 23; and Derek C. Bok and John T. Dunlop, *Labor and the American Community* (New York: Simon and Schuster, 1970), 425–26.

4. In its report to the 11th Biennial Convention of AFL-CIO, COPE reported "voter turnout exceeded 50 percent" among union membership and families, compared with 38 percent turnout nationally, as cited in Caddy, *The Hundred Million Dollar Payoff,* 15. See also Bok and Dunlop, *Labor and the American Community,* for a discussion of registration and voting by union members.

5. Michael Malbin, "Of Mountains and Molehills: PACs, Campaigns, and Public Policy," in *Parties, Interest Groups, and Campaign Finance Laws,* ed. Michael Malbin, (Washington, D.C.: American Enterprise Institute, 1980), 152–83.

6. Federal Election Commission, *Dollar Politics,* 3rd ed. (Washington, DC: Congressional Quarterly, 1982), 47.

7. The reports are issued annually by the AFL-CIO Committee on Political Education. See appendix.

8. See R.B. Freeman, "What Unions Do to National Legislation": National Bureau of Economic Research Working Paper (Forthcoming) for a complete discussion based on the "minimum winning coalition" theory of W. Riker, *The Theory of Political Coalitions* (New Haven: Yale University Press, 1962).

9. For a study showing no indirect benefit, see Henry Farber, "Unions and the Minimum Wage," *Report of the Minimum Wage Study Commission,* Vol. VI (Washington, D.C.: Government Printing Office, June 1981), 105–34.

10. Richard Caves and Daniel Esty, "Market Structure and Political Influence: New Data on Political Expenditures, Activity, and Success": Harvard Institute of Economic Research Discussion Paper No. 844 (1981).

11. Jay Hamilton (Harvard University) estimated the impact of the COPE ratings of U.S. Senators in twenty-five 1980 Senate races on contributions from labor and all other political action committees. His estimates show that a one-point increase in a Senator's COPE rating raised labor's contribution to him *relative* to those of his opponent by $2,773 while reducing other PAC contributions by $2,669. The impact of COPE was highly significant in the equations for union contributions but only modestly significant in the equation for other PAC contributions. For analyses of the effect of COPE and other interest group ratings on spending, see Jay Hamilton, "PAC'ing the U.S. Senate in 1980: An Econometric Study of the Contributions of Political Action Committees" (Undergraduate thesis, Harvard College, 1983).

12. Bok and Dunlop, *Labor and the American Community,* 424.

13. Frances Turner, "The Labor Law Reform Bill, 1977–1978: An Analysis of Its Defeat" (Harvard University, 1982) provides a useful history of the bill as well as an analysis of the failure

to beat the cloture amendment. For newspaper and magazine reports, see *Business Week:* 7 February, 1977, 28–29; 2 May, 1977, 34–35; 7 November, 1977, 86; 13 February, 1978, 31–32; 6 March, 1978, 32; 22 May, 1978, 64; 14 August, 1978, 80; *Fortune:* 31 July, 1978, 80–82; *Newsweek:* 20 March, 1978, 57–58; *Time:* 11 April, 1977, 55; *U.S. News and World Report:* 7 March, 1977, 88; 11 April, 1977, 93; 25 July, 1977, 77–78.

14. Cited in "The Big Guns Aim at Labor Law Reform," *Business Week,* 13 February, 1978, 32.

15. Also cited in "The Big Guns," 32.

16. These figures are from *U.S. News and World Report,* 7 March, 1977, 88, and *Fortune,* July 1978, 80.

Chapter 14

1. *New York Times,* 6 January, 1970, p. 1.

2. *New York Times,* 2 May, 1981, p. 26.

3. The text of the Landrum-Griffin Act, officially titled the Labor-Management Reporting and Disclosure Act of 1959 (73 Stat. 519), can be found in Archibald Cox and Derek C. Bok, *1966 Statutory Supplement: Labor Law Cases and Materials* (Brooklyn, N.Y.: The Fountain Press, 1966), 75–102.

4. Turnover is not, of course, a perfect indicator of democracy. Some changes result from retirement and death, and in others a ruling group replaces one office-holder with another without any outside challenge. On the other hand, a lack of turnover might reflect the approval of the vast majority of the members of an enlightened incumbent's performance.

5. See Leon Applebaum, "Officer Turnover and Salary Structures in Local Unions," *Industrial and Labor Relations Review* 20 (January 1966): 224–30; Leon Applebaum and Harry R. Blaine, "Compensation and Turnover of Union Officers," *Industrial Relations* 14 (May 1975): 156–57; and Department of Labor, Bureau of Labor Statistics, *Directory of National Unions and Employee Associations, 1973* (Washington, D.C.: Government Printing Office, 1974), 62.

6. See "Local Union Democracy: Fresh Local Mandate in the USWA Comes Every Three Years," *Steel Labor* 44, no. 6 (June 1979): 8–9.

7. For data on the turnover of national union leaders, see Martin Estey, *The Unions: Structure, Development and Management* 3rd ed., (New York: Harcourt Brace Jovanovich, 1981), 62–63; Marvin Snowbarger and Sam Pintz, "Landrum-Griffin and Union President Turnover," *Industrial Relations* 9 (October 1970): 475–76; Marcus Sandver, "Officer Turnover in National Unions: A Time Series Analysis" *Bulletin of Business Research* 53 (Ohio State University, Center for Business and Economic Research, January 1978).

8. Figure provided by the Bureau of Labor Statistics.

9. Leonard R. Sayles and George Strauss, *The Local Union* (New York: Harcourt, Brace and World, 1967), 147.

10. Jack Barbash, *American Unions: Structure, Government and Politics* (New York: Random House, 1967), 143.

11. Sayles and Strauss, *The Local Union,* p. 1.

12. See Benjamin Civiletti, *Testimony before the Permanent Subcommittee on Investigations of the Senate Committee on Governmental Affairs,* Labor-Management Racketeering Hearings, 95th Cong., 2d Sess., April 1978.

13. Derek C. Bok and John T. Dunlop, *Labor and the American Community* (New York: Simon and Schuster, 1970), 69.

14. Irwin Ross, "How Lawless are Big Companies?" *Fortune,* 103 (1 December, 1980): 57–64.

15. Ross, "How Lawless Are Big Companies?" p. 62.

16. "Summary Overview of the State of the Art Regarding Information Gathering Techniques and Level of Knowledge in Three Areas Concerning Crimes Against Business" (New York: American Management Associations, 1977).

Notes

17. These figures obtained by dividing workers on strike and work time lost by our estimates of the proportion of all workers who are either union members or members of associations.

18. These data are from *Analysis of Work Stoppages, 1980*, Bulletin 2120, (Department of Labor, Bureau of Labor Statistics, March 1982). We have taken decade averages from table 1 and evidence on contract status from table 8. Data for earlier years are taken from predecessor Bulletins to 2120. We have estimated the likelihood of a strike during negotiations in the union sector by multiplying our estimated percentage of union workers involved in a strike by the proportion of workers involved in strikes as part of negotiations (about 80 percent) by three (since the vast majority of contracts are for three years). This yields .27 as the frequency of strikes during negotiations, which in turn implies one strike every 3.7 negotiations. For related discussions, see Sean Flaherty, "Contract Status and the Economic Determinants of Strike Activity," *Industrial Relations* 22, no. 1 (Winter 1983): 20–30; and Bruce E. Kaufman, "The Propensity to Strike in American Manufacturing," *Proceedings of the Thirtieth Annual Winter Meeting* p. 419–26 of the *Industrial Relations Research Association*, New York City, December 28–30, 1977.

19. See Douglas Hibbs, "Industrial Conflict in Advanced Industrial Societies," *American Political Science Review* 70, no. 4 (December 1976): 1033–58.

20. See John A. Ackerman, "The Impact of the Coal Strike of 1977–1978," *Industrial and Labor Relations Review* 36 (October 1982): 175–88. The quote is from page 175. Earlier work is given in Donald Cullen, *National Emergency Strikes* (Ithaca: New York School of Industrial and Labor Relations, 1968).

21. For a quantitative analysis see George R. Neuman and Melvin W. Reder, "Output and Strike Activity in U.S. Manufacturing: How Large are the Losses?" (Paper presented at the National Bureau of Economic Research Conference on the Economics of Trade Unions, 7 May, 1983.) This study probably understates the output loss due to strikes because the Commerce Department "adjusts" the data to smooth it, as is described in Neumann and Reder, p. 15.

22. For Hicks's theory see John R. Hicks, *The Theory of Wages*, 2d American ed., (New York: St. Martin's Press, 1963). For evidence on the cyclical nature of strikes, see F. S. O'Brien, "Industrial Conflict and Business Fluctuations: A Comment," *Journal of Political Economy* 73, no. 6 (December 1965): 650–54; A. Rees, "Industrial Conflict and Business Fluctuations," *Journal of Political Economy* 60, no. 5 (October 1952); 371–82; and R. Weintraub, "Prosperity Versus Strikes: An Empirical Approach," *Industrial and Labor Relations Review* 19, no. 1 (October 1965): 231–38. For a dissenting view, see G. W. Scully, "Business Cycles and Industrial Strike Activity," *Journal of Business* 44, no. 4 (October 1971): 359–74. Also see M. Shalev, "Trade Unions and Economic Analysis: The Case of Industrial Conflict," *Journal of Labor Research* 1, no. 1 (Spring 1980): 133–74; and B. Kaufman, "Bargaining Theory, Inflation, and Cyclical Strike Activity in Manufacturing," *Industrial and Labor Relations Review* 34, no. 3 (April 1981): 333–55. The first econometric effort at explaining strikes is O. Ashenfelter and G. E. Johnson, "Bargaining Theory, Trade Unions, and Industrial Strike Activity," *American Economic Review* 59 (March 1969): 35–49.

Chapter 15

1. Unionization figures are from the U.S. Department of Labor, Bureau of Labor Statistics, *Handbook of Labor Statistics* 1978, updated.

2. See the *Annual Report of the National Labor Relations Board* (Washington D.C.: U.S. Government Printing Office, 1950–1980) for various years.

3. Formally, if B_i is the estimated impact of the ith factor on unionization we attribute B_i X_i of the change to the change in X_i. Note that our analysis uses a linear probability model. More complex functional forms, such as the logistic, will yield comparable results.

4. Percentage of the civilian labor force organized in 1952: U.S., 33 percent; Canada, 21 percent; in 1982: U.S., 24 percent; Canada, 31 percent. The U.S. data are from the *Handbook of Labor Statistics* 1980 and a telephone interview with George Rubin, BLS, April 20, 1982. The

Canadian data are from George V. Haythorne, "Canada: Industrial Relations—Internal and External Pressures" (Ottawa, September 1982, mimeographed).

5. In 1956 13 percent of public sector workers were organized; in 1980 23 percent. Source: *Handbook of Labor Statistics* 1981.

6. See Henry S. Farer and Daniel H. Saks, "Why Workers Want Unions: The Role of Relative Wages and Job Characteristics," *Journal of Political Economy* 88 (April 1980): 349–69.

7. Our calculation of the .7 elasticity is based on Paula Voos, *Labor Union Organizing Programs 1954–1977*, (Ph.D. diss., Harvard University, May 1982), table 3–2. The dollars spent per nonunion worker are from Voos, table 1–3; they indicate a 30 percent decline. To obtain the estimate in the text we multiply the 30 percent decline by the 0.7 elasticity, yielding 21 percent. Twenty-one percent of the 0.7 point decline is 0.15 points.

8. *Annual Report of the National Labor Relations Board*, vols. 16 and 44 (Washington, D.C.: Government Printing Office, 1954 and 1980).

9. The differential success of unions in elections contested by several unions can be interpreted differently. It is possible that two or more unions contest an election only when workers are extremely eager to organize. Then the decline in the proportion of elections contested by unions represents a decline in worker interest, not organizing activity. As we have used the figures simply to check the plausibility of Voos's estimates, we do not pursue the alternative interpretation here.

10. The AFL-CIO News estimates about 1500 practitioners (see *AFL-CIO News* 28, no. 2 (January 15, 1983): 1.

11. For texts of most of the major U.S. labor laws, see Archibald Cox and Derek C. Bok, *1966 Statutory Supplement: Labor Law Cases and Materials* (Brooklyn, N.Y.: The Foundation Press, 1966). Section 8(a)(3) of the National Labor Relations Act is on pages 43–44.

12. See Paul Weiler, "Promises to Keep: Securing Workers' Rights to Self-organization under the NLRA," *Harvard Law Review* 96, no. 8 (June 1983): 1769–1827 for a detailed discussion of illegal management activities. To obtain the estimated number of cases of discharge deemed meritorious, we applied the proportion of all employer unfair labor practices deemed meritorious in 1980 (39 percent) to the number of 8(a)(3) charges.

13. In one decision in which it decided to weaken the regulation of campaigns—Shopping Kart Food Market, Inc. 228 LLRB 1311 (1977)—the Board cited the Getman-Goldberg-Herman study.

14. In the study cited in table 15–4, Seeber and Cooke explain virtually all of the decline in union success in NLRB elections with a very different indicator, the proportion of elections that are "consent" elections.

15. See R. B. Freeman, "The Simple Economics of Declining Union Density": NBER Working Paper (Forthcoming).

16. The first study examining the ability of unions victorious in representation elections to negotiate collective agreements is Richard Prosten, "The Longest Season: Union Organizing in the Last Decade, a/k/a How Come One Team Has to Play with Its Shoelaces Tied Together?" *Proceedings of the Thirty-First Annual Winter Meeting of the Industrial Relations Research Association*, December 1978, 240–49. This study examined 2,658 elections. The second study focused on large units, covering 160 elections. It was conducted by Charles McDonald, AFL-CIO Organizing Division.

17. Figures are from *Annual Report of the National Labor Relations Board* for various years. For an analysis of decertifications, see Daniel A. Gerard, "The Impact of Union Campaigning in Decertification Elections: Getman, Goldberg and Herman Revisited" (Undergraduate thesis, Harvard College, March 1982).

18. Membership figures are from the Bureau of Labor Statistics, *Directory of National Unions and Employee Associations, 1979*, Bulletin 2079 (Washington D.C.: Government Printing Office, 1980), p. 59, and earlier editions.

19. We have made several estimates of attrition using variants of the following formula: attrition rate = (change in union membership minus gains through NLRB elections)/union membership in initial period. All of our estimates range from 3 to 5 percent. See R. B. Freeman, "The Simple Economics of Declining Union Density."

20. For derivation and discussion of this formula, see R. B. Freeman, "The Simple Economics of Declining Union Density."

21. This is obtained by setting the change in membership equal to zero in the difference equation: union share $(t) = (1 - \text{attrition rate})$ union share $(t-1)$ + new gains in membership

Notes

from NLRB elections divided by the workforce and solving for the stable union share. In this formula t indicates a year.

22. David Ellwood and Glenn Fine, "Impact of Right-to-Work Laws on Union Organizing": National Bureau of Economic Research Working Paper No. 1116 (May 1983). See R. B. Freeman and J. L. Medoff, "New Estimates of Private Sector Unionism in the U.S.," *Industrial and Labor Relations Review* 32 (January 1979): table 6, for number of workers covered by collective bargaining but not union members.

23. Harrison Lauer, "The Effect of Police Unions," (Undergraduate thesis, Harvard College, May 1981).

24. George Barnett, Presidential address delivered at the Forty-Fifth Annual Meeting of the American Economic Association, Cincinnati, Ohio, December 29, 1932.

25. For a history of unionism in this period see Phillip Taft, *The A.F. of L. in the Time of Gompers* (New York: Harper, 1957).

26. The first economist to study the spurt phenomenon seriously is James A. Davis, "The Theory of Union Growth," *Quarterly Journal of Economics* 55 (August 1941): 611–37. For other statements of the pattern, see John T. Dunlop, "The Development of Labor Organization: A Theoretical Framework," in *Insights Into Labor Issues*, R. A. Lester and J. Shister, eds., (New York: Macmillan, 1948), 163–93; and Walter Galenson, *The CIO Challenge to the AFL* (Cambridge, Mass.: Harvard University Press, 1960), 641–42.

27. See R. B. Freeman, "The Effect of Demographic Factors on Age-Earnings Profiles," *Journal of Human Resources* 14 (Summer 1979). See also R. B. Freeman, "Career Patterns of College Graduates in a Declining Job Market": National Bureau of Economic Research Working Paper No. 750 (1981).

INDEX

Abraham, Katharine G., 124, 126, 128, 273n5, n7
Ackerman, John A., 281n20
Aetna Life Insurance Company, 76, 273n10
Affirmative action, 134
AFL-CIO, 26, 34, 37–38, 40, 191, 198, 203–4, 234, 240, 242, 264n15, 282n10; Committee on Political Education of, 38, 192–95, 197, 199, 201, 254–55, 279n4, n7, n11; executive council of, 211; Industrial Union Department of, 76; Policy Goal on pension fund investment of, 75
A. G. Becker Company, 76
Age: exit behavior differences by, 98; fringe benefits and, 70, 73; unionization rates by, 30–31; wage differences by, 48; see also Older workers; Seniority; Younger workers
Airlines industry: legislation affecting, 199; wage concessions in, 56
Alexander, Kenneth, 270n10
Allen, Steven G., 166–68, 268n3, 277n4
Alpert, William T., 70, 269n14
Amalgamated Butchers, 35
Amalgamated Clothing Workers, 83
Amalgamated Food and Allied Workers Union, 273n1
American Association of University Professors, 244
American Economic Association, 244
American Federation of Labor, 229, 244; see also AFL-CIO
American Federation of State, County, and Municipal Employees, 244
American Management Associations, 215
American Medical Association, 32
American Motors, 267n24
"American shop" employers, 244
Andrews, Emily S., 269n18
Annual Survey of Manufacturers, 253
Antitrust violations, 214, 215
Antos, J., 263n2
Applebaum, Leon, 280n5
Apprenticeship programs, 164
Arbitration, 11, 20; exit behavior and, 104–9
Ashenfelter, Orley, 265n1, n9, 281n22
Aspin, Leslie, 235
Atherton, Wallace N., 261n7
Attrition, 240–42

Automatic progression of wages, 81
Automobile industry, 52; production cutbacks in, 111; wage concessions in, 56; see also United Auto Workers

Baby boom generation, 244
Bakke, E. Wight, 270n14
Bankruptcy, 117, 121
Barbash, Jack, 212, 264n14, 280n10
Barber, Randy, 75, 267n2, 269n19
Barnett, George, 283
"Battle of the Running Bulls," 4
Beal, Edwin F., 264n18
Beer, Michael, 262n12
Begin, James P., 264n18
Benefit programs, see Fringe benefits
Berger, Chris J., 128, 140, 273n6, 274n5
Berman, Michael, 147
Bernstein, Merton C., 264n19
B. F. Goodrich, 231
"Birmingham" geographic differential, 83
Blacks: exit behavior of, 97–98; seniority policies and, 134–35; unionization rate of, 30; wages of, 50; see also Race
Blaine, Harry R., 280n5
Blau, Francine, 100, 126
Block, Farrell, 196
Block, Richard N., 107, 234, 272n14
Bok, Derek C., 162, 192, 202, 214, 261n2, 262 n10, n21, 264n11, 276n1, 277n5, 279n3, n12, 280n3, n13, 282n11
Bonuses, 65
Borjas, George, 139, 267n2, 274n2
Bourdon, Clinton C., 227n15
Bourdreau, John W., 140, 274n5
Bowen, William G., 266n15
Boyle, Tony, 178
Brett, Jeanne M., 275n12
Bribery, 214, 215
Bricklayers, Masons, and Plasterers, 35
Brotslaw, Irving, 147
Brown, Charles, 100, 166, 167, 272n18, 277 n14
Bureau of the Census, 119, 171, 263n6; see also Current Population Surveys
Bureau of Labor Statistics, 56, 106, 116, 172, 216, 222, 267n26, 271n13, 272n6, 273n4,

Index

Index

Index

Product market conditions, 52; givebacks and, 55
Professional Nurses Association, 244
Profitability, 181–90, 248; cartelization and, 188–89; market sector and, 184–88; reduction in, 22
Profit maximization, 107
Promotions: of nonunion workers, 154; seniority and, 122, 126–28
Prosten, Richard, 234, 282n16
Protection, selling of, 214
Public Accommodation Act (1964), 18, 192
Public goods, 8–10
Public sector employees, unionization of, 227, 243, 244

Quality of Employment Survey (QES), 29, 47, 62, 66, 67, 71–73, 88, 105, 127, 138, 140, 142–44, 209, 210, 228, 259, 268n5, 270n15, 271n7, 273n8, 274n6
Quality of Working Conditions Survey, 148
"Quality of Working Life," 248
Quantitative analysis, 23
Quasi-rent return on capital, 182
Quit rates, see Exit behavior

Race: exit behavior differences by, 97; membership participation by, 208; and unionization rates, 29–30; wage differences by, 50
Railroads, 199
Railway Labor Act, 199, 200
Raimon, R., 100
Reder, Melvin W., 262n11, 281n21
Rees, Albert, 58, 266n15, n22, 267n27, 281 n22
Region: unionization rates by, 31; wage differences by, 50
Rehiring, 117
Report on Congress (COPE), 194
Republican Party, 41, 195, 197, 203
Retail Clerks International Union, 35
Reuther, Walter, 213
Reynolds, Lloyd G., 15, 261n2, 262n17, n19, 264n18
Rifkin, Jeremy, 75, 267n2, 269n19
"Right-to-work" laws, 31, 203, 242–43, 263n9
Riker, W., 279n8
Roomkin, Myron, 234
Ross, Irwin, 280n14, n15
Ruback, Richard, 184, 278n5
Rubberworkers Union, 38
Rubin, George, 36, 264n12, n15, 281n4
Rubin, Paul H., 196
Rustin, Bayard, 134, 135, 263n5

Saks, Daniel H., 88, 262n1, 263n4, n7, 270 n15, 282n6
Salinger, Michael, 187, 278n7
San, Gee, 266n16
Sandver, Marcus, 280n7
Sayles, Leonard R., 212, 213, 280n9, n11
Scanlon Plan, 189, 279n11
Schriesheim, Chester A., 147
Schuster, Michael, 176, 277n17
Scully, G. W., 281n22
Sears Roebuck, 76
Secondary labor force, 30, 160, 161
Seeber, R., 234, 282n14
Segal, Martin E., 266n15
Senate, U.S., 191, 194, 203, 204; Committee on Government Affairs, Permanent Subcommittee on Investigations of, 214; see also Congress
Seniority, 20, 21, 122–35; exit behavior and, 107; fringe benefits and, 65, 69, 122, 129–31; layoffs and, 115, 117, 122–26; membership participation and, 208; of nonunion workers, 154; promotions and, 122, 126–28; wages and, 131–33
Sex: exit behavior differences by, 97; membership participation by, 208; and unionization rates, 28; wage differences by, 50
Shalev, M., 281n22
Sheflin, Neil, 277n9
Sheler, Jeffrey L., 194
Sick leave, 65–66
Silberman, Jonathan I., 196
Simon, Herbert, 10, 262n10
Simons, Henry C., 43, 161, 192, 261n1, 262 n20, 265n2, 279n3
Single-employer bargaining, 38, 39
Single rates for wages, 79–81
Slichter, Sumner H., 15, 82, 116, 157, 164, 174, 261n2, 262n13, n16, 270nn7–9, 272 n8, 276n16, 277n3, n5
SMSAs (Standard Metropolitan Statistical Areas), 93, 158, 159
Smith, Adam, 3
Smith, Daniel, 268n9, 269n21
Smith, F. J., 147
Snowbarger, Marvin, 280n7
Social organization, 17–18, 247
Solnick, Loren M., 157, 268n6, 276n17
Somers, Gerald G., 40, 270n8
South, unionization rates in, 31
Stafford, Frank P., 265n6
Stagflation, 58
Standard Industrial Classification (SIC), 264 n13
State agencies, 42
Steel industry: layoffs in, 111; rate standardization in, 83
Steiber, Jack, 270n8
Stock market, 184